Computer-Aided Design: Concepts and Applications

Computer-Aided Design: Concepts and Applications

Edited by
Gilbert Knowles

Larsen & Keller
www.larsen-keller.com

Computer-Aided Design: Concepts and Applications
Edited by Gilbert Knowles
ISBN: 978-1-63549-678-9 (Hardback)

Published by Larsen and Keller Education,
5 Penn Plaza,
19th Floor,
New York, NY 10001, USA

Cataloging-in-Publication Data

Computer-aided design : concepts and applications / edited by Gilbert Knowles.
    p. cm.
Includes bibliographical references and index.
ISBN 978-1-63549-678-9
1. Computer-aided design. 2. Computer-aided engineering. I. Knowles, Gilbert.
TA174 .C66 2018
620.004 2--dc23

For more information regarding Larsen and Keller Education and its products, please visit the publisher's website www.larsen-keller.com

Table of Contents

Preface

Computer-aided design refers to the process of using computer systems to create, modify, optimize and analyze design. These systems have been applied to enhance communication, efficiently increase design, enhance design quality, increase manufacturing operations, etc. The computer-aided design is used in aerospace industry, prosthetics, shipbuilding, architectural design, advertising, animations, automotive, etc. Such selected concepts that redefine CAD have been presented in this book. The topics covered in it deal with the core aspects of the area. It includes in-depth information about the use of this technology in the present day scenario. The textbook will provide comprehensive knowledge to the readers.

To facilitate a deeper understanding of the contents of this book a short introduction of every chapter is written below:

Chapter 1- The use of computers to conceptualize and create designs is known as computer-aided design. The output generated by computer-aided design is usually in the form of electronic files for print and machining. The chapter on computer-aided design offers an insightful focus, keeping in mind the complex subject matter.

Chapter 2- Computer-aided engineering is used to assist in engineering analysis tasks. It includes optimization, multibody dynamics, finite element analysis and computational fluid dynamics. The chapter strategically encompasses and incorporates the major subdisciplines of computer-aided design, providing a complete understanding.

Chapter 3- Three-dimensional computer graphics are three-dimensional depictions of data. The algorithms used in 3D computer graphics are the same as 2D computer vector graphics in the wire-frame model and the raster display. Some of the softwares used in 3D modeling are polygonal modeling, virtual actor, digital sculpting, etc. This chapter is an overview of the subject matter incorporating all the major aspects of computer-aided design.

Chapter 4- The method used to map three-dimensional points on a two-dimensional plane is termed as 3D projection. 3D reconstruction, anaglyph 3D, game engine and medical animation are important applications of computer-aided design. Applications of computer-aided design are best understood in confluence with the major topics listed in the following chapter. The topics discussed in the chapter are of great importance to broaden the existing knowledge on computer-aided design.

Chapter 5- The various computer-aided design software are Blender, BRL-CAD, Archimedes, FreeCAD, OpenSCAD, SolveSpace, LibreCAD and Magic. Blender is a software that is used to create visual effects and animation movies. Some of the features of Blender are texturing, ringing and skinning, fluid and smoke simulation, 3D modeling and video editing. The topics elaborated in this chapter will help in gaining a better perspective about the various computer-aided design softwares.

Chapter 6- Circuits cloud is a cloud computing based application that is available online. It is used to design electronic circuits. CircuitMaker, Electric, gEDA, KiCad, and PCB are the other software mentioned in this section. Computer-aided design is best understood in confluence with the major topics listed in the following chapter.

Chapter 7- The topics discussed in the chapter are of great importance to broaden the existing knowledge of CAD file formats. The file format used in Autodesk 3ds max 3D modeling and rendering software is known as 3DS. Additive manufacturing file format, COLLADA, KernelCAD and PLY are other file formats discussed in this section. The aspects elucidated in this chapter are of vital importance, and provide a better understanding of computer-aided design.

Finally, I would like to thank the entire team involved in the inception of this book for their valuable time and contribution. This book would not have been possible without their efforts. I would also like to thank my friends and family for their constant support.

Editor

An Introduction to Computer-Aided Design

The use of computers to conceptualize and create designs is known as computer-aided design. The output generated by computer-aided design is usually in the form of electronic files for print and machining. The chapter on computer-aided design offers an insightful focus, keeping in mind the complex subject matter.

Computer-Aided Design

Computer-aided design (CAD) is the use of computer systems (or workstations) to aid in the creation, modification, analysis, or optimization of a design. CAD software is used to increase the productivity of the designer, improve the quality of design, improve communications through documentation, and to create a database for manufacturing. CAD output is often in the form of electronic files for print, machining, or other manufacturing operations. The term CADD (for *Computer Aided Design and Drafting*) is also used.

Its use in designing electronic systems is known as electronic design automation, or EDA. In mechanical design it is known as mechanical design automation (MDA) or computer-aided drafting (CAD), which includes the process of creating a technical drawing with the use of computer software.

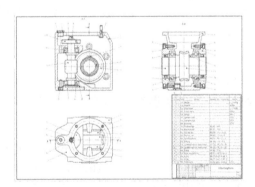

Example: 2D CAD drawing

Example: 3D CAD model

CAD software for mechanical design uses either vector-based graphics to depict the objects of traditional drafting, or may also produce raster graphics showing the overall appearance of designed objects. However, it involves more than just shapes. As in the manual drafting of technical and engineering drawings, the output of CAD must convey information, such as materials, processes, dimensions, and tolerances, according to application-specific conventions.

CAD may be used to design curves and figures in two-dimensional (2D) space; or curves, surfaces, and solids in three-dimensional (3D) space.

CAD is an important industrial art extensively used in many applications, including automotive, shipbuilding, and aerospace industries, industrial and architectural design, prosthetics, and many more. CAD is also widely used to produce computer animation for special effects in movies, advertising and technical manuals, often called DCC digital content creation. The modern ubiquity and power of computers means that even perfume bottles and shampoo dispensers are designed using techniques unheard of by engineers of the 1960s. Because of its enormous economic importance, CAD has been a major driving force for research in computational geometry, computer graphics (both hardware and software), and discrete differential geometry.

The design of geometric models for object shapes, in particular, is occasionally called *computer-aided geometric design* (*CAGD*).

Overview of CAD Software

Starting around the mid 1970s, as computer aided design systems began to provide more capability than just an ability to reproduce manual drafting with electronic drafting, the cost benefit for companies to switch to CAD became apparent. The benefits of CAD systems over manual drafting are the capabilities one often takes for granted from computer systems today; automated generation of Bill of Material, auto layout in integrated circuits, interference checking, and many others. Eventually CAD provided the designer with the ability to perform engineering calculations. During this transition, calculations were still performed either by hand or by those individuals who could run computer programs. CAD was a revolutionary change in the engineering industry, where draftsmen, designers and engineering roles begin to merge. It did not eliminate departments, as much as it merged departments and empowered draftsman, designers and engineers. CAD is just another example of the pervasive effect computers were beginning to have on industry. Current computer-aided design software packages range from 2D vector-based drafting systems to 3D solid and surface modelers. Modern CAD packages can also frequently allow rotations in three dimensions, allowing viewing of a designed object from any desired angle, even from the inside looking out. Some CAD software is capable of dynamic mathematical modeling, in which case it may be marketed as CAD.

CAD technology is used in the design of tools and machinery and in the drafting and design of all types of buildings, from small residential types (houses) to the largest commercial and industrial structures (hospitals and factories).

CAD is mainly used for detailed engineering of 3D models and/or 2D drawings of physical components, but it is also used throughout the engineering process from conceptual design and layout of products, through strength and dynamic analysis of assemblies to definition of manufacturing methods of components. It can also be used to design objects. Furthermore, many CAD applications now offer advanced rendering and animation capabilities so engineers can better visualize their product designs. 4D BIM is a type of virtual construction engineering simulation incorporating time or schedule related information for project management.

CAD has become an especially important technology within the scope of computer-aided technologies, with benefits such as lower product development costs and a greatly shortened design cycle. CAD enables designers to layout and develop work on screen, print it out and save it for future editing, saving time on their drawings.

Uses

Computer-aided design is one of the many tools used by engineers and designers and is used in many ways depending on the profession of the user and the type of software in question.

CAD is one part of the whole Digital Product Development (DPD) activity within the Product Life-cycle Management (PLM) processes, and as such is used together with other tools, which are either integrated modules or stand-alone products, such as:

- Computer-aided engineering (CAE) and Finite element analysis (FEA)

- Computer-aided manufacturing (CAM) including instructions to Computer Numerical Control (CNC) machines

- Photorealistic rendering and Motion Simulation.

- Document management and revision control using Product Data Management (PDM).

CAD is also used for the accurate creation of photo simulations that are often required in the preparation of Environmental Impact Reports, in which computer-aided designs of intended buildings are superimposed into photographs of existing environments to represent what that locale will be like, where the proposed facilities are allowed to be built. Potential blockage of view corridors and shadow studies are also frequently analyzed through the use of CAD.

CAD has been proven to be useful to engineers as well. Using four properties which are history, features, parameterization, and high level constraints. The construction history can be used to look back into the model's personal features and work on the single area rather than the whole model. Parameters and constraints can be used to determine the size, shape, and other properties of the different modeling elements. The features in the CAD system can be used for the variety of tools for measurement such as tensile strength, yield strength, electrical or electro-magnetic properties. Also its stress, strain, timing or how the element gets affected in certain temperatures, etc.

Types

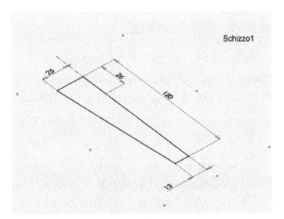

A simple procedure

There are several different types of CAD, each requiring the operator to think differently about how to use them and design their virtual components in a different manner for each.

There are many producers of the lower-end 2D systems, including a number of free and open source programs. These provide an approach to the drawing process without all the fuss over scale and placement on the drawing sheet that accompanied hand drafting, since these can be adjusted as required during the creation of the final draft.

3D wireframe is basically an extension of 2D drafting (not often used today). Each line has to be manually inserted into the drawing. The final product has no mass properties associated with it and cannot have features directly added to it, such as holes. The operator approaches these in a similar fashion to the 2D systems, although many 3D systems allow using the wireframe model to make the final engineering drawing views.

3D "dumb" solids are created in a way analogous to manipulations of real world objects (not often used today). Basic three-dimensional geometric forms (prisms, cylinders, spheres, and so on) have solid volumes added or subtracted from them, as if assembling or cutting real-world objects. Two-dimensional projected views can easily be generated from the models. Basic 3D solids don't usually include tools to easily allow motion of components, set limits to their motion, or identify interference between components.

There are two types of *3D Solid Modeling*

1. *Parametric modeling* allows the operator to use what is referred to as "design intent". The objects and features created are modifiable. Any future modifications can be made by changing how the original part was created. If a feature was intended to be located from the center of the part, the operator should locate it from the center of the model. The feature could be located using any geometric object already available in the part, but this random placement would defeat the design intent. If the operator designs the part as it functions the parametric modeler is able to make changes to the part while maintaining geometric and functional relationships.

2. *Direct or Explicit modeling* provide the ability to edit geometry without a history tree. With direct modeling once a sketch is used to create geometry the sketch is incorporated into the new geometry and the designer just modifies the geometry without needing the original sketch. As with parametric modeling, direct modeling has the ability to include relationships between selected geometry (e.g., tangency, concentricity).

Top end systems offer the capabilities to incorporate more organic, aesthetics and ergonomic features into designs. Freeform surface modeling is often combined with solids to allow the designer to create products that fit the human form and visual requirements as well as they interface with the machine.

Technology

Originally software for Computer-Aided Design systems was developed with computer languages such as Fortran, ALGOL but with the advancement of object-oriented programming methods this has radically changed. Typical modern parametric feature based modeler and freeform surface systems are built around a number of key C modules with their own APIs. A CAD system can be seen as built up from the interaction of a graphical user interface (GUI) with NURBS geometry and/or boundary representation (B-rep) data via a geometric modeling kernel. A geometry constraint engine may also be employed to manage the associative relationships between geometry, such as wireframe geometry in a sketch or components in an assembly.

A CAD model of a computer mouse.

Unexpected capabilities of these associative relationships have led to a new form of prototyping called digital prototyping. In contrast to physical prototypes, which entail manufacturing time in the design. That said, CAD models can be generated by a computer after the physical prototype has been scanned using an industrial CT scanning machine. Depending on the nature of the business, digital or physical prototypes can be initially chosen according to specific needs.

Today, CAD systems exist for all the major platforms (Windows, Linux, UNIX and Mac OS X); some packages even support multiple platforms.

Right now, no special hardware is required for most CAD software. However, some CAD systems can do graphically and computationally intensive tasks, so a modern graphics card, high speed (and possibly multiple) CPUs and large amounts of RAM may be recommended.

The human-machine interface is generally via a computer mouse but can also be via a pen and digitizing graphics tablet. Manipulation of the view of the model on the screen is also sometimes done with the use of a Spacemouse/SpaceBall. Some systems also support stereoscopic glasses for viewing the 3D model.Technologies which in the past were limited to larger installations or specialist applications have become available to a wide group of users.These include the CAVE or HMD's and interactive devices like motion-sensing technology.

Software

CAD model of the TexiBot showing aircraft nose wheel and landing gear fully engaged

CAD software enables engineers and architects to design, inspect and manage engineering projects within an integrated graphical user interface (GUI) on a personal computer system. Most applications support solid modeling with boundary representation (B-Rep) and NURBS geometry, and enable the same to be published in a variety of formats. A geometric modeling kernel is a software component that provides solid modeling and surface modeling features to CAD applications.

Based on market statistics, commercial software from Autodesk, Dassault Systems, Siemens PLM Software and PTC dominate the CAD industry. The following is a list of major CAD applications, grouped by usage statistics.

Commercial	
• Autodesk AutoCAD	• TurboCAD
• Autodesk Inventor	• IronCAD
• Bricsys BricsCAD	• MEDUSA
• Dassault CATIA	• ProgeCAD
• Dassault SolidWorks	• SpaceClaim
• Kubotek KeyCreator	• PunchCAD
• Siemens NX	• Rhinoceros 3D
• Siemens Solid Edge	• VariCAD
• PTC PTC Creo (formerly known as Pro/ENGINEER)	• VectorWorks
• Trimble SketchUp	• Cobalt
• AgiliCity Modelur	• RoutCad RoutCad
	• SketchUp
Freeware and open source	**CAD Kernels**
• 123D	• Parasolid by Siemens
• LibreCAD	• ACIS by Spatial
• FreeCAD	• ShapeManager by Autodesk
• BRL-CAD	• Open CASCADE
• OpenSCAD	• C3D by C3D Labs
• NanoCAD	
• QCad	

History

Designers have long used computers for their calculations. Digital computers were used in power system analysis or optimization as early as "Proto-whirlwind" in 1949. Circuit design theory, or power network methodology would be algebraic, symbolic, and often vector-based. Examples of problems being solved in the mid-1940s to 50s include, Servo motors controlled by generated pulse (1949), The digital computer with built-in compute operations to automatically co-ordinate transforms to compute radar related vectors (1951) and the essentially graphic mathematical process of forming a shape with a digital machine tool (1952). These were accomplished with the use of computer software. The man credited with coining the term CAD. Douglas T. Ross stated "As soon as I saw the interactive display equipment," [being used by radar operators 1953] it would be just what his data reduction group needed. With the Lincoln Lab people, they were the only ones who used the big,complex display systems put in for the pre-SAGE, Cape Cod system. But "we used it for our own personal workstation." The designers of these very early computers built utility programs so that programmers could debug programs using flow charts on a display scope with logical switches that could be opened and closed during the debugging session. They found that they could create electronic symbols and geometric figures to be used to create simple circuit diagrams and flow charts. They made the pleasant discovery that an object once drawn could be reproduced at will, its orientation, Linkage [flux, mechanical, lexical scoping] or scale changed. This suggested numerous possibilities to them. It took ten years of interdisciplinary development work before SKETCHPAD sitting on evolving math libraries emerged from MIT's labs. Additional developments were carried out in the 1960s within the aircraft, automotive, industrial control and electronics industries in the area of 3D surface construction, NC programming and design analysis, most of it independent of one another and often not publicly published until much later. Some of the mathematical description work on curves was developed in the early 1940s by Robert Issac Newton from Pawtucket, Rhode Island. Robert A. Heinlein in his 1957 novel *The Door into Summer* suggested the possibility of a robotic *Drafting Dan*. However, probably the most important work on polynomial curves and sculptured surface was done by Pierre Bézier, Paul de Casteljau (Citroen), Steven Anson Coons (MIT, Ford), James Ferguson (Boeing), Carl de Boor (GM), Birkhoff (GM) and Garibedian (GM) in the 1960s and W. Gordon (GM) and R. Riesenfeld in the 1970s.

The invention of the 3D CAD/CAM is attributed to a French engineer, Pierre Bezier (Arts et Métiers ParisTech, Renault). After his mathematical work concerning surfaces, he developed UNISURF, between 1966 and 1968, to ease the design of parts and tools for the automotive industry. Then, UNISURF became the working base for the following generations of CAD software.

It is argued that a turning point was the development of the SKETCHPAD system at MIT by Ivan Sutherland (who later created a graphics technology company with Dr. David Evans). The distinctive feature of SKETCHPAD was that it allowed the designer to interact with his computer graphically: the design can be fed into the computer by drawing on a CRT monitor with a light pen. Effectively, it was a prototype of graphical user interface, an indispensable feature of modern CAD. Sutherland presented his paper Sketchpad: A Man-Machine Graphical Communication System in 1963 at a Joint Computer Conference having worked on it as his PhD thesis paper for a few years. Quoting, "For drawings where motion of the drawing, or analysis of a drawn problem is of value to the user, Sketchpad excels. For highly repetitive drawings or drawings where accuracy is required, Sketchpad is sufficiently faster than conventional techniques to be worthwhile. For drawings which merely communicate with shops, it is probably better to use conventional paper and pencil." Over time efforts would be directed toward the goal of having the designers drawings communicate not just with shops but with the shop tool itself. This goal would be a long time arriving.

The first commercial applications of CAD were in large companies in the automotive and aerospace industries, as well as in electronics. Only large corporations could afford the computers capable of performing the calculations. Notable company projects were, a joint project of GM (Dr. Patrick J.Hanratty) and IBM (Sam Matsa, Doug Ross's MIT APT research assistant) to develop a prototype system for design engineers DAC-1 (Design Augmented by Computer) 1964; Lockheed projects; Bell GRAPHIC 1 and Renault.

One of the most influential events in the development of CAD was the founding of MCS (Manufacturing and Consulting Services Inc.) in 1971 by Dr. P. J. Hanratty, who wrote the system ADAM (Automated Drafting And Machining) but more importantly supplied code to companies such as McDonnell Douglas (Unigraphics), Computervision (CADDS), Calma, Gerber, Autotrol and Control Data.

As computers became more affordable, the application areas have gradually expanded. The development of CAD software for personal desktop computers was the impetus for almost universal application in all areas of construction.

Other key points in the 1960s and 1970s would be the foundation of CAD systems United Computing, Intergraph, IBM, Intergraph IGDS in 1974 (which led to Bentley Systems MicroStation in 1984).

CAD implementations have evolved dramatically since then. Initially, with 3D in the 1970s, it was typically limited to producing drawings similar to hand-drafted drawings. Advances in programming and computer hardware, notably solid modeling in the 1980s, have allowed more versatile applications of computers in design activities.

Key products for 1981 were the solid modelling packages - Romulus (ShapeData) and Uni-Solid (Unigraphics) based on PADL-2 and the release of the surface modeler CATIA (Dassault Systemes). Autodesk was founded 1982 by John Walker, which led to the 2D system AutoCAD. The next milestone was the release of Pro/ENGINEER in 1987, which heralded greater usage of feature-based modeling methods and parametric linking of the parameters of features. Also of importance to the development of CAD was the development of the B-rep solid modeling kernels (engines for manipulating geometrically and topologically consistent 3D objects) Parasolid (ShapeData) and ACIS (Spatial Technology Inc.) at the end of the 1980s and beginning of the 1990s, both inspired by the work of Ian Braid. This led to the release of mid-range packages such as SolidWorks and Tri-Spective (later known as IRONCAD) in 1995, Solid Edge (then Intergraph) in 1996 and Autodesk Inventor in 1999. An independent geometric modeling kernel has been evolving in Russia since the 1990s. Nikolay Golovanov joined ASCON Company in 1994 from the Kolomna Engineering Design Bureau and began development of C3D – the geometric kernel of the Russian popular CAD system, KOMPAS-3D. Nowadays, C3D (C3D Labs) is the most valued Russian CAD product in the category of "components", i.e. products designed for integration in the end-user CAD systems of Russian and global vendors.

Vector Graphics

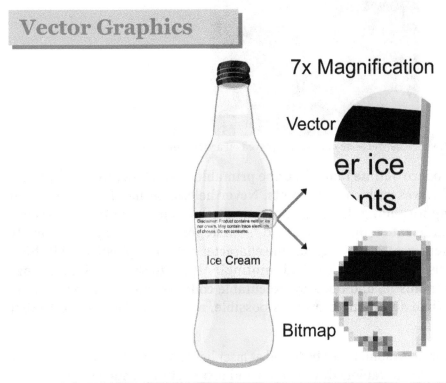

Example showing effect of vector graphics versus raster graphics

Vector graphics is the use of polygons to represent images in computer graphics. Vector graphics are based on vectors, which lead through locations called control points or nodes. Each of these points has a definite position on the x- and y-axes of the work plane and determines the direction of the path; further, each path may be assigned various attributes, including such values as stroke color, shape, curve, thickness, and fill.

Overview

One of the first uses of vector graphic displays was the US SAGE air defense system. Vector graphics systems were only retired from U.S. en route air traffic control in 1999, and are likely still in use in military and specialised systems. Vector graphics were also used on the TX-2 at the MIT Lincoln Laboratory by computer graphics pioneer Ivan Sutherland to run his program Sketchpad in 1963.

Subsequent vector graphics systems, most of which iterated through dynamically modifiable stored lists of drawing instructions, include the IBM 2250, Imlac PDS-1, and DEC GT40. There was a home gaming system that used vector graphics called Vectrex as well as various arcade games like *Asteroids*, *Space Wars* and many cinematronics titles such as *Rip-Off*, and *Tail Gunner* using vector monitors. Storage scope displays, such as the Tektronix 4014, could display vector images but not modify them without first erasing the display.

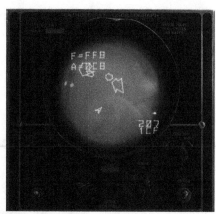

A free software *Asteroids*-like video game played on a vector monitor

In computer typography, modern outline fonts describe printable characters (glyphs) by cubic or quadratic mathematical curves with control points. Nevertheless, bitmap fonts are still in use. Converting outlines requires filling them in; converting to bitmaps is not trivial, because bitmaps often don't have sufficient resolution to avoid "stairstepping" ("aliasing"), especially with smaller visible character sizes. Processing outline character data in sophisticated fashion to create satisfactory bitmaps for rendering is called "hinting". Although the term implies suggestion, the process is deterministic, and done by executable code, essentially a special-purpose computer language. While automatic hinting is possible, results can be inferior to that done by experts.

Modern vector graphics displays can sometimes be found at laser light shows, where two fast-moving X-Y mirrors position the beam to rapidly draw shapes and text as straight and curved strokes on a screen.

Vector graphics can be created in form using a pen plotter, a special type of printer that uses a series of ballpoint and felt-tip pens on a servo-driven mount that moves horizontally across the paper, with the plotter moving the paper back and forth through its paper path for vertical movement. Although a typical plot might easily require a few thousand paper motions, back and forth, the paper doesn't slip. In a tiny roll-fed plotter made by Alps in Japan, teeth on thin sprockets indented the paper near its edges on the first pass, and maintained registration on subsequent passes.

Some Hewlett-Packard pen plotters had two-axis pen carriers and stationery paper (plot size was limited). However, the moving-paper H-P plotters had grit wheels (akin to machine-shop grinding wheels) which, on the first pass, indented the paper surface, and collectively maintained registration.

Present-day vector graphic files such as engineering drawings are typically printed as bitmaps, after vector-to-raster conversion.

The term "vector graphics" is mainly used today in the context of two-dimensional computer graphics. It is one of several modes an artist can use to create an image on a raster display. Vector graphics can be uploaded to online databases for other designers to download and manipulate, speeding up the creative process. Other modes include text, multimedia, and 3D rendering. Virtually all modern 3D rendering is done using extensions of 2D vector graphics techniques. Plotters used in technical drawing still draw vectors directly to paper.

This vector-based image of a round four-color swirl displays several unique features of vector graphics versus raster graphics: there is no aliasing along the rounded edge which results in digital artifacts, the color gradients are all smooth, and the user can resize the image infinitely without losing any quality.

Standards

The World Wide Web Consortium (W3C) standard for vector graphics is Scalable Vector Graphics (SVG). The standard is complex and has been relatively slow to be established at least in part owing to commercial interests. Many web browsers now have some support for rendering SVG data, but full implementations of the standard are still comparatively rare.

In recent years, SVG has become a significant format that is completely independent of the resolution of the rendering device, typically a printer or display monitor. SVG files are essentially printable text that describes both straight and curved paths, as well as other attributes. Rendering SVG requires conversion to raster format at a resolution appropriate for the current task. SVG is also a format for animated graphics.

There is also a version of SVG for mobile phones. In particular, the specific format for mobile phones is called SVGT (SVG Tiny version). These images can count links and also exploit anti-aliasing. They can also be displayed as wallpaper.

Conversion

Original reference photo before vectorization

Detail can be added to or removed from vector art.

From Raster

Modern displays and printers are raster devices; vector formats have to be converted to raster format (bitmaps – pixel arrays) before they can be rendered (displayed or printed). The size of the bitmap/raster-format file generated by the conversion will depend on the resolution required, but the size of the vector file generating the bitmap/raster file will always remain the same. Thus, it is easy to convert from a vector file to a range of bitmap/raster file formats but it is much more difficult to go in the opposite direction, especially if subsequent editing of the vector picture is required. It might be an advantage to save an image created from a vector source file as a bitmap/raster format, because different systems have different (and incompatible) vector formats, and some might not support vector graphics at all. However, once a file is converted from the vector format, it is likely to be bigger, and it loses the advantage of scalability without loss of resolution. It will also no longer be possible to edit individual parts of the image as discrete objects. The file size of a vector graphic image depends on the number of graphic elements it contains; it is a list of descriptions.

Printing

Vector art is ideal for printing since the art is made from a series of mathematical curves, it will print very crisply even when resized. For instance, one can print a vector logo on a small sheet of copy paper, and then enlarge the same vector logo to billboard size and keep the same crisp quality. A low-resolution raster graphic would blur or pixelate excessively if it were enlarged from business card size to billboard size. (The precise resolution of a raster graphic necessary for high-quality results depends on the viewing distance; e.g., a billboard may still appear to be of high quality even at low resolution if the viewing distance is great enough.)

If we regard typographic characters as images, then the same considerations that we have made for graphics apply even to composition of written text for printing (typesetting). Older character sets were stored as bitmaps. Therefore, to achieve maximum print quality they had to be used at a given resolution only; these font formats are said to be non-scalable. High quality typography is nowadays based on character drawings (fonts) which are typically stored as vector graphics, and as such are scalable to any size. Examples of these vector formats for characters are Postscript fonts and TrueType fonts.

Operation

Advantages to this style of drawing over raster graphics:

- This minimal amount of information translates to a much smaller file size compared to large raster images (the size of representation does not depend on the dimensions of the object), though a vector graphic with a small file size is often said to lack detail compared with a real world photo.

- Correspondingly, one can infinitely zoom in on e.g., a circle arc, and it remains smooth. On the other hand, a polygon representing a curve will reveal being not really curved.

- On zooming in, lines and curves need not get wider proportionally. Often the width is either not increased or less than proportional. On the other hand, irregular curves represented by simple geometric shapes may be made proportionally wider when zooming in, to keep them looking smooth and not like these geometric shapes.

- The parameters of objects are stored and can be later modified. This means that moving, scaling, rotating, filling etc. doesn't degrade the quality of a drawing. Moreover, it is usual to specify the dimensions in device-independent units, which results in the best possible rasterization on raster devices.

- From a 3-D perspective, rendering shadows is also much more realistic with vector graphics, as shadows can be abstracted into the rays of light from which they are formed. This allows for photo realistic images and renderings.

For example, consider a circle of radius r. The main pieces of information a program needs in order to draw this circle are

1. an indication that what is to be drawn is a circle
2. the radius r
3. the location of the center point of the circle
4. stroke line style and color (possibly transparent)
5. fill style and color (possibly transparent)

Vector formats are not always appropriate in graphics work and also have numerous disadvantages. For example, devices such as cameras and scanners produce essentially continuous-tone raster graphics that are impractical to convert into vectors, and so for this type of work, an image editor will operate on the pixels rather than on drawing objects defined by mathematical expressions. Comprehensive graphics tools will combine images from vector and raster sources, and may provide editing tools for both, since some parts of an image could come from a camera source, and others could have been drawn using vector tools.

Some authors have criticized the term *vector graphics* as being confusing. In particular, *vector graphics* does not simply refer to graphics described by Euclidean vectors. Some authors have proposed to use *object-oriented graphics* instead. However this term can also be confusing as it can be read as any kind of graphics implemented using object-oriented programming.

Typical Primitive Objects

Any particular vector file format supports only some kinds of primitive objects. Nearly all vector file formats support simple and fast-rendering primitive objects:

- Lines, polylines and polygons
- Bézier curves and bezigons
- Circles and ellipses

Most vector file formats support

- Text (in computer font formats such as TrueType where each letter is created from Bézier curves) or quadratics.
- Color gradients

- Often, a bitmap image is considered as a primitive object. From the conceptual view, it behaves as a rectangle.

A few vector file formats support more complex objects as primitives:

- Many computer-aided design applications support splines and other curves, such as:
  - o   Catmull–Rom splines
  - o   NURBS
- iterated function systems
- superellipses and superellipsoids
- metaballs
- etc.

If an image stored in one vector file format is converted to another file format that supports all the primitive objects used in that particular image, then the conversion can be lossless.

Vector Operations

Vector graphics editors typically allow translation, rotation, movement (without rotation), mirroring, stretching, skewing, affine transformations, changing of z-order (loosely, what's in front of what) and combination of primitives into more complex objects.

More sophisticated transformations include set operations on closed shapes (union, difference, intersection, etc.).

Vector graphics are ideal for simple or composite drawings that need to be device-independent, or do not need to achieve photo-realism. For example, the PostScript and PDF page description languages use a vector graphics model.

Polygon

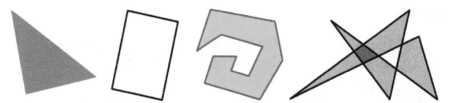

Some polygons of different kinds: open (excluding its boundary), boundary only (excluding interior), closed (including both boundary and interior), and self-intersecting.

In elementary geometry, a polygon is a plane figure that is bounded by a finite chain of straight line segments closing in a loop to form a closed polygonal chain or *circuit*. These segments are called its *edges* or *sides*, and the points where two edges meet are the polygon's *vertices* (singular: vertex) or *corners*. The interior of the polygon is sometimes called its *body*. An n-gon is a polygon with n sides; for example, a triangle is a 3-gon. A polygon is a 2-dimensional example of the more general polytope in any number of dimensions.

The basic geometrical notion of a polygon has been adapted in various ways to suit particular purposes. Mathematicians are often concerned only with the bounding closed polygonal chain and with simple polygons which do not self-intersect, and they often define a polygon accordingly. A polygonal boundary may be allowed to intersect itself, creating star polygons and other self-intersecting polygons. These and other generalizations of polygons are described below.

Classification

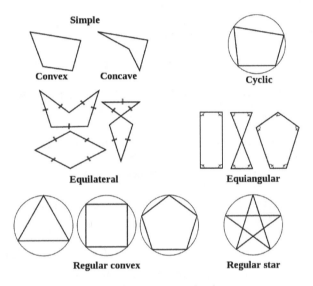

Some different types of polygon

Number of Sides

Polygons are primarily classified by the number of sides.

Convexity and Non-convexity

Polygons may be characterized by their convexity or type of non-convexity:

- Convex: any line drawn through the polygon (and not tangent to an edge or corner) meets its boundary exactly twice. As a consequence, all its interior angles are less than 180°. Equivalently, any line segment with endpoints on the boundary passes through only interior points between its endpoints.

- Non-convex: a line may be found which meets its boundary more than twice. Equivalently, there exists a line segment between two boundary points that passes outside the polygon.

- Simple: the boundary of the polygon does not cross itself. All convex polygons are simple.

- Concave. Non-convex and simple. There is at least one interior angle greater than 180°.

- Star-shaped: the whole interior is visible from at least one point, without crossing any edge. The polygon must be simple, and may be convex or concave.

- Self-intersecting: the boundary of the polygon crosses itself. Branko Grünbaum calls these coptic, though this term does not seem to be widely used. The term *complex* is sometimes used in contrast to *simple*, but this usage risks confusion with the idea of a *complex polygon* as one which exists in the complex Hilbert plane consisting of two complex dimensions.

- Star polygon: a polygon which self-intersects in a regular way. A polygon cannot be both a star and star-shaped.

Equality and Symmetry

- Equiangular: all corner angles are equal.

- Cyclic: all corners lie on a single circle, called the circumcircle.

- Isogonal or vertex-transitive: all corners lie within the same symmetry orbit. The polygon is also cyclic and equiangular.

- Equilateral: all edges are of the same length. The polygon need not be convex.

- Tangential: all sides are tangent to an inscribed circle.

- Isotoxal or edge-transitive: all sides lie within the same symmetry orbit. The polygon is also equilateral and tangential.

- Regular: the polygon is both *isogonal* and *isotoxal*. Equivalently, it is both *cyclic* and *equilateral*, or both *equilateral* and *equiangular*. A non-convex regular polygon is called a *regular star polygon*.

Miscellaneous

- Rectilinear: the polygon's sides meet at right angles, i.e., all its interior angles are 90 or 270 degrees.

- Monotone with respect to a given line *L*: every line orthogonal to L intersects the polygon not more than twice.

Properties and Formulas

Euclidean geometry is assumed throughout.

Angles

Any polygon has as many corners as it has sides. Each corner has several angles. The two most important ones are:

- Interior angle – The sum of the interior angles of a simple n-gon is $(n-2)\pi$ radians or $(n-2) \times 180$ degrees. This is because any simple n-gon (having n sides) can be considered to be made up of $(n-2)$ triangles, each of which has an angle sum of π radians or 180 degrees. The measure of any interior angle of a convex regular n-gon is $\left(1-\frac{2}{n}\right)\pi$ radians or $180-\frac{360}{n}$ degrees. The interior angles of regular star polygons were first studied by Poinsot, in the same paper in which he describes the four regular star polyhedra: for a regular $\frac{p}{q}$-gon (a p-gon with central density q), each interior angle is $\frac{\pi(p-2q)}{p}$ radians or $\frac{180(p-2q)}{p}$ degrees.

- Exterior angle – The exterior angle is the supplementary angle to the interior angle. Tracing around a convex n-gon, the angle "turned" at a corner is the exterior or external angle. Tracing all the way around the polygon makes one full turn, so the sum of the exterior angles must be 360°. This argument can be generalized to concave simple polygons, if external angles that turn in the opposite direction are subtracted from the total turned. Tracing around an n-gon in general, the sum of the exterior angles (the total amount one rotates at the vertices) can be any integer multiple d of 360°, e.g. 720° for a pentagram and 0° for an angular "eight" or antiparallelogram, where d is the density or starriness of the polygon.

Area and Centroid

Simple Polygons

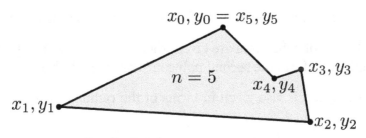

Coordinates of a non-convex pentagon.

For a non-self-intersecting (simple) polygon with n vertices x_i, y_i ($i = 1$ to n), the signed area and the Cartesian coordinates of the centroid are given by:

$$A = \frac{1}{2}\sum_{i=0}^{n-1}(x_i y_{i+1} - x_{i+1}y_i),$$

$$16A^2 = \sum_{i=1}^{n}\sum_{j=1}^{n}\begin{vmatrix} Q_{i,j} & Q_{i,j+1} \\ Q_{i+1,j} & Q_{i+1,j+1} \end{vmatrix},$$

where $Q_{i,j}$ is the squared distance between (x_i, y_i) and (x_j, y_j); and

$$C_x = \frac{1}{6A}\sum_{i=0}^{n-1}(x_i + x_{i+1})(x_i y_{i+1} - x_{i+1}y_i),$$

$$C_y = \frac{1}{6A}\sum_{i=0}^{n-1}(y_i + y_{i+1})(x_i y_{i+1} - x_{i+1}y_i).$$

To close the polygon, the first and last vertices are the same, i.e., $x_n, y_n = x_0, y_0$. The vertices must be ordered according to positive or negative orientation (counterclockwise or clockwise, respectively); if they are ordered negatively, the value given by the area formula will be negative but correct in absolute value, but when calculating C_x and C_y, the signed value of A (which in this case is negative) should be used. This is commonly called the shoelace formula or Surveyor's formula.

The area A of a simple polygon can also be computed if the lengths of the sides, $a_1, a_2, ..., a_n$ and the exterior angles, $\theta_1, \theta_2, ..., \theta_n$ are known, from:

$$A = \frac{1}{2}(a_1[a_2 \sin(\theta_1) + a_3 \sin(\theta_1 + \theta_2) + \cdots + a_{n-1} \sin(\theta_1 + \theta_2 + \cdots + \theta_{n-2})]$$
$$+ a_2[a_3 \sin(\theta_2) + a_4 \sin(\theta_2 + \theta_3) + \cdots + a_{n-1} \sin(\theta_2 + \cdots + \theta_{n-2})]$$
$$+ \cdots + a_{n-2}[a_{n-1} \sin(\theta_{n-2})]).$$

The formula was described by Lopshits in 1963.

If the polygon can be drawn on an equally spaced grid such that all its vertices are grid points, Pick's theorem gives a simple formula for the polygon's area based on the numbers of interior and boundary grid points: the former number plus one-half the latter number, minus 1.

In every polygon with perimeter p and area A, the isoperimetric inequality $p^2 > 4\pi A$ holds.

If any two simple polygons of equal area are given, then the first can be cut into polygonal pieces which can be reassembled to form the second polygon. This is the Bolyai–Gerwien theorem.

The area of a regular polygon is also given in terms of the radius r of its inscribed circle and its perimeter p by

$$A = \tfrac{1}{2} \cdot p \cdot r.$$

This radius is also termed its apothem and is often represented as a.

The area of a regular n-gon with side s inscribed in a unit circle is

$$A = \frac{ns}{4}\sqrt{4 - s^2}.$$

The area of a regular n-gon in terms of the radius R of its circumscribed circle and its perimeter p is given by

$$A = \frac{R}{2} \cdot p \cdot \sqrt{1 - \tfrac{p^2}{4n^2R^2}}.$$

The area of a regular n-gon inscribed in a unit-radius circle, with side s and interior angle α, can also be expressed trigonometrically as

$$A = \frac{ns^2}{4}\cot\frac{\pi}{n} = \frac{ns^2}{4}\cot\frac{\alpha}{n-2} = n \cdot \sin\frac{\pi}{n} \cdot \cos\frac{\pi}{n} = n \cdot \sin\frac{\alpha}{n-2} \cdot \cos\frac{\alpha}{n-2}.$$

The lengths of the sides of a polygon do not in general determine the area. However, if the polygon is cyclic the sides *do* determine the area.

Of all n-gons with given sides, the one with the largest area is cyclic. Of all n-gons with a given perimeter, the one with the largest area is regular (and therefore cyclic).

Self-intersecting Polygons

The area of a self-intersecting polygon can be defined in two different ways, each of which gives a different answer:

- Using the above methods for simple polygons, we allow that particular regions within the polygon may have their area multiplied by a factor which we call the *density* of the region. For example, the central convex pentagon in the center of a pentagram has density 2. The two triangular regions of a cross-quadrilateral (like a figure 8) have opposite-signed densities, and adding their areas together can give a total area of zero for the whole figure.

- Considering the enclosed regions as point sets, we can find the area of the enclosed point set. This corresponds to the area of the plane covered by the polygon, or to the area of one or more simple polygons having the same outline as the self-intersecting one. In the case of the cross-quadrilateral, it is treated as two simple triangles.

Generalizations of Polygons

The idea of a polygon has been generalized in various ways. Some of the more important include:

- A spherical polygon is a circuit of arcs of great circles (sides) and vertices on the surface of a sphere. It allows the digon, a polygon having only two sides and two corners, which is impossible in a flat plane. Spherical polygons play an important role in cartography (map making) and in Wythoff's construction of the uniform polyhedra.

- A skew polygon does not lie in a flat plane, but zigzags in three (or more) dimensions. The Petrie polygons of the regular polytopes are well known examples.

- An apeirogon is an infinite sequence of sides and angles, which is not closed but has no ends because it extends indefinitely in both directions.

- A skew apeirogon is an infinite sequence of sides and angles that do not lie in a flat plane.

- A complex polygon is a configuration analogous to an ordinary polygon, which exists in the complex plane of two real and two imaginary dimensions.

- An abstract polygon is an algebraic partially ordered set representing the various elements (sides, vertices, etc.) and their connectivity. A real geometric polygon is said to be a *realization* of the associated abstract polygon. Depending on the mapping, all the generalizations described here can be realized.

- A polyhedron is a three-dimensional solid bounded by flat polygonal faces, analogous to a polygon in two dimensions. The corresponding shapes in four or higher dimensions are called polytopes.

Naming Polygons

The word "polygon" comes from Late Latin *polygōnum* (a noun), from Greek (*polygōnon/ polugōnon*), noun use of neuter of (*polygōnos/polugōnos*, the masculine adjective), meaning "many-angled". Individual polygons are named (and sometimes classified) according to the number of sides, combining a Greek-derived numerical prefix with the suffix *-gon*, e.g. *pentagon*, *dodecagon*. The triangle, quadrilateral and nonagon are exceptions.

Beyond decagons (10-sided) and dodecagons (12-sided), mathematicians generally use numerical notation, for example 17-gon and 257-gon.

Exceptions exist for side counts that are more easily expressed in verbal form (e.g. 20 and 30), or are used by non-mathematicians. Some special polygons also have their own names; for example the regular star pentagon is also known as the pentagram.

Polygon names and miscellaneous properties		
Name	**Edges**	**Properties**
monogon	1	Not generally recognised as a polygon, although some disciplines such as graph theory sometimes use the term.
digon	2	Not generally recognised as a polygon in the Euclidean plane, although it can exist as a spherical polygon.
triangle (or trigon)	3	The simplest polygon which can exist in the Euclidean plane. Can tile the plane.
quadrilateral (or tetragon)	4	The simplest polygon which can cross itself; the simplest polygon which can be concave; the simplest polygon which can be non-cyclic. Can tile the plane.
pentagon	5	The simplest polygon which can exist as a regular star. A star pentagon is known as a pentagram or pentacle.
hexagon	6	Can tile the plane.
heptagon (or septagon)	7	The simplest polygon such that the regular form is not constructible with compass and straightedge. However, it can be constructed using a Neusis construction.
octagon	8	
nonagon (or enneagon)	9	"Nonagon" mixes Latin [*novem* = 9] with Greek, "enneagon" is pure Greek.
decagon	10	
hendecagon (or undecagon)	11	The simplest polygon such that the regular form cannot be constructed with compass, straightedge, and angle trisector.
dodecagon (or duodecagon)	12	
tridecagon (or triskaidecagon)	13	
tetradecagon (or tetrakaidecagon)	14	
pentadecagon (or pentakaidecagon)	15	
hexadecagon (or hexakaidecagon)	16	
heptadecagon (or heptakaidecagon)	17	Constructible polygon
octadecagon (or octakaidecagon)	18	

enneadecagon (or enneakaideca-gon)	19	
icosagon	20	
icositetragon (or icosikaitetragon)	24	
triacontagon	30	
tetracontagon (or tessaracontagon)	40	
pentacontagon (or pentecontagon)	50	
hexacontagon (or hexecontagon)	60	
heptacontagon (or hebdomeconta-gon)	70	
octacontagon (or ogdoëcontagon)	80	
enneacontagon (or enenecontagon)	90	
hectogon (or hecatontagon)	100	
	257	Constructible polygon
chiliagon	1000	Philosophers including René Descartes, Immanuel Kant, David Hume, have used the chiliagon as an example in discussions.
myriagon	10,000	Used as an example in some philosophical discussions, for example in Descartes' *Meditations on First Philosophy*
	65,537	Constructible polygon
megagon	1,000,000	As with René Descartes' example of the chiliagon, the million-sided polygon has been used as an illustration of a well-defined concept that cannot be visualised. The megagon is also used as an illustration of the convergence of regular polygons to a circle.
apeirogon	∞	A degenerate polygon of infinitely many sides.

Constructing Higher Names

To construct the name of a polygon with more than 20 and less than 100 edges, combine the prefixes as follows. The "kai" term applies to 13-gons and higher was used by Kepler, and advocated by John H. Conway for clarity to concatenated prefix numbers in the naming of quasiregular polyhedra.

Tens		*and*	Ones		final suffix
			1	-hena-	
20	icosi- (icosa- when alone)		2	-di-	
30	triaconta- (or triconta-)		3	-tri-	
40	tetraconta- (or tessaraconta-)		4	-tetra-	
50	pentaconta- (or penteconta-)	-kai-	5	-penta-	-gon
60	hexaconta- (or hexeconta-)		6	-hexa-	
70	heptaconta- (or hebdomeconta-)		7	-hepta-	
80	octaconta- (or ogdoëconta-)		8	-octa-	
90	enneaconta- (or eneneconta-)		9	-ennea-	

History

Polygons have been known since ancient times. The regular polygons were known to the ancient Greeks, with the pentagram, a non-convex regular polygon (star polygon), appearing as early as the 7th century B.C. on a krater by Aristonothos, found at Caere and now in the Capitoline Museum.

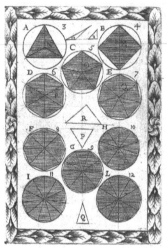

Historical image of polygons (1699)

The first known systematic study of non-convex polygons in general was made by Thomas Bradwardine in the 14th century.

In 1952, Geoffrey Colin Shephard generalized the idea of polygons to the complex plane, where each real dimension is accompanied by an imaginary one, to create complex polygons.

Polygons in Nature

The Giant's Causeway, in Northern Ireland

Polygons appear in rock formations, most commonly as the flat facets of crystals, where the angles between the sides depend on the type of mineral from which the crystal is made.

Regular hexagons can occur when the cooling of lava forms areas of tightly packed columns of basalt, which may be seen at the Giant's Causeway in Northern Ireland, or at the Devil's Postpile in California.

In biology, the surface of the wax honeycomb made by bees is an array of hexagons, and the sides and base of each cell are also polygons.

Polygons in Computer Graphics

In computer graphics, a polygon is a primitive used in modelling and rendering. They are defined in a database, containing arrays of vertices (the coordinates of the geometrical vertices, as well as other attributes of the polygon, such as color, shading and texture), connectivity information, and materials.

Naming conventions differ from those of mathematicians:

- A simple polygon is convex, planar, more easily handled by algorithms and hardware.

- a concave polygon is a simple polygon having at least one interior angle greater than 180°.

- A complex polygon may have arbitrary topology including holes, requiring more advanced algorithms (often systems will tesselate these into simple polygons).

Any surface is modelled as a tessellation called polygon mesh. If a square mesh has $n + 1$ points (vertices) per side, there are n squared squares in the mesh, or $2n$ squared triangles since there are two triangles in a square. There are $(n + 1)^2 / 2(n^2)$ vertices per triangle. Where n is large, this approaches one half. Or, each vertex inside the square mesh connects four edges (lines).

The imaging system calls up the structure of polygons needed for the scene to be created from the database. This is transferred to active memory and finally, to the display system (screen, TV monitors etc.) so that the scene can be viewed. During this process, the imaging system renders polygons in correct perspective ready for transmission of the processed data to the display system. Although polygons are two-dimensional, through the system computer they are placed in a visual scene in the correct three-dimensional orientation.

In computer graphics and computational geometry, it is often necessary to determine whether a given point $P = (x_o, y_o)$ lies inside a simple polygon given by a sequence of line segments. This is called the Point in polygon test.

Vector Graphics Editor

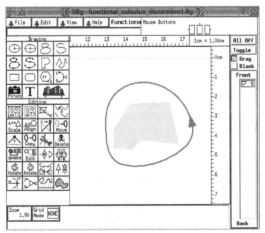

A screenshot of the xfig vector graphics editor

A vector graphics editor is a computer program that allows users to compose and edit vector graphics images interactively on a computer and save them in one of many popular vector graphics formats, such as EPS, PDF, WMF, SVG, or VML.

Vector Editors versus Bitmap Editors

Vector editors are often contrasted with bitmap editors, and their capabilities complement each other. Vector editors are often better for page layout, typography, logos, sharp-edged artistic illustrations (e.g. cartoons, clip art, complex geometric patterns), technical illustrations, diagramming and flowcharting. Bitmap editors are more suitable for retouching, photo processing, photorealistic illustrations, collage, and illustrations drawn by hand with a pen tablet. Recent versions of bitmap editors such as GIMP and Adobe Photoshop support vector tools (e.g. editable paths), and vector editors such as Adobe Fireworks, Adobe FreeHand, Adobe Illustrator, Affinity Designer, Animatron, Artboard, Autodesk Graphic (formerly iDraw), CorelDRAW, Sketch, Inkscape, sK1 or Xara Photo & Graphic Designer have adopted raster effects that were once limited to bitmap editors (e.g. blurring).

Specialized Features

Some vector editors support animation, while others (e.g. Adobe Flash, Animatron or Synfig Studio) are specifically geared towards producing animated graphics. Generally, vector graphics are more suitable for animation, though there are raster-based animation tools as well.

Vector editors are closely related to desktop publishing software such as Adobe InDesign or Scribus, which also usually include some vector drawing tools (usually less powerful than those in standalone vector editors). Modern vector editors are capable of, and often preferable for, designing unique documents (like flyers or brochures) of up to a few pages; it's only for longer or more standardized documents that the page layout programs are more suitable.

Special vector editors are used for computer-assisted drafting. These are not suitable for artistic or decorative graphics, but are rich in tools and object libraries used to ensure precision and standards compliance of drawings and blueprints.

Finally, 3D computer graphics software such as Maya, Blender or 3D Studio Max can also be thought of as an extension of the traditional 2D vector editors, as they share some common concepts and tools.

Image Tracing

In computer graphics, image tracing, raster-to-vector conversion or vectorization is the conversion of raster graphics into vector graphics.

Background

An image does not have any structure: it is just a collection of marks on paper, grains in film, or pixels in a bitmap. While such an image is useful, it has some limits. If the image is magnified enough, its artifacts appear. The halftone dots, film grains and pixels become apparent. Images of sharp edges become fuzzy or jagged.

Ideally, a vector image does not have the same problem. Edges are represented as a mathematical lines or curves, and they can be magnified thousands of times — until the precision of the numbers becomes an issue.

This image illustrates the difference between bitmap and vector images. The bitmap image is composed of a fixed set of pixels, while the vector image is composed of a fixed set of shapes. In the picture, scaling the bitmap reveals the pixels while scaling the vector image preserves the shapes.

The task in vectorization is to convert a two-dimensional image into a two-dimensional vector representation of the image. It is not examining the image and attempting to recognize or extract a three-dimensional model which may be depicted; i.e. it is not a vision system. For most applications, vectorization also does not involve optical character recognition; characters are treated as lines, curves, or filled objects without attaching any significance to them. In vectorization the shape of the character is preserved, so artistic embellishments remain.

Synthetic images such as maps, cartoons, logos, clip art, and technical drawings are suitable for vectorization. Those images could have been originally made as vector images because they are based on geometric shapes or drawn with simple curves.

Continuous tone photographs (such as live portraits) are not good candidates for vectorization.

The input to vectorization is an image, but an image may come in many forms such as a photograph, a drawing on paper, or one of several raster file formats. Programs that do raster-to-vector conversion may accept bitmap formats such as TIFF, BMP and PNG.

The output is a vector file format. Common vector formats are SVG, DXF, EPS, EMF and AI.

Vectorization can be used to update images or recover work. Personal computers often come with a simple paint program that produces a bitmap output file. These programs allow users to make simple illustrations by adding text, drawing outlines, and filling outline with a specific color. Only the results of these operations (the pixels) are saved in the resulting bitmap; the drawing and filling operations are discarded. Vectorization can be used to recapture some of the information that was lost.

Vectorization is also used to recover information that was originally in a vector format but has been lost or has become unavailable. A company may have commissioned a logo from a graphic arts firm. Although the graphics firm used a vector format, the client company may not have received a copy of that format. The company may then acquire a vector format by scanning and vectorizing a paper copy of the logo.

Process

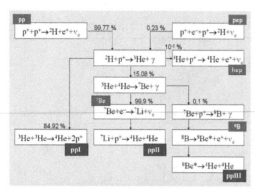
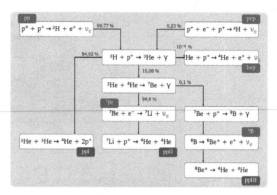

Original PNG file (37 kB)   Hand converted to SVG (9 kB)

Vectorization starts with an image.

Manual

The image can be vectorized manually. A person could look at the image, make some measurements, and then write the output file by hand. That was the case for the vectorization of a technical illustration about neutrinos. The illustration has a few geometric shapes and a lot of text; it was relatively easy to convert the shapes, and the SVG vector format allows the text (even subscripts and superscripts) to be entered easily.

The original image did not have any curves (except for the text), so the conversion is straightforward. Curves make the conversion more complicated. Manual vectorization of complicated shapes can be facilitated by the tracing function built into some vector graphics editing programs.

If the image is not yet in machine readable form, then has to be scanned into a usable file format.

Once there is a machine-readable bitmap, the image can be imported into a graphics editing program (such as Adobe Illustrator, CorelDRAW, or Inkscape). Then a person can manually trace the elements of the image using the program's editing features. Curves in the original image can be approximated with lines, arcs, and Bézier curves. An illustration program allows spline knots to be adjusted for a close fit. Manual vectorization is possible, but it can be tedious.

Although graphics drawing programs have been around for a long time, artists may find the freehand drawing facilities are awkward even when a drawing tablet is used. Instead of using a program, Pepper (2005) recommends making an initial sketch on paper. Instead of scanning the sketch and tracing it freehand in the computer, Pepper states: "Those proficient with a graphic tablet and stylus could make the following changes directly in CorelDRAW by using a scan of the sketch as an underlay and drawing over it. I prefer to use pen and ink, and a light table"; most of the final image was traced by hand in ink. Later the line-drawing image was scanned at 600 dpi, cleaned up in a paint program, and then automatically traced with a program. Once the black and white image was in the graphics program, some other elements were added and the figure was colored.

Similarly, Ploch (2005) recreated a design from a digital photograph. The JPEG was imported and some "basic shapes" were traced by hand and colored in the graphics drawing program; more complex shapes were handled differently. Ploch used a bitmap editor to remove the background and crop the more complex image components. He then printed the image and traced it by hand onto tracing paper to get a clean black and white line drawing. That drawing was scanned and then vectorized with a program.

Automatic

There are programs that automate the vectorization process. Example programs are Adobe Streamline (discontinued), Corel's PowerTRACE, and Potrace. Some of these programs have a command line interface while others are interactive that allow the user to adjust the conversion settings and view the result. Adobe Streamline is not only an interactive program, but it also allows a user to manually edit the input bitmap and the output curves. Corel's PowerTRACE is accessed through CorelDRAW; CorelDRAW can be used to modify the input bitmap and edit the output curves. Adobe Illustrator has a facility to trace individual curves.

Automated programs can have mixed results. A program (PowerTRACE) was used to convert a PNG map to SVG. The program did a good job on the map boundaries (the most tedious task in the tracing) and the settings dropped out all the text (small objects). The text was manually re-inserted.

Map in PNG format (13 kB)

Map after automated conversion and touch up to re-add the labels and adjust colors. (18 kB)

Other conversions may not go as well. The results depend on having high-quality scans, reasonable settings, and good algorithms.

Scanned images often have a lot of noise. The bitmap image may need a lot of work to clean it up. Erase stray marks and fill in lines and areas.

Corel advice: Put image on a light table, cover with vellum (tracing paper), and then manually ink the desired outlines. Then scan the vellum and use automated raster-to-vector conversion program on that scan.

Options

There are many different image styles and possibilities, and no single vectorization method works well on all images. Consequently, vectorization programs have many options that influence the result.

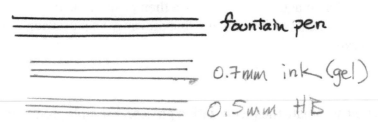

Although these lines may look solid, they are far from perfect. The lines were drawn on vellum with a fountain pen, a 0.7 mm gel pen, and a 0.5 mm HB pencil. The images was scanned at 600 pixels per inch with 24-bit RGB. The line widths end up being 10 to 14 pixels wide. The ink colors are not uniform and have specular reflections that put light pixels within the lines. The pencil lines also have interior defects due to the roughness (tooth) of the paper. The scan also has some unsharp masking artifacts.

One issue is what the predominant shapes are. If the image is of a fill-in form, then it will probably have just vertical and horizontal lines of a constant width. The program's vectorization should take that into account. On the other hand, a CAD drawing may have lines at any angle, there may be curved lines, and there may be several line weights (thick for objects and thin for dimension lines). Instead of (or in addition to) curves, the image may contain outlines filled with the same color. Adobe Streamline allows users to select a combination of line recognition (horizontal and vertical lines), centerline recognition, or outline recognition. Streamline also allows outline shapes that are small to be thrown out; the notion is such small shapes are noise. The user may set the noise level between 0 and 1000; an outline that has fewer pixels than that setting is discarded.

Another issue is the number of colors in the image. Even images that were created as black on white drawings may end up with many shades of gray. Some line-drawing routines employ anti-aliasing; a pixel completely covered by the line will be black, but a pixel that is only partially covered will be gray. If the original image is on paper and is scanned, there is a similar result: edge pixels will be gray. Sometimes images are compressed (e.g., JPEG images), and the compression will introduce gray levels.

Many of the vectorization programs will group same-color pixels into lines, curves, or outlined shapes. If each possible color is grouped into its own object, there can be an enormous number of objects. Instead, the user is asked to select a finite number of colors (usually less than 256), the image is reduced to using that many colors (this step is color quantization), and then the vectorization is done on the reduced image. For continuous tone images such as photographs, the result of color quantization is posterization. Gradient fills will also be posterized.

Reducing the number of colors in an image is often aided with a histogram. The most common colors may be selected as the representatives, and other colors are mapped to their closest representative. When the number of colors is set to two, the user may be asked to make threshold and contrast setting. A contrast setting looks for significant changes in pixel color rather than a particular color; consequently, it may ignore the gradual color variations in a gradient fill. Once the outline has been extracted, the user could manually reintroduce the gradient fill.

The vectorization program will want to group a region of the same color into a single object. It can clearly do that by making the region boundary exactly follow the pixel boundaries, but the result will be a boundary of often short orthogonal lines. The resulting conversion will also have the same pixelation problems that a bitmap has when it is magnified. Instead, the vectorization program needs to approximate the region boundary with lines and curves that closely follow the pixel boundaries but are not exactly the pixel boundaries. A tolerance parameter tells the program how closely it should follow the pixel boundaries.

The end result of many vectorization programs are curves consisting of cubic Bézier curves. A region boundary is approximated with several curve segments. To keep a curve smooth, the joints of two curves is constrained so the tangents match. One problem is determining where a curve bends so sharply that it should not be smooth. The smooth portions of a curve are then approximated with a Bézier curve fitting procedure. Successive division may be used. Such a fitting procedure tries to fit the curve with a single cubic curve; if the fit is acceptable, then the procedure stops. Otherwise, it selects some advantageous point along the curve and breaks the curve into two parts. It then fits the parts while keeping the joint tangent. If the fit is still unacceptable, then it breaks the curve into more parts.

Some vectorizers are standalone programs, but many have interactive interfaces that allow a user to adjust the program parameters and quickly see the result. PowerTRACE, for example, can display the original image and preview the converted image so the user may compare them; the program also reports information such as the number of curves.

Example

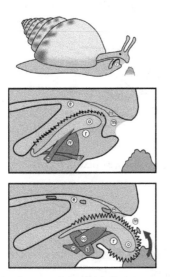

Original artwork in PNG format; 115 kB.

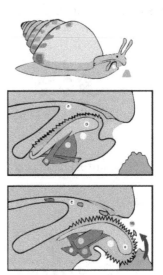

Traced with PowerTRACE using detailed logo, smoothing 40, detail +2.5; result: 50 colors, 94 curves, 2452 nodes, 96 kB.

On the right is an illustration showing the operation of the radula in mollusks. The upper portion is mostly a one-pen-width filled outline diagram, but it has a mesh gradient fill along the bottom of the shell and along the bottom of food. It also has some artistic brushes on the upper left of the shell. The bottom portion of the illustration has four line weights and some small characters; the color fill is simple except for a gradient at the jagged lines.

The 531×879 pixel image was traced; 50 colors were used. Most (if not all) lines were lost; they were turned into black regions, and their effective line widths vary. The black outline around the blue food in upper part disappeared. The gradient fills and brushed spots were lost to color quantization/posterization; some brush spots disappeared. Some letters survived the vectorization with distortion, but most letters were discarded. Losing the letters is not a big issue; post conversion editing would want to delete the annotation and replace it with text rather than curves. Thin lines crossing at a shallow angle made filled regions, and intersecting outlines of filled region became confused; see lower right corner. The tracing also has some odd features. Many black outlines touch, so they become a large, complicated, object rather than just outlines for specific regions. Instead of just background, a rectangular white region separates the two outlined rectangles. The objects labeled *op*, *rp*, and *rr* are not simple layered shapes; the desired result would have *rr* overlaid by *rp* which is overlaid by *op*.

Usage Domains

- In computer-aided design (CAD) drawings (blueprints etc.) are scanned, vectorized and written as CAD files in a process called *paper-to-CAD conversion* or *drawing conversion*.

- In geographic information systems (GIS) satellite or aerial images are vectorized to create maps.

- In graphic design and photography, graphics can be vectorized for easier usage and resizing.

- Vectorization is often the first step in OCR solutions for handwritten text or signatures.

Vectorization is effective on single colored, non gradient input data, like signatures.

Signature of Christopher Columbus as JPEG image (1,308 × 481 pixel), 63 kB

Vectorized two-color (black & white) variant of the signature of Christopher Columbus, 19 kB

Continuous Tone Images

Vectorization is usually inappropriate for continuous tone images such as portraits. The result is often poor. For example, many different image tracing algorithms were applied to a 25 kB JPEG image. The resulting vector images are at least a factor of ten larger and may have pronounced posterization effects when a small number of colors are used.

| A photograph in JPEG format, 25 KB | The photograph at left vectorized with *RaveGrid*, 1.64 MB | Same photograph vectorized with AutoTrace in the Delineate GUI, 677 KB | Same photograph vectorized with Inkscape's "Trace Bitmap" function, based on potrace, 1.05 MB |

Scalable Vector Graphics

Scalable Vector Graphics (SVG) is an XML-based vector image format for two-dimensional graphics with support for interactivity and animation. The SVG specification is an open standard developed by the World Wide Web Consortium (W3C) since 1999.

SVG images and their behaviors are defined in XML text files. This means that they can be searched, indexed, scripted, and compressed. As XML files, SVG images can be created and edited with any text editor, as well as with drawing software.

All major modern web browsers—including Mozilla Firefox, Internet Explorer, Google Chrome, Opera, Safari, and Microsoft Edge—have SVG rendering support.

Overview

SVG has been in development within the World Wide Web Consortium (W3C) since 1999, after six competing proposals for vector graphics languages had been submitted to the consortium during 1998. The early SVG Working Group decided not to develop any of the commercial submissions, but to create a new markup language that was informed by but not really based on any of them.

SVG allows three types of graphic objects: vector graphic shapes such as paths and outlines consisting of straight lines and curves, bitmap images, and text. Graphical objects can be grouped, styled, transformed and composited into previously rendered objects. The feature set includes nested transformations, clipping paths, alpha masks, filter effects and template objects. SVG drawings can be interactive and can include animation, defined in the SVG XML elements or via scripting that accesses the SVG Document Object Model (DOM). SVG uses CSS for styling and JavaScript for scripting. Text, including internationalization and localization, appearing in plain text within the SVG DOM enhances the accessibility of SVG graphics.

The SVG specification was updated to version 1.1 in 2011. There are two 'Mobile SVG Profiles,' SVG Tiny and SVG Basic, meant for mobile devices with reduced computational and display capabilities. Scalable Vector Graphics 2 became a W3C Candidate Recommendation on 15 September 2016. SVG 2 incorporates several new features in addition to those of SVG 1.1 and SVG Tiny 1.2.

Printing

Though the SVG Specification primarily focuses on vector graphics markup language, its design includes the basic capabilities of a page description language like Adobe's PDF. It contains provisions for rich graphics, and is compatible with CSS for styling purposes. SVG has the information needed to place each glyph and image in a chosen location on a printed page.

Scripting and Animation

SVG drawings can be dynamic and interactive. Time-based modifications to the elements can be described in SMIL, or can be programmed in a scripting language (e.g. ECMAScript or JavaScript). The W3C explicitly recommends SMIL as the standard for animation in SVG.

A rich set of event handlers such as *onmouseover* and *onclick* can be assigned to any SVG graphical object.

Compression

SVG images, being XML, contain many repeated fragments of text, so they are well suited for lossless data compression algorithms. When an SVG image has been compressed with the industry standard gzip algorithm, it is referred to as an "SVGZ" image and uses the corresponding .svgz filename extension. Conforming SVG 1.1 viewers will display compressed images. An SVGZ file is typically 20 to 50 percent of the original size. W3C provides SVGZ files to test for conformance.

Development History

SVG was developed by the W3C SVG Working Group starting in 1998, after six competing vector graphics submissions were received that year:

- Web Schematics, from CCLRC

- PGML, from Adobe, IBM, Netscape, and Sun

- VML, by Autodesk, Hewlett-Packard, Macromedia, and Microsoft

- Hyper Graphics Markup Language, by Orange, PCSL, and PRP

- WebCGM, from Boeing, CCLRC, Inso, JISC, and Xerox

- DrawML, from Excosoft

The working group was chaired at the time by Chris Lilley of the W3C.

Version 1.x

- SVG 1.0 became a W3C Recommendation on 4 September 2001.

- SVG 1.1 became a W3C Recommendation on 14 January 2003. The SVG 1.1 specification is modularized in order to allow subsets to be defined as profiles. Apart from this, there is very little difference between SVG 1.1 and SVG 1.0.

    o SVG Tiny and SVG Basic (the Mobile SVG Profiles) became W3C Recommendations on 14 January 2003. These are described as profiles of SVG 1.1.

- SVG Tiny 1.2 became a W3C Recommendation on 22 December 2008. It was initially drafted as a profile of the planned SVG Full 1.2 (which has since been dropped in favor of SVG 2), but was later refactored as a standalone specification.

- SVG 1.1 Second Edition, which includes all the errata and clarifications, but no new features to the original SVG 1.1 was released on 16 August 2011.

Version 2.x

- SVG 2 will completely rework draft 1.2, with more integration with new web features such as CSS, HTML5, and WOFF.

Mobile Profiles

Because of industry demand, two mobile profiles were introduced with SVG 1.1: *SVG Tiny* (SVGT) and *SVG Basic* (SVGB).

These are subsets of the full SVG standard, mainly intended for user agents with limited capabilities. In particular, SVG Tiny was defined for highly restricted mobile devices such as cellphones; it does not support styling or scripting. SVG Basic was defined for higher-level mobile devices, such as smartphones.

In 2003, the 3GPP, an international telecommunications standards group, adopted SVG Tiny as the mandatory vector graphics media format for next-generation phones. SVGT is the required vector graphics format and support of SVGB is optional for Multimedia Messaging Service (MMS) and Packet-switched Streaming Service. It was later added as required format for vector graphics in 3GPP IP Multimedia Subsystem (IMS).

Differences from Non-mobile SVG

Neither mobile profile includes support for the full Document Object Model (DOM), while only SVG Basic has optional support for scripting, but because they are fully compatible subsets of the full standard, most SVG graphics can still be rendered by devices which only support the mobile profiles.

SVGT 1.2 adds a microDOM (μDOM), styling and scripting.

Related Work

The MPEG-4 Part 20 standard - *Lightweight Application Scene Representation (LASeR) and*

Simple Aggregation Format (SAF) is based on SVG Tiny. It was developed by MPEG (ISO/IEC JTC1/SC29/WG11) and published as ISO/IEC 14496-20:2006. SVG capabilities are enhanced in MPEG-4 Part 20 with key features for mobile services, such as dynamic updates, binary encoding, state-of-art font representation. SVG was also accommodated in MPEG-4 Part 11, in the Extensible MPEG-4 Textual (XMT) format - a textual representation of the MPEG-4 multimedia content using XML.

Functionality

The SVG 1.1 specification defines 14 functional areas or feature sets:

Paths

> Simple or compound shape outlines are drawn with curved or straight lines that can be filled in, outlined, or used as a clipping path. Paths have a compact coding.

> For example, M (for "move to") precedes initial numeric x and y coordinates, and L (for "line to") precedes a point to which a line should be drawn. Further command letters (C, S, Q, T, and A) precede data that is used to draw various Bézier and elliptical curves. Z is used to close a path.

> In all cases, absolute coordinates follow capital letter commands and relative coordinates are used after the equivalent lower-case letters.

Basic shapes

> Straight-line paths and paths made up of a series of connected straight-line segments (polylines), as well as closed polygons, circles, and ellipses can be drawn. Rectangles and round-cornered rectangles are also standard elements.

Text

> Unicode character text included in an SVG file is expressed as XML character data. Many visual effects are possible, and the SVG specification automatically handles bidirectional text (for composing a combination of English and Arabic text, for example), vertical text (as Chinese was historically written) and characters along a curved path (such as the text around the edge of the Great Seal of the United States).

Painting

> SVG shapes can be filled and/or outlined (painted with a color, a gradient, or a pattern). Fills may be opaque, or have any degree of transparency.

> "Markers" are line-end features, such as arrowheads, or symbols that can appear at the vertices of a polygon.

Color

> Colors can be applied to all visible SVG elements, either directly or via `fill`, `stroke`, and other properties. Colors are specified in the same way as in CSS2, i.e. using names like `black`

or `blue`, in hexadecimal such as `#2f0` or `#22ff00`, in decimal like `rgb(255,255,127)`, or as percentages of the form `rgb(100%,100%,50%)`.

Gradients and patterns

SVG shapes can be filled or outlined with solid colors as above, or with color gradients or with repeating patterns. Color gradients can be linear or radial (circular), and can involve any number of colors as well as repeats. Opacity gradients can also be specified. Patterns are based on predefined raster or vector graphic objects, which can be repeated in x and/or y directions. Gradients and patterns can be animated and scripted.

Since 2008, there has been discussion among professional users of SVG that either gradient meshes or preferably diffusion curves could usefully be added to the SVG specification. It is said that a "simple representation [using diffusion curves] is capable of representing even very subtle shading effects" and that "Diffusion curve images are comparable both in quality and coding efficiency with gradient meshes, but are simpler to create (according to several artists who have used both tools), and can be captured from bitmaps fully automatically." The current draft of SVG 2 includes gradient meshes.

Clipping, masking and compositing

Graphic elements, including text, paths, basic shapes and combinations of these, can be used as outlines to define both *inside* and *outside* regions that can be painted (with colors, gradients and patterns) independently. Fully opaque *clipping paths* and semi-transparent *masks* are *composited* together to calculate the color and opacity of every pixel of the final image, using alpha blending.

Interactivity

SVG images can interact with users in many ways. In addition to hyperlinks as mentioned below, any part of an SVG image can be made receptive to user interface events such as changes in focus, mouse clicks, scrolling or zooming the image and other pointer, keyboard and document events. Event handlers may start, stop or alter animations as well as trigger scripts in response to such events.

Linking

SVG images can contain hyperlinks to other documents, using XLink. Through the use of the `<view>` element or a fragment identifier, URLs can link to SVG files that change the visible area of the document. This allows for creating specific view states that are used to zoom in/out of a specific area or to limit the view to a specific element. This is helpful when creating sprites. XLink support in combination with the `<use>` element also allow linking to and re-using internal and external elements. This allows to do more with less markup and makes for cleaner code.

Scripting

All aspects of an SVG document can be accessed and manipulated using scripts in a similar way to HTML. The default scripting language is ECMAScript (closely related to JavaScript) and there are defined Document Object Model (DOM) objects for every SVG element and attribute. Scripts are enclosed in <script> elements. They can run in response to pointer events, keyboard events and document events as required.

Animation

SVG content can be animated using the built-in animation elements such as <animate>, <animateMotion> and <animateColor>. Content can be animated by manipulating the DOM using ECMAScript and the scripting language's built-in timers. SVG animation has been designed to be compatible with current and future versions of Synchronized Multimedia Integration Language (SMIL). Animations can be continuous, they can loop and repeat, and they can respond to user events, as mentioned above.

Fonts

As with HTML and CSS, text in SVG may reference external font files, such as system fonts. If the required font files do not exist on the machine where the SVG file is rendered, the text may not appear as intended. To overcome this limitation, text can be displayed in an *SVG font*, where the required glyphs are defined in SVG as a font that is then referenced from the <text> element.

Metadata

In accord with the W3C's Semantic Web initiative, SVG allows authors to provide metadata about SVG content. The main facility is the <metadata> element, where the document can be described using Dublin Core metadata properties (e.g. title, creator/ author, subject, description, etc.). Other metadata schemas may also be used. In addition, SVG defines <title> and <desc> elements where authors may also provide plain-text descriptive material within an SVG image to help indexing, searching and retrieval by a number of means.

An SVG document can define components including shapes, gradients etc., and use them repeatedly. SVG images can also contain raster graphics, such as PNG and JPEG images, and further SVG images.

Example

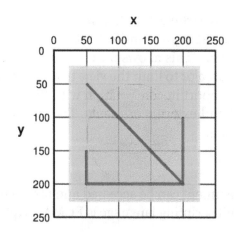

This code will produce the shapes shown in the image (excluding the grid):

```
<?xml version="1.0" encoding="UTF-8" ?>

<svg xmlns="http://www.w3.org/2000/svg" version="1.1">

   <rect  x="25"  y="25"  width="200"  height="200"  fill="lime"  stroke-width="4"
stroke="pink" />

  <circle cx="125" cy="125" r="75" fill="orange" />

  <polyline points="50,150 50,200 200,200 200,100" stroke="red" stroke-width="4"
fill="none" />

  <line x1="50" y1="50" x2="200" y2="200" stroke="blue" stroke-width="4" />

</svg>
```

SVG on the Web

The use of SVG on the web was limited by the lack of support in older versions of Internet Explorer (IE). Many web sites that serve SVG images, such as Wikipedia, also provide the images in a raster format, either automatically by HTTP content negotiation or by allowing the user directly to choose the file.

SVG exported from KOMPAS-Graphic

Google announced on 31 August 2010 that it had started to index SVG content on the web, whether it is in standalone files or embedded in HTML, and that users would begin to see such content listed among their search results. It was announced on 8 December 2010 that Google Image Search would also begin indexing SVG files. On 28 January 2011, it was discovered that Google was allowing Image Search results to be restricted exclusively to SVG files. This feature was announced officially on 11 February 2011.

Native Browser Support

Konqueror was the first browser to support SVG in release version 3.2 in February 2004. As of 2011, all major desktop browsers, and many minor ones, have some level of SVG support. Other browsers' implementations are not yet complete.

Some earlier versions of Firefox (e.g. versions between 1.5 and 3.6), as well as a smattering of other now-outdated web browsers capable of displaying SVG graphics, needed them embedded in <object> or <iframe> elements to display them integrated as parts of an HTML webpage instead of using the standard way of integrating images with `<img>`. However, SVG images may be included in XHTML pages using XML namespaces.

Tim Berners-Lee, the inventor of the World Wide Web, has been critical of (earlier versions of) Internet Explorer for its failure to support SVG.

- Opera (since 8.0) has support for the SVG 1.1 Tiny specification while Opera 9 includes SVG 1.1 Basic support and some of SVG 1.1 Full. Opera 9.5 has partial SVG Tiny 1.2 support. It also supports SVGZ (compressed SVG).

- Browsers based on the Gecko layout engine (such as Firefox, Flock, Camino, and SeaMonkey) all have had incomplete support for the SVG 1.1 Full specification since 2005. The Mozilla site has an overview of the modules which are supported in Firefox and of the modules which are in progress in the development. Gecko 1.9, included in Firefox 3.0, adds support for more of the SVG specification (including filters).

- Pale Moon, which uses the Goanna layout engine (a fork of the Gecko engine), supports SVG.

- Browsers based on WebKit (such as Apple's Safari, Google Chrome, and The Omni Group's OmniWeb) have had incomplete support for the SVG 1.1 Full specification since 2006.

- Amaya has partial SVG support.

- Internet Explorer 8 and older versions do not support SVG. IE9 (released 14 March 2011) supports the basic SVG feature set. IE10 extended SVG support by adding SVG 1.1 filters.

- Microsoft Edge supports much of SVG 1.1.

- The Maxthon Cloud Browser also supports SVG.

There are several advantages to native and full support: plugins are not needed, SVG can be freely mixed with other content in a single document, and rendering and scripting become considerably more reliable.

Plug-in Browser Support

Internet Explorer, up to and including IE8, was the only major browser not to provide native SVG support. IE8 and older require a plug-in to render SVG content. There are a number of plug-ins available to assist, including:

- Ample SDK Open-Source JavaScript GUI Framework provides partial support for SVG 1.1, SMIL, DOM and style scripting in Internet Explorer (5.5 - 8.0) too. It is not dependent on any plugins and relies on presence of alternative Vector Graphics format VML in Internet Explorer.

- Batik, a widely deployed Java plugin

- Google Chrome Frame from Google can support all web elements supported by WebKit, including SVG 1.0 and partially SVG 1.1. (*discontinued*)

- GPAC, targets SVGT 1.2

- Adobe SVG Viewer from Adobe Systems plugin supports most of SVG 1.0/1.1. (*discontinued*)

- Corel SVG Viewer (*discontinued*)

- Raphaël is another JavaScript library that takes advantage of the intersection between VML's and SVG's features to create vector graphics and animate them.

- Renesis Player for Internet Explorer from examotion GmbH, supports SVG 1.1 on IE 6 and 7 (*discontinued*)

- SVG Web is a JavaScript library for Web developers, targeted at Internet Explorer and dependent on the presence of an installed Adobe Flash plugin on the client machine. SVG Web provides partial support for SVG 1.1, SVG Animation (SMIL), Fonts, Video and Audio, DOM and style scripting.

On 5 January 2010, a senior manager of the Internet Explorer team at Microsoft announced on his official blog that Microsoft had just requested to join the SVG Working Group of the W3C in order to "take part in ensuring future versions of the SVG spec will meet the needs of developers and end users," although no plans for SVG support in Internet Explorer were mentioned at that time. Internet Explorer 9 beta supported a basic SVG feature set based on the SVG 1.1 W3C recommendation. Functionality has been implemented for most of the SVG document structure, interactivity through scripting and styling inline and through CSS. The presentation elements, attributes and DOM interfaces that have been implemented include basic shapes, colors, filling, gradients, patterns, paths and text.

Mobile Support

SVG Tiny (SVGT) 1.1 and 1.2 are mobile profiles for SVG. SVGT 1.2 includes some features not found in SVG 1.1, including non-scaling strokes, which are supported by some SVG 1.1 implementations, such as Opera, Firefox and WebKit. As shared code bases between desktop and mobile browsers increased, the use of SVG 1.1 over SVGT 1.2 also increased.

Support for SVG may be limited to SVGT on older or more limited smart phones, or may be primarily limited by their respective operating system. Adobe Flash Lite has optionally supported SVG Tiny since version 1.1. At the SVG Open 2005 conference, Sun demonstrated a mobile implementation of SVG Tiny 1.1 for the Connected Limited Device Configuration (CLDC) platform.

Mobiles that use Opera Mobile, as well as the iPhone's built in browser, also include SVG support. However, even though it used the WebKit engine, the Android built-in browser did not support SVG prior to v3.0 (Honeycomb). Prior to v3.0, Firefox Mobile 4.0b2 (beta) for Android was the first browser running under Android to support SVG by default.

The level of SVG Tiny support available varies from mobile to mobile, depending on the SVG engine installed. Many newer mobile products support additional features beyond SVG Tiny 1.1, like gradient and opacity; this is sometimes referred as "SVGT 1.1+", though there is no such standard.

Rim's BlackBerry has built-in support for SVG Tiny 1.1 since version 5.0. Support continues for WebKit-based BlackBerry Torch browser in OS 6 and 7.

Nokia's S60 platform has built-in support for SVG. For example, icons are generally rendered using the platform's SVG engine. Nokia has also led the JSR 226: Scalable 2D Vector Graphics API expert group that defines Java ME API for SVG presentation and manipulation. This API has been implemented in S60 Platform 3rd Edition Feature Pack 1 and onward. Some Series 40 phones also support SVG (such as Nokia 6280).

Most Sony Ericsson phones beginning with K700 (by release date) support SVG Tiny 1.1. Phones beginning with K750 also support such features as opacity and gradients. Phones with Sony Ericsson Java Platform-8 have support for JSR 226.

Windows Phone has supported SVG since version 7.5

SVG is also supported on various mobile devices from Motorola, Samsung, LG, and Siemens mobile/BenQ-Siemens. eSVG, an SVG rendering library mainly written for embedded devices, is available on some mobile platforms.

OpenVG is an API designed for hardware-accelerated 2D vector graphics. Its primary platforms are handheld devices, mobile phones, gaming or media consoles, and consumer electronic devices including operating systems with Gallium3D based graphics drivers.

Online SVG Converters

This is an incomplete list of web applications that can convert SVG files to raster image formats (this process is known as rasterization), or raster images to SVG (this process is known as image tracing or vectorization) - without the need of installing a desktop software or browser plug-in.

- Autotracer.org. Online raster image vectorizer using the AutoTrace library. BMP, GIF, JPEG, or PNG to DXF, EPS, PDF, or SVG. Upload limit: 1MB.

- FileFormat.info - Converts SVG to PNG, JPEG, TIFF. Output resolution can be specified. No batch processing. Upload limit: 5MB.

- Online-Convert - Converts to/from BMP, EPS, GIF, HDR, ICO, JPEG, PNG, SVG, TGA, TIFF, WBMP, WebP. No batch processing. The output (e. g. image size) is customizable; the conversion to SVG is handled by Potrace.

- SVGConv - Converts SVG to JPEG, PNG, GIF, BMP, TGA, TIFF, PDF, PS, EPS. Allows the user to customize the output (like image size, background color) and has batch processing features (converting multiple files in a single step). Upload limit: 10MB

- SVG2Android - Converts SVG to an Android VectorDrawable (introduced in API 21)

- Free Online Converter - Converts most raster images to SVG via tracing. When converting from raster images such as PNG to SVG or JPG to SVG, converter will convert the forms and objects in black-and-white images in vector graphics form. The conversion to SVG is handled by Potrace.

Application Support

SVG images can be produced by the use of a vector graphics editor, such as Inkscape, Adobe Illustrator, Adobe Flash Professional or CorelDRAW, and rendered to common raster image formats such as PNG using the same software. Inkscape uses a (built-in) potrace to import raster image formats.

Software can be programmed to render SVG images by using a library such as librsvg used by GNOME since 2000, or Batik. SVG images can also be rendered to any desired popular image format by using the free software command-line utility ImageMagick (which also uses librsvg under the hood).

Other uses for SVG include embedding for use in word processing (e.g. with LibreOffice) and desktop publishing (e.g. Scribus), plotting graphs (e.g. gnuplot), and importing paths (e.g. for use in GIMP or Blender). Microsoft Office 2016 added support for importing and editing SVG images in January 2017. The Uniform Type Identifier for SVG used by Apple is `public.svg-image` and conforms to `public.image` and `public.xml`.

Raster Graphics

In computer graphics, a raster graphics or bitmap image is a dot matrix data structure, representing a generally rectangular grid of pixels, or points of color, viewable via a monitor, paper, or other display medium. Raster images are stored in image files with varying formats.

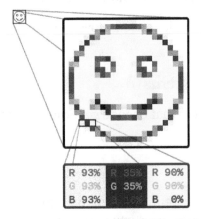

The smiley face in the top left corner is a raster image. When enlarged, individual pixels appear as squares. Zooming in further, they can be analyzed, with their colors constructed by adding the values for red, green and blue.

A bitmap, a single-bit raster, corresponds bit-for-bit with an image displayed on a screen, generally in the same format used for storage in the display's video memory, or maybe as a device-independent bitmap. A raster is technically characterized by the width and height of the image in pixels and by the number of bits per pixel (or color depth, which determines the number of colors it can represent).

The printing and prepress industries know raster graphics as contones (from "continuous tones"). The opposite to contones is "line work", usually implemented as vector graphics in digital systems.

Etymology

The word "raster" has its origins in the Latin *rastrum* (a rake), which is derived from *radere* (to scrape). It originates from the raster scan of cathode ray tube (CRT) video monitors, which paint the image line by line by magnetically steering a focused electron beam. By association, it can also refer to a rectangular grid of pixels. The word rastrum is now used to refer to a device for drawing musical staff lines.

Applications

Computer Displays

Most modern computers have bitmapped displays, where each on-screen pixel directly corresponds to a small number of bits in memory. The screen is refreshed simply by scanning through pixels and coloring them according to each set of bits. The refresh procedure, being speed critical, is often implemented by dedicated circuitry, often as a part of a graphics processing unit. An early scanned display with raster computer graphics was invented in the late 1960s by A. Michael Noll at Bell Labs, but its patent application filed February 5, 1970 was abandoned at the Supreme Court in 1977 over the issue of the patentability of computer software.

Image Storage

Most computer images are stored in raster graphics formats or compressed variations, including GIF, JPEG, and PNG, which are popular on the World Wide Web.

Three-dimensional voxel raster graphics are employed in video games and are also used in medical imaging such as MRI scanners.

Geographic Information Systems

GIS programs commonly use rasters that encode geographic data in the pixel values as well as the pixel locations.

Resolution

Raster graphics are resolution dependent, meaning they cannot scale up to an arbitrary resolution without loss of apparent quality. This property contrasts with the capabilities of vector graphics, which easily scale up to the quality of the device rendering them. Raster graphics deal more practically than vector graphics with photographs and photo-realistic images, while vector graphics often serve better for typesetting or for graphic design. Modern computer-monitors typically display about 72 to 130 pixels per inch (PPI), and some modern consumer printers can resolve 2400 dots per inch (DPI) or more; determining the most appropriate image resolution for a given printer-resolution can pose difficulties, since printed output may have a greater level of detail than a viewer can discern on a monitor. Typically, a resolution of 150 to 300 PPI works well for 4-color process (CMYK) printing.

However, for printing technologies that perform color mixing through dithering (halftone) rather than through overprinting (virtually all home/office inkjet and laser printers), printer DPI and image PPI have a very different meaning, and this can be misleading. Because, through the dithering process, the printer builds a single image pixel out of several printer dots to increase color depth, the printer's DPI setting must be set far higher than the desired PPI to ensure sufficient color depth without sacrificing image resolution. Thus, for instance, printing an image at 250 PPI may actually require a printer setting of 1200 DPI.

Raster-based Image Editors

Raster-based image editors, such as Painter, Photoshop, Paint.NET, MS Paint, and GIMP, revolve around editing pixels, unlike vector-based image editors, such as Xfig, CorelDRAW, Adobe Illustrator, or Inkscape, which revolve around editing lines and shapes (vectors). When an image is rendered in a raster-based image editor, the image is composed of millions of pixels. At its core, a raster image editor works by manipulating each individual pixel. Most pixel-based image editors work using the RGB color model, but some also allow the use of other color models such as the CMYK color model.

Dot Matrix

A dot matrix is a 2-dimensional patterned array, used to represent characters, symbols and images. Every type of modern technology uses dot matrices for display of information, including cell phones, televisions, and printers. They are also used in textiles with sewing, knitting, and weaving.

An alternate form of information display using lines and curves is known as a vector display, was used with early computing devices such as air traffic control radar displays and pen-based plotters but is no longer used. Electronic vector displays were typically monochrome only, and either don't fill in the interiors of closed vector shapes, or shape-filling is slow, time-consuming, and often non-uniform, as on pen-based plotters.

Dot matrix pattern woven into fabric in 1858, using punched cards on a Jacquard loom

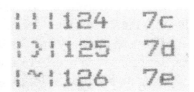

Close-up view of dot matrix text produced by an impact printer

"Bling Bling": Dot matrix-style skywriting

In printers, the dots are usually the darkened areas of the paper. In displays, the dots may light up, as in an LED, CRT, or plasma display, or darken, as in an LCD.

Usage in Printers

As an impact printer, the term mainly refers to low-resolution impact printers, with a column of 8, 9 or 24 "pins" hitting an ink-impregnated fabric ribbon, like a typewriter ribbon, onto the paper. It was originally contrasted with both daisy wheel printers and line printers that used fixed-shape embossed metal or plastic stamps to mark paper.

However, almost all modern computer printers also create their output as matrices of dots, but use a different technology like laser printing or inkjet printing, and are not called dot matrix printers. Impact printers survive where multi-part forms are needed, as the pins can impress dots through multiple layers of paper to make a carbonless copy, for security purposes.

All types of electronic printers typically generate image data as a two-step process. First the information to be printed is converted into a dot matrix using a raster image processor, and the output is a dot matrix referred to as a raster image, which is a complete full-page rendering of the information to be printed. Raster image processing may occur in either the printer itself using a page description language such as Adobe Postscript, or may be performed by printer driver software installed on the user's computer.

Early 1980s impact printers used a simple form of internal raster image processing, using low-resolution built-in bitmap fonts to render raw character data sent from the computer, and only capable of storing enough dot matrix data for one printed line at a time. External raster image processing was possible such as to print a graphical image, but was commonly extremely slow and data was sent one line at a time to the impact printer.

Depending on the printer technology the dot size or grid shape may not be uniform. Some printers are capable of producing smaller dots and will intermesh the small dots within the corners larger ones for antialiasing. Some printers have a fixed resolution across the printhead but with much smaller micro-stepping for the mechanical paper feed, resulting in non-uniform dot-overlapping printing resolutions like 600×1200 dpi.

A dot matrix is useful for marking materials other than paper. In manufacturing industry, many product marking applications use dot matrix inkjet or impact methods. This can also be used to print 2D matrix codes, e.g. Datamatrix.

Usage in Computers

Although the output of modern computers is generally all in the form of dot matrices (technically speaking), computers may internally store data as either a dot matrix or as a vector pattern of lines and curves. Vector data encoding requires less memory and less data storage, in situations where the shapes may need to be resized, as with font typefaces. For maximum image quality using only dot matrix fonts, it would be necessary to store a separate dot matrix pattern for the many different potential point sizes that might be used. Instead, a single group of vector shapes is used to render all the specific dot matrix patterns needed for the current display or printing task.

LED Matrix

An LED matrix or LED display is a large, low-resolution form of dot-matrix display, useful both for industrial and commercial information displays as well as for hobbyist human–machine interfaces. It consists of a 2-D diode matrix with their cathodes joined in rows and their anodes joined in columns (or vice versa). By controlling the flow of electricity through each row and column pair it is possible to control each LED individually. By multiplexing, scanning across rows, quickly flashing the LEDs on and off, it is possible to create characters or pictures to display information to the user. By varying the pulse rate per LED, the display can approximate levels of brightness.

Multi-colored LEDs or RGB-colored LEDs permit use as a full-color image display. The refresh rate is typically fast enough to prevent the human eye from detecting the flicker.

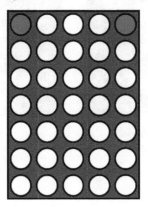

A LED matrix display scanning by rows to make the letter W

The primary difference between a common LED matrix and an OLED display is the large, low resolution dots. The OLED monitor functionally works the same, except there are many times more dots, and they are all much smaller, allowing for greater detail in the displayed patterns.

Color Depth

Color depth or colour depth, also known as bit depth, is either the number of bits used to indicate the color of a single pixel, in a bitmapped image or video frame buffer, or the number of bits used for each color component of a single pixel. For consumer video standards, such as High Efficiency Video Coding (H.265), the bit depth specifies the number of bits used for each color component. When referring to a pixel the concept can be defined as bits per pixel (bpp), which specifies the number of bits used. When referring to a color component the concept can be defined as bits per component, bits per channel, bits per color (all three abbreviated bpc), and also bits per pixel component, bits per color channel or bits per sample (bps). Color depth is only one aspect of color representation, expressing how finely *levels* of color can be expressed (a.k.a. color precision); the other aspect is how *broad* a range of colors can be expressed (the gamut). The definition of both color precision and gamut is accomplished with a color encoding specification which assigns a digital code value to a location in a color space.

Comparison: same image on five different color depths (bits).
Different looks (color/greyscale/black-and-white ... dithering), but also different file sizes.

32 bit.png 4,294,967,296 colors	8 bit.png 256 colors	4 bit.png 16 colors
98 KB	37 KB (-62%)	13 KB (-87%)

2 bit.png 4 colors
6 KB (-94%)

1 bit.png 2 colors
4 KB (-96%)

Indexed Color

With the relatively low color depth, the stored value is typically a number representing the index into a color map or palette (a form of vector quantization). The colors available in the palette itself may be fixed by the hardware or modifiable within the limits of the hardware (for instance, both color Macintosh systems and VGA-equipped IBM-PCs typically ran at 8-bit due to limited VRAM, but while the best VGA systems only offered an 18-bit (262,144 color) palette from which colors could be chosen, all color Macintosh video hardware offered a 24-bit (16 million color) palette). Modifiable palettes are sometimes referred to as pseudocolor palettes.

- 1-bit color (2^1 = 2 colors): monochrome, often black and white, compact Macintoshes, Atari ST.

- 2-bit color (2^2 = 4 colors): CGA, gray-scale early NeXTstation, color Macintoshes, Atari ST.

- 3-bit color (2^3 = 8 colors): many early home computers with TV displays, including the ZX Spectrum and BBC Micro

- 4-bit color (2^4 = 16 colors): as used by EGA and by the least common denominator VGA standard at higher resolution, color Macintoshes, Atari ST, Commodore 64, Amstrad CPC.

- 5-bit color (2^5 = 32 colors): Original Amiga chipset

- 6-bit color (2^6 = 64 colors): Original Amiga chipset

- 8-bit color (2^8 = 256 colors): most early color Unix workstations, VGA at low resolution, Super VGA, color Macintoshes, Atari TT, Amiga AGA chipset, Falcon030, Acorn Archimedes.

- 12-bit color (2^{12} = 4096 colors): some Silicon Graphics systems, Color NeXTstation systems, and Amiga systems in HAM mode.

Old graphics chips, particularly those used in home computers and video game consoles, often feature an additional level of palette mapping for individual sprites and tiles in order to increase the maximum number of simultaneously displayed colors, while minimizing use of then-expensive memory (& bandwidth). For example, in the ZX Spectrum, the picture is stored in a two-color format, but these two colors can be separately defined for each rectangular block of 8x8 pixels.

Direct Color

A typical computer monitor and video card may offer 8 bits of color precision (256 output levels) per R/G/B color channel, for an overall 24-bit color space (or 32-bit space, with alpha transparency bits, which have little bearing on the color precision), though earlier standards offered 6 bits per channel (64 levels) or less; the DVD-Video and Blu-ray Disc standards support video with a bit depth of 8-bits per color YCbCr with 4:2:0 chroma subsampling.

8-bit Color

A very limited but true direct color system, there are 3 bits (8 possible levels) for each of the R and G components, and the two remaining bits in the byte pixel to the B component (four levels), enabling 256 ($8 \times 8 \times 4$) different colors. The normal human eye is less sensitive to the blue component than to the red or green (two thirds of the eye's receptors process the longer wavelengths), so it is assigned one bit less than the others. Used, amongst others, in the MSX2 system series of computers in the early to mid 1990s.

Do not confuse with an indexed color depth of 8bpp (although it can be simulated in such systems by selecting the adequate table).

High Color (15/16-bit)

High color supports 15/16-bit for three RGB colors. In 16-bit direct color, there can be 4 bits (16 possible levels) for each of the R, G, and B components, plus optionally 4 bits for alpha (transparency), enabling 4,096 ($16 \times 16 \times 16$) different colors with 16 levels of transparency. Or in some systems there can be 5 bits per color component and 1 bit of alpha (32768 colors, just fully transparent or not); or there can be 5 bits for red, 6 bits for green, and 5 bits for blue, for 65536 colors with no transparency. These color depths are sometimes used in small devices with a color display, such as mobile telephones.

Variants with 5 or more bits per color component are sometimes called high color, which is sometimes considered sufficient to display photographic images.

18-bit

Almost all of the least expensive LCDs (such as typical twisted nematic types) provide 18-bit color ($64 \times 64 \times 64 = 262,144$ combinations) to achieve faster color transition times, and use either dithering or frame rate control to approximate 24-bit-per-pixel true color, or throw away 6 bits of color information entirely. More expensive LCDs (typically IPS) can display 24-bit or greater color depth.

True Color (24-bit)

True color supports 24-bit for three RGB colors. It provides a method of representing and storing graphical-image information (especially in computer processing) in an RGB color space such that a very large number of colors, shades, and hues can be displayed in an image, such as in high-quality photographic images or complex graphics. Usually, true color is defined to mean 256 shades of red, green, and blue, for a total of 2^{24}, or alternately 256^3, or 16,777,216 color variations. The human eye can discriminate up to ten million colors. Color processing in the eye occurs through retinal cone cells which are of three types, although not corresponding to red, green and blue hues.

"True color" can also refer to an RGB display-mode that does not need a color look-up table (CLUT).

For each pixel, generally one byte is used for each channel while the fourth byte (if present) is used either as an alpha channel, data, or ignored. Byte order is usually either RGB or BGR. Some systems exist with more than 8 bits per channel, and these are often also referred to as true color (for example a 48-bit true-color scanner).

Even with true color, monochromatic images, which are restricted to 256 levels, owing to their single channel, can sometimes still reveal visible banding artifacts.

True color, like other RGB color models, cannot express colors outside of the gamut of its RGB color space (generally sRGB).

Macintosh systems refer to 24-bit color as "millions of colors".

RGBA color space, or 32-bit color, is a variant of true color in which the additional 8 bits are allocated to transparency and indicate how transparent the element is to which the color is assigned, when overlaid on other elements.

Deep Color (30/36/48-bit)

Deep color consists of a billion or more colors. The xvYCC, sRGB, and YCbCr color spaces can be used with deep color systems.

Deep color supports 30/36/48 bits per pixel across three RGB colors, also referred to as 10/12/16 bits per channel/color/component/sample. With an alpha channel of the same precision this becomes 40/48/64 bits per pixel. Video cards with 10 bits per component (30-bit color RGB), started coming to market in the late 1990s. An early example was the Radius ThunderPower card for the Macintosh, which included extensions for QuickDraw and Adobe Photoshop plugins to support editing 30-bit images.

Systems using more than 24 bits in a 32-bit pixel for actual color data exist, but most of them opt for a 30-bit implementation with two bits of padding so that they can have an even 10 bits of color for each channel, similar to many HiColor systems. 10-bit professional video displays are actually providing 10 bits per color channel, and use a value of 95 for black and 685 for white; the values from 685 to 1023 are used for "whiter than white" images like glare, specular highlights, and similar details.

While some high-end graphics workstation systems and the accessories marketed toward use with such systems, as from SGI, have always used more than 8 bits per channel, such as 12 or 16 (36-bit or 48-bit color), such color depths have only worked their way into the general market more recently.

As bit depths climb above 8 bits per channel, some systems use the extra bits to store more intensity range than can be displayed all at once, as in high dynamic range imaging (HDRI). Floating point numbers are numbers in excess of 'full' white and black. This allows an image to accurately depict the intensity of the sun and deep shadows in the same color space for less distortion after intensive editing. Various models describe these ranges, many employing 32-bit accuracy per channel. In 1999 Industrial Light & Magic released the OpenEXR image file format as an open standard that supports 16-bit-per-channel half-precision floating-point numbers.

High Efficiency Video Coding (HEVC) defines the Main 10 profile which allows for a bit depth of 8-bits to 10-bits per sample with 4:2:0 chroma subsampling. 8-bits per sample allows for 256 shades per primary color (a total of 16.78 million colors) while 10-bits per sample allows for 1024 shades per primary color (a total of 1.07 billion colors). The Main 10 profile was added at the October 2012 HEVC meeting based on proposal JCTVC-K0109 which proposed that a 10-bit profile be added to HEVC for consumer applications. The proposal stated that this was to allow for improved video quality and to support the Rec. 2020 color space that will be used by UHDTV. The second version of HEVC has five profiles that allow for a bit depth of 8-bits to 16-bits per sample.

Industry Support

The HDMI 1.3 specification defines bit depths of 30 bits (1.073 billion colors), 36 bits (68.71 billion colors), and 48 bits (281.5 trillion colors). In that regard, the Nvidia Quadro graphics cards manufactured after 2006 support 30-bit deep color as do some models of the Radeon HD 5900 series such as the HD 5970. The ATI FireGL V7350 graphics card supports 40-bit and 48-bit color.

The DisplayPort specification also supports color depths greater than 24 bpp.

At WinHEC 2008, Microsoft announced that color depths of 30 bits and 48 bits would be supported in Windows 7, along with the wide color gamut scRGB (which can be converted to xvYCC output).

Television Color

Virtually all television displays and computer displays form images by varying the strength of just three primary colors: red, green, and blue. For example, bright yellow is formed by roughly equal red and green contributions, with little or no blue contribution.

Increasing the number of color primaries can increase the color gamut that a display can reproduce, although whether this results in a difference to the human eye is not yet proven, since humans are trichromats. Recent technologies such as Texas Instruments's *BrilliantColor* augment the typical red, green, and blue channels with up to three other primaries: cyan, magenta and yellow. Mitsubishi and Samsung, among others, use this technology in some TV sets to extend the range of displayable colors. The Sharp Aquos line of televisions has introduced Quattron technology, which augments the usual RGB pixel components with a yellow subpixel.

Analog CRTs, whether color or monochrome, use continuous voltage signals which do not have a fixed number of intensities.

References

- "SVG specification, "Clipping, Masking and Compositing"". World Wide Web Consortium. 14 January 2003. Retrieved 19 October 2009

- Matick, R.; Ling, D. T.; Gupta, S.; Dill, F. (2006) [1984], "All points addressable raster display memory", IBM Journal of Research and Development, 28 (4): 379, retrieved 2013-09-28

- Selinger, Peter (2001–2013). "Potrace – Transforming bitmaps into vector graphics". SourceForge project Potrace. Retrieved 2014-01-29

- Bach, Michael; Meigen, Thomas; Strasburger, Hans (1997). "Raster-scan cathode-ray tubes for vision research – limits of resolution in space, time and intensity, and some solutions". Spatial Vision. 10 (4): 403–14. PMID 9176948. doi:10.1163/156856897X00311

- Claus Kühnel (2001). BASCOM Programming of Microcontrollers with Ease: An Introduction by Program Examples. Universal Publishers. pp. 114–119. ISBN 978-1-58112-671-6

- Fog, Agner (2010-02-16). "Calling conventions for different C++ compilers and operating systems: Chapter 3, Data Representation" (PDF). Retrieved 2010-08-30

- Ben Waggoner (2002). Compression for great digital video: power tips, techniques, and common sense. Focal Press. p. 34. ISBN 978-1-57820-111-2

- Capin, Tolga (15 June 2009). "Mobile SVG Profiles: SVG Tiny and SVG Basic". World Wide Web Consortium. Retrieved 24 October 2010

- Gatter, Mark (2004). Getting It Right in Print: Digital Pre-press for Graphic Designers. Laurence King Publishing. p. 31. ISBN 978-1-85669-421-6

- Dengler, Patrick (8 July 2010). "Getting to SVG 2.0: A report from the SVG Working Group Face-to-Face (May 24th – June 1st 2010)". Microsoft Developer Network. Microsoft. Retrieved 26 August 2010

- D. B. Judd and G. Wyszecki (1975). Color in Business, Science and Industry. Wiley Series in Pure and Applied Optics (third ed.). New York: Wiley-Interscience. pp. 388. ISBN 0-471-45212-2

- "SVG Open 2005 Conference and Exhibition - Proceedings - Cartoon Oriented User Interfaces". svgopen.org. Retrieved 29 August 2010

- Noll, A. Michael (March 1971). "Scanned-Display Computer Graphics". Communications of the ACM. 14 (3): 143–150. doi:10.1145/362566.362567

- G.J. Sullivan; J.-R. Ohm; W.-J. Han; T. Wiegand (2012-05-25). "Overview of the High Efficiency Video Coding (HEVC) Standard" (PDF). IEEE Transactions on Circuits and Systems for Video Technology. Retrieved 2013-05-18

2

Subdisciplines of Computer-Aided Design

Computer-aided engineering is used to assist in engineering analysis tasks. It includes optimization, multibody dynamics, finite element analysis and computational fluid dynamics. The chapter strategically encompasses and incorporates the major subdisciplines of computer-aided design, providing a complete understanding.

Computer-Aided Engineering

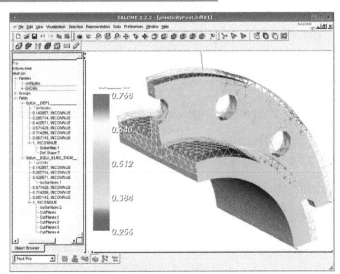

Nonlinear static analysis of a 3D structure subjected to plastic deformations

Computer-aided engineering (CAE) is the broad usage of computer software to aid in engineering analysis tasks. It includes finite element analysis (FEA), computational fluid dynamics (CFD), multibody dynamics (MBD), and optimization.

Overview

Software tools that have been developed to support these activities are considered CAE tools. CAE tools are being used, for example, to analyze the robustness and performance of components and assemblies. The term encompasses simulation, validation, and optimization of products and manufacturing tools. In the future, CAE systems will be major providers of information to help support design teams in decision making. Computer-aided engineering is used in many fields such as automotive, aviation, space, and shipbuilding industries.

In regard to information networks, CAE systems are individually considered a single node on a total information network and each node may interact with other nodes on the network.

CAE systems can provide support to businesses. This is achieved by the use of reference architectures and their ability to place information views on the business process. Reference architecture is the basis from which information model, especially product and manufacturing models.

The term CAE has also been used by some in the past to describe the use of computer technology within engineering in a broader sense than just engineering analysis. It was in this context that the term was coined by Jason Lemon, founder of SDRC in the late 1970s. This definition is however better known today by the terms CAx and PLM.

CAE Fields and Phases

CAE areas covered include:

- Stress analysis on components and assemblies using Finite Element Analysis (FEA);
- Thermal and fluid flow analysis Computational fluid dynamics (CFD);
- Multibody dynamics (MBD) and Kinematics;
- Analysis tools for process simulation for operations such as casting, molding, and die press forming.
- Optimization of the product or process.

In general, there are three phases in any computer-aided engineering task:

- Pre-processing – defining the model and environmental factors to be applied to it. (typically a finite element model, but facet, voxel and thin sheet methods are also used)
- Analysis solver (usually performed on high powered computers)
- Post-processing of results (using visualization tools)

This cycle is iterated, often many times, either manually or with the use of commercial optimization software.

CAE in the Automotive Industry

CAE tools are very widely used in the automotive industry. In fact, their use has enabled the automakers to reduce product development cost and time while improving the safety, comfort, and durability of the vehicles they produce. The predictive capability of CAE tools has progressed to the point where much of the design verification is now done using computer simulations rather than physical prototype testing. CAE dependability is based upon all proper assumptions as inputs and must identify critical inputs (BJ). Even though there have been many advances in CAE, and it is widely used in the engineering field, physical testing is still a must. It is used for verification and model updating, to accurately define loads and boundary conditions and for final prototype sign-off.

The Future of CAE in the Product Development Process

Even though CAE has built a strong reputation as verification, troubleshooting and analysis tool, there is still a perception that sufficiently accurate results come rather late in the design cycle to really drive the design. This can expected to become a problem as modern products become ever more complex. They include smart systems, which leads to an increased need for multi-physics analysis including controls, and contain new lightweight materials, to which engineers are often less familiar. CAE software companies and manufacturers are constantly looking for tools and process improvements to change this situation. On the software side, they are constantly looking to develop more powerful solvers, better use computer resources and include engineering knowledge in pre- and post-processing. On the process side, they try to achieve a better alignment between 3D CAE, 1D System Simulation and physical testing. This should increase modeling realism and calculation speed. On top of that, they try to better integrate CAE in the overall product lifecycle management. In this way, they can connect product design with product use, which is an absolute must for smart products. Such an enhanced engineering process is also referred to as predictive engineering analytics.

Computer-Aided Software Engineering

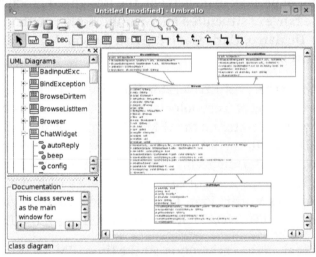

Example of a CASE tool.

Computer-aided software engineering (CASE) is the domain of software tools used to design and implement applications. CASE tools are similar to and were partly inspired by computer-aided design (CAD) tools used for designing hardware products. CASE tools are used for developing high-quality, defect-free, and maintainable software. CASE software is often associated with methods for the development of information systems together with automated tools that can be used in the software development process.

History

The Information System Design and Optimization System (ISDOS) project, started in 1968 at the University of Michigan, initiated a great deal of interest in the whole concept of using computer systems to help analysts in the very difficult process of analysing requirements and developing systems. Several papers by Daniel Teichroew fired a whole generation of enthusiasts with the potential of automated systems development. His Problem Statement Language / Problem Statement Analyzer (PSL/PSA) tool was a CASE tool although it predated the term.

Another major thread emerged as a logical extension to the data dictionary of a database. By extending the range of metadata held, the attributes of an application could be held within a dictionary and used at runtime. This "active dictionary" became the precursor to the more modern model-driven engineering capability. However, the active dictionary did not provide a graphical representation of any of the metadata. It was the linking of the concept of a dictionary holding analysts' metadata, as derived from the use of an integrated set of techniques, together with the graphical representation of such data that gave rise to the earlier versions of CASE.

The term was originally coined by software company Nastec Corporation of Southfield, Michigan in 1982 with their original integrated graphics and text editor GraphiText, which also was the first microcomputer-based system to use hyperlinks to cross-reference text strings in documents—an early forerunner of today's web page link. GraphiText's successor product, DesignAid, was the first microprocessor-based tool to logically and semantically evaluate software and system design diagrams and build a data dictionary.

Under the direction of Albert F. Case, Jr. vice president for product management and consulting, and Vaughn Frick, director of product management, the DesignAid product suite was expanded to support analysis of a wide range of structured analysis and design methodologies, including those of Ed Yourdon and Tom DeMarco, Chris Gane & Trish Sarson, Ward-Mellor (real-time) SA/SD and Warnier-Orr (data driven).

The next entrant into the market was Excelerator from Index Technology in Cambridge, Mass. While DesignAid ran on Convergent Technologies and later Burroughs Ngen networked microcomputers, Index launched Excelerator on the IBM PC/AT platform. While, at the time of launch, and for several years, the IBM platform did not support networking or a centralized database as did the Convergent Technologies or Burroughs machines, the allure of IBM was strong, and Excelerator came to prominence. Hot on the heels of Excelerator were a rash of offerings from companies such as Knowledgeware (James Martin, Fran Tarkenton and Don Addington), Texas Instrument's IEF and Andersen Consulting's FOUNDATION toolset (DESIGN/1, INSTALL/1, FCP).

CASE tools were at their peak in the early 1990s. At the time IBM had proposed AD/Cycle, which was an alliance of software vendors centered on IBM's Software repository using IBM DB2 in mainframe and OS/2:

> The application development tools can be from several sources: from IBM, from vendors, and from the customers themselves. IBM has entered into relationships with Bachman Information Systems, Index Technology Corporation, and Knowledgeware wherein selected products from these vendors will be marketed through an IBM complementary marketing program to provide offerings that will help to achieve complete life-cycle coverage.

With the decline of the mainframe, AD/Cycle and the Big CASE tools died off, opening the market for the mainstream CASE tools of today. Many of the leaders of the CASE market of the early 1990s ended up being purchased by Computer Associates, including IEW, IEF, ADW, Cayenne, and Learmonth & Burchett Management Systems (LBMS). The other trend that led to the evolution of CASE tools was the rise of object-oriented methods and tools. Most of the various tool vendors added some support for object-oriented methods and tools. In addition new products arose that were designed from the bottom up to support the object-oriented approach. Andersen developed its project Eagle as an alternative to Foundation. Several of the thought leaders in object-oriented development each developed their own methodology and CASE tool set: Jacobsen, Rumbaugh, Booch, etc. Eventually, these diverse tool sets and methods were consolidated via standards led by the Object Management Group (OMG). The OMG's Unified Modelling Language (UML) is currently widely accepted as the industry standard for object-oriented modeling.

CASE Software

A. Fuggetta classified CASE software into 3 categories:

1. *Tools* support specific tasks in the software life-cycle.

2. *Workbenches* combine two or more tools focused on a specific part of the software life-cycle.

3. *Environments* combine two or more tools or workbenches and support the complete software life-cycle.

Tools

CASE tools supports specific tasks in the software development life-cycle. They can be divided into the following categories:

1. Business and Analysis modeling. Graphical modeling tools. E.g., E/R modeling, object modeling, etc.

2. Development. Design and construction phases of the life-cycle. Debugging environments. E.g., GNU Debugger.

3. Verification and validation. Analyze code and specifications for correctness, performance, etc.

4. Configuration management. Control the check-in and check-out of repository objects and files. E.g., SCCS, CMS.

5. Metrics and measurement. Analyze code for complexity, modularity (e.g., no "go to's"), performance, etc.

6. Project management. Manage project plans, task assignments, scheduling.

Another common way to distinguish CASE tools is the distinction between Upper CASE and Lower CASE. Upper CASE Tools support business and analysis modeling. They support traditional diagrammatic languages such as ER diagrams, Data flow diagram, Structure charts, Decision Trees, Decision tables, etc. Lower CASE Tools support development activities, such as physical design, debugging, construction, testing, component integration, maintenance, and reverse engineering. All other activities span the entire life-cycle and apply equally to upper and lower CASE.

Workbenches

Workbenches integrate two or more CASE tools and support specific software-process activities. Hence they achieve:

*   a homogeneous and consistent interface (presentation integration).

*   seamless integration of tools and tool chains (control and data integration).

An example workbench is Microsoft's Visual Basic programming environment. It incorporates several development tools: a GUI builder, smart code editor, debugger, etc. Most commercial CASE products tended to be such workbenches that seamlessly integrated two or more tools. Workbenches also can be classified in the same manner as tools; as focusing on Analysis, Development, Verification, etc. as well as being focused on upper case, lower case, or processes such as configuration management that span the complete life-cycle.

Environments

An environment is a collection of CASE tools or workbenches that attempts to support the complete software process. This contrasts with tools that focus on one specific task or a specific part of the life-cycle. CASE environments are classified by Fuggetta as follows:

1. Toolkits. Loosely coupled collections of tools. These typically build on operating system workbenches such as the Unix Programmer's Workbench or the VMS VAX set. They typically perform integration via piping or some other basic mechanism to share data and pass control. The strength of easy integration is also one of the drawbacks. Simple passing of parameters via technologies such as shell scripting can't provide the kind of sophisticated integration that a common repository database can.

2. Fourth generation. These environments are also known as 4GL standing for fourth generation language environments due to the fact that the early environments were designed around specific languages such as Visual Basic. They were the first environments to provide deep integration of multiple tools. Typically these environments were focused on specific types of applications. For example, user-interface driven applications that did standard atomic transactions to a relational database. Examples are Informix 4GL, and Focus.

3. Language-centered. Environments based on a single often object-oriented language such as the Symbolics Lisp Genera environment or VisualWorks Smalltalk from Parcplace. In these environments all the operating system resources were objects in the object-oriented language. This provides powerful debugging and graphical opportunities but the code developed is mostly limited to the specific language. For this reason, these environments were mostly a niche within CASE. Their use was mostly for prototyping and R&D projects. A common core idea for these environments was the model-view-controller user interface that facilitated keeping multiple presentations of the same design consistent with the underlying model. The MVC architecture was adopted by the other types of CASE environments as well as many of the applications that were built with them.

4. Integrated. These environments are an example of what most IT people tend to think of first when they think of CASE. Environments such as IBM's AD/Cycle, Andersen Consulting's FOUNDATION, the ICL CADES system, and DEC Cohesion. These environments attempt to cover the complete life-cycle from analysis to maintenance and provide an integrated database repository for storing all artifacts of the software process. The integrated software repository was the defining feature for these kinds of tools. They provided multiple different design models as well as support for code in heterogenous languages. One of the main goals for these types of environments was "round trip engineering": being able to make changes at the design level and have those automatically be reflected

in the code and vice versa. These environments were also typically associated with a particular methodology for software development. For example, the FOUNDATION CASE suite from Andersen was closely tied to the Andersen Method/1 methodology.

5. Process-centered. This is the most ambitious type of integration. These environments attempt to not just formally specify the analysis and design objects of the software process but the actual process itself and to use that formal process to control and guide software projects. Examples are East, Enterprise II, Process Wise, Process Weaver, and Arcadia. These environments were by definition tied to some methodology since the software process itself is part of the environment and can control many aspects of tool invocation.

In practice, the distinction between workbenches and environments was flexible. Visual Basic for example was a programming workbench but was also considered a 4GL environment by many. The features that distinguished workbenches from environments were deep integration via a shared repository or common language and some kind of methodology (integrated and process-centered environments) or domain (4GL) specificity.

Major CASE Risk Factors

Some of the most significant risk factors for organizations adopting CASE technology include:

- Inadequate standardization. Organizations usually have to tailor and adopt methodologies and tools to their specific requirements. Doing so may require significant effort to integrate both divergent technologies as well as divergent methods. For example, before the adoption of the UML standard the diagram conventions and methods for designing object-oriented models were vastly different among followers of Jacobsen, Booch, and Rumbaugh.

- Unrealistic expectations. The proponents of CASE technology—especially vendors marketing expensive tool sets—often hype expectations that the new approach will be a silver bullet that solves all problems. In reality no such technology can do that and if organizations approach CASE with unrealistic expectations they will inevitably be disappointed.

- Inadequate training. As with any new technology, CASE requires time to train people in how to use the tools and to get up to speed with them. CASE projects can fail if practitioners are not given adequate time for training or if the first project attempted with the new technology is itself highly mission critical and fraught with risk.

- Inadequate process control. CASE provides significant new capabilities to utilize new types of tools in innovative ways. Without the proper process guidance and controls these new capabilities can cause significant new problems as well.

Computer-aided Process Planning

Computer-aided process planning (CAPP) is the use of computer technology to aid in the process planning of a part or product, in manufacturing. CAPP is the link between CAD and CAM in that it provides for the planning of the process to be used in producing a designed part.

CAPP is a linkage between the CAD and CAM module. It provides for the planning of the process to be used in producing a designed part. Process planning is concerned with determining the sequence of individual manufacturing operations needed to produce a given part or product. The resulting operation sequence is documented on a form typically referred to as a route sheet (also called as process sheet/method sheet) containing a listing of the production operations and associated machine tools for a work part or assembly. Process planning in manufacturing also refers to the planning of use of blanks, spare parts, packaging material, user instructions (manuals) etc.

The term "computer-aided production planning" is used in different contexts on different parts of the production process; to some extent CAPP overlaps with the term "PIC" (production and inventory control).

Process planning translates design information into the process steps and instructions to efficiently and effectively manufacture products. As the design process is supported by many computer-aided tools, computer-aided process planning (CAPP) has evolved to simplify and improve process planning and achieve more effective use of manufacturing resources. process planning is of two types as:

1. generative type computer aided process planning.

2. variant type process planning.

Process planning encompasses the activities and functions to prepare a detailed set of plans and instructions to produce a part. The planning begins with engineering drawings, specifications, parts or material lists and a forecast of demand. The results of the planning are:

• Routings which specify operations, operation sequences, work centers, standards, tooling and fixtures. This routing becomes a major input to the manufacturing resource planning system to define operations for production activity control purposes and define required resources for capacity requirements planning purposes.

• Process plans which typically provide more detailed, step-by-step work instructions including dimensions related to individual operations, machining parameters, set-up instructions, and quality assurance checkpoints.

• Fabrication and assembly drawings to support manufacture (as opposed to engineering drawings to define the part).

Keneth Crow stated that "Manual process planning is based on a manufacturing engineer's experience and knowledge of production facilities, equipment, their capabilities, processes, and tooling. Process planning is very time-consuming and the results vary based on the person doing the planning".

According to Engelke, the need for CAPP is greater with an increased number of different types of parts being manufactured, and with a more complex manufacturing process.

Computer-aided process planning initially evolved as a means to electronically store a process plan once it was created, retrieve it, modify it for a new part and print the plan. Other capabilities were table-driven cost and standard estimating systems, for sales representatives to create customer quotations and estimate delivery time.

Future Development

Generative or dynamic CAPP is the main focus of development, the ability to automatically generate production plans for new products, or dynamically update production plans on the basis of resource availability. Generative CAPP will probably use iterative methods, where simple production plans are applied to automatic CAD/CAM development to refine the initial production plan.

A Generative CAPP system was developed at Beijing No. 1 Machine Tool Plant (BYJC) in Beijing, China as part of a UNDP project (DG/CRP/87/027) from 1989–1995. The project was reported in "Machine Design Magazine; New Trends" May 9, 1994, P.22-23. The system was demonstrated to the CASA/SME Leadership in Excellence for Applications Development (LEAD) Award committee in July 1995. The committee awarded BYJC the LEAD Award in 1995 for this achievement. In order to accomplish Generative CAPP, modifications were made to the CAD, PDM, ERP, and CAM systems. In addition, a Manufacturing Execution System (MES) was built to handle the scheduling of tools, personnel, supply, and logistics, as well as maintain shop floor production capabilities.

Generative CAPP systems are built on a factory's production capabilities and capacities. In Discrete Manufacturing, Art-to-Part validations have been performed often, but when considering highly volatile engineering designs, and multiple manufacturing operations with multiple tooling options, the decisions tables become longer and the vector matrices more complex. BYJC builds CNC machine tools and Flexible Manufacturing Systems (FMS) to customer specifications. Few are duplicates. The Generative CAPP System is based on the unique capabilities and capacities needed to produce those specific products at BYJC. Unlike a Variant Process Planning system that modifies existing plans, each process plan could be defined automatically, independent of past routings. As improvements are made to production efficiencies, the improvements are automatically incorporated into the current production mix. This generative system is a key component of the CAPP system for the Agile Manufacturing environment.

In order to achieve the Generative CAPP system, components were built to meet needed capabilities:

1. Shop floor manufacturing abilities of BYJC were defined. It was determined that there are 46 major operations and 84 dependent operations the shop floor could execute to produce the product mix. These operations are manufacturing primitive operations. As new manufacturing capabilities are incorporated into the factory's repertoire, they need to be accommodated in the spectrum of operations.

2. These factory operations are then used to define the features for the Feature Based Design extensions that are incorporated into the CAD system.

3. The combination of these feature extensions and the parametric data associated with them became part of the data that is passed from the CAD system to the modified PDM system as the data set content for the specific product, assembly, or part.

4. The ERP system was modified to handle the manufacturing abilities for each tool on the shop floor. This is an extension to the normal feeds and speeds that the ERP system has the

capability of maintaining about each tool. In addition, personnel records are also enhanced to note special characteristics, talents, and education of each employee should it become relevant in the manufacturing process.

5. A Manufacturing Execution System (MES) was created. The MES's major component is an expert/artificial intelligent system that matches the engineering feature objects from the PDM system against the tooling, personnel, material, transportation needs, etc. needed to manufacture them in the ERP system. Once physical components are identified, the items are scheduled. The scheduling is continuously updated based on the real time conditions of the enterprise. Ultimately, the parameters for this system were based on:

    a. Expenditures

    b. Time

    c. Physical dimensions

    d. Availability

The parameters are used to produce multidimensional differential equations. Solving the partial differential equations will produce the optimum process and production planning at the time when the solution was generated. Solutions had the flexibility to change over time based on the ability to satisfy agile manufacturing criteria. Execution planning can be dynamic and accommodate changing conditions.

The system allows new products to be brought on line quickly based on their manufacturability. The more sophisticated CAD/CAM, PDM and ERP systems have the base work already incorporated into them for Generative Computer Aided Process Planning. The task of building and implementing the MES system still requires identifying the capabilities that exist within a given establishment, and exploiting them to the fullest potential. The system created is highly specific, the concepts can be extrapolated to other enterprises.

Traditional CAPP methods that optimize plans in a linear manner have not been able to satisfy the need for flexible planning, so new dynamic systems will explore all possible combinations of production processes, and then generate plans according to available machining resources. For example, K.S. Lee et al. states that "By considering the multi-selection tasks simultaneously, a specially designed genetic algorithm searches through the entire solution space to identify the optimal plan".

Computer-aided Manufacturing

Computer-aided manufacturing (CAM) is the use of software to control machine tools and related ones in the manufacturing of workpieces. This is not the only definition for CAM, but it is the most common; CAM may also refer to the use of a computer to assist in all operations of a manufacturing plant, including planning, management, transportation and storage. Its primary purpose is to create a faster production process and components and tooling with more precise dimensions and material consistency, which in some cases, uses only the required amount of raw material (thus minimizing waste), while simultaneously reducing energy consumption. CAM is now a system used in schools and lower educational purposes. CAM is a subsequent comput-er-aided process after computer-aided design (CAD) and sometimes computer-aided engineer-ing (CAE), as the model generated in CAD and verified in CAE can be input into CAM software, which then controls the machine tool. CAM is used in many schools alongside computer-aided design (CAD) to create objects.

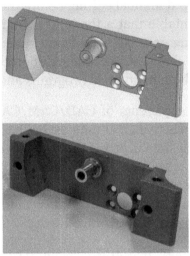

CAD model and CNC machined part

Overview

Chrome-cobalt disc with crowns for dental implants, manufactured using WorkNC CAM

Traditionally, CAM has been considered as a numerical control (NC) programming tool, where in two-dimensional (2-D) or three-dimensional (3-D) models of components generated in CADAs with other "Computer-Aided" technologies, CAM does not eliminate the need for skilled profes-sionals such as manufacturing engineers, NC programmers, or machinists. CAM, in fact, lever-ages both the value of the most skilled manufacturing professionals through advanced produc-tivity tools, while building the skills of new professionals through visualization, simulation and optimization tools.

History

Early commercial applications of CAM was in large companies in the automotive and aerospace industries, for example Pierre Béziers work developing the CAD/CAM application UNISURF in the 1960s for car body design and tooling at Renault.

Historically, CAM software was seen to have several shortcomings that necessitated an overly high level of involvement by skilled CNC machinists. Fallows created the first CAD software but this had severe shortcomings and was promptly taken back into the developing stage. CAM software would output code for the least capable machine, as each machine tool control added on to the standard G-code set for increased flexibility. In some cases, such as improperly set up CAM software or specific tools, the CNC machine required manual editing before the program will run properly. None of these issues were so insurmountable that a thoughtful engineer or skilled machine operator could not overcome for prototyping or small production runs; G-Code is a simple language. In high production or high precision shops, a different set of problems were encountered where an experienced CNC machinist must both hand-code programs and run CAM software.

Integration of CAD with other components of CAD/CAM/CAE Product lifecycle management (PLM) environment requires an effective CAD data exchange. Usually it had been necessary to force the CAD operator to export the data in one of the common data formats, such as IGES or STL or Parasolid formats that are supported by a wide variety of software. The output from the CAM software is usually a simple text file of G-code/M-codes, sometimes many thousands of commands long, that is then transferred to a machine tool using a direct numerical control (DNC) program or in modern Controllers using a common USB Storage Device.

CAM packages could not, and still cannot, reason as a machinist can. They could not optimize toolpaths to the extent required of mass production. Users would select the type of tool, machining process and paths to be used. While an engineer may have a working knowledge of G-code programming, small optimization and wear issues compound over time. Mass-produced items that require machining are often initially created through casting or some other non-machine method. This enables hand-written, short, and highly optimized G-code that could not be produced in a CAM package.

At least in the United States, there is a shortage of young, skilled machinists entering the workforce able to perform at the extremes of manufacturing; high precision and mass production. As CAM software and machines become more complicated, the skills required of a machinist or machine operator advance to approach that of a computer programmer and engineer rather than eliminating the CNC machinist from the workforce.

Typical areas of concern:

- High Speed Machining, including streamlining of tool paths
- Multi-function Machining
- 5 Axis Machining
- Feature recognition and machining
- Automation of Machining processes
- Ease of Use

Overcoming Historical Shortcomings

Over time, the historical shortcomings of CAM are being attenuated, both by providers of niche solutions and by providers of high-end solutions. This is occurring primarily in three arenas:

1. Ease of usage

2. Manufacturing complexity

3. Integration with PLM and the extended enterprise

Ease in use

For the user who is just getting started as a CAM user, out-of-the-box capabilities providing Process Wizards, templates, libraries, machine tool kits, automated feature based machining and job function specific tailorable user interfaces build user confidence and speed the learning curve.

User confidence is further built on 3D visualization through a closer integration with the 3D CAD environment, including error-avoiding simulations and optimizations.

Manufacturing complexity

The manufacturing environment is increasingly complex. The need for CAM and PLM tools by buMs are NC programmer or machinist is similar to the need for computer assistance by the pilot of modern aircraft systems. The modern machinery cannot be properly used without this assistance.

Today's CAM systems support the full range of machine tools including: turning, 5 axis machining and wire EDM. Today's CAM user can easily generate streamlined tool paths, optimized tool axis tilt for higher feed rates, better tool life and surface finish and optimized Z axis depth cuts as well as driving non-cutting operations such as the specification of probing motions.

Integration with PLM and the extended enterpriseLM to integrate manufacturing with enterprise operations from concept through field support of the finished product.

To ensure ease of use appropriate to user objectives, modern CAM solutions are scalable from a stand-alone CAM system to a fully integrated multi-CAD 3D solution-set. These solutions are created to meet the full needs of manufacturing personnel including part planning, shop documentation, resource management and data management and exchange. To prevent these solutions from detailed tool specific information a dedicated tool management.

Machining Process

Most machining progresses through many stages, each of which is implemented by a variety of basic and sophisticated strategies, depending on the material and the software available.

Roughing

This process begins with raw stock, known as billet, and cuts it very roughly to shape of the final model. In milling, the result often gives the appearance of terraces, because the strategy has taken advantage of the ability to cut the model horizontally. Common strategies are zig-zag clearing, offset clearing, plunge roughing, rest-roughing.

Semi-f

This process begins with a roughed part that unevenly approximates the model and cuts to within a fixed offset distance from the model. The semi-finishing pass must leave a small amount of material so the tool can cut accurately while finishing, but not so little that the tool and material deflect instead of sending. Common strategies are raster passes, water-line passes, constant step-over passes, pencil milling.

Finishing

Finishing involves a slow pass across the material in very fine steps to produce the finished part. In finishing, the step between one pass and another is minimal. Feed rates are low and spindle speeds are raised to produce an accurate surface.

Contour milling

In milling applications on hardware with five or more axes, a separate finishing process called contouring can be performed. Instead of stepping down in fine-grained increments to approximate a surface, the work piece is rotated to make the cutting surfaces of the tool tangent to the ideal part features. This produces an excellent surface finish with high dimensional accuracy.

Software: Large Vendors

The top 20 largest CAM software companies, by direct revenues in year 2015, are sorted by global revenues:

- Dassault Systèmes: CATIA

- Siemens AG: NX CAM

- Vero Software part of HEXAGON: AlphaCAM, EdgeCAM, Machining Strategist, PEPS, SurfCAM, VISI, WorkNC / Dental

- Autodesk Inc.: HSM (Works, Express, Inventor), PowerMill, PartMaker | FeatureCAM, ArtCAM, Fusion 360

- Geometric Ltd.: CAMWorks

- OPEN MIND Technologies: hyperMill

- Tebis Technische Informationssysteme AG: Tebis

- CNC Software Inc.: MasterCAM

- 3D Systems: Cimatron, GibbsCAM

- PTC: Creo

- CGTech: VERICUT

- Missler Software: TopSolid

- SPRUT Technology Ltd.:SprutCAM, SprutCAM Robot

- SAI Software: FlexiSign

- Gravotech Group: TYPE3

- MecSoft Corporation: VisualCAD/CAM, RhinoCAM, VisualCAM for SOLIDWORKS, Free-Mill

- C&G Systems: cam-tool

- SolidCAM GmbH: SolidCAM

- NTT Data Engineering Systems: Space-E (based on the Catia system)

- BobCAD-CAM Inc.: BobCAD-CAM

References

- Coronel, Carlos; Morris, Steven (February 4, 2014). Database Systems: Design, Implementation, & Management. Cengage Learning. pp. 695–700. ISBN 1285196147. Retrieved 25 November 2014

- Saracoglu, B. O. (2006). "Identification of Technology Performance Criteria for CAD/CAM/CAE/CIM/CAL in Shipbuilding Industry". doi:10.1109/PICMET.2006.296739

- Alfonso Fuggetta (December 1993). "A classification of CASE technology". Computer. 26 (12): 25–38. doi:10.1109/2.247645. Retrieved 2009-03-14

- Engelke, William D. (1987), "How to Integrate CAD/CAM Systems: Management and Technology",P.237-238. CRC press. ISBN 0-8247-7658-5

- Van der Auweraer, Herman; Anthonis, Jan; De Bruyne, Stijn; Leuridan, Jan (2012). "Virtual engineering at work: the challenges for designing mechatronic products". Engineering with computers. 29 (3): 389–408. doi:10.1007/s00366-012-0286-6

- Seong Wook Cho; Seung Wook Kim; Jin-Pyo Park; Sang Wook Yang; Young Choi (2011). "Engineering collaboration framework with CAE analysis data". International Journal of Precision Engineering and Manufacturing. 12

- Boothroyd, Geoffrey; Knight, Winston Anthony (2006). Fundamentals of machining and machine tools (3rd ed.). CRC Press. p. 401. ISBN 978-1-57444-659-3

3

An Overview of 3D Computer Graphics

Three-dimensional computer graphics are three-dimensional depictions of data. The algorithms used in 3D computer graphics are the same as 2D computer vector graphics in the wire-frame model and the raster display. Some of the softwares used in 3D modeling are polygonal modeling, virtual actor, digital sculpting, etc. This chapter is an overview of the subject matter incorporating all the major aspects of computer-aided design.

3D Computer Graphics

Three-dimensional computer graphics (3D computer graphics, in contrast to 2D computer graphics) are graphics that use a three-dimensional representation of geometric data (often Cartesian) that is stored in the computer for the purposes of performing calculations and rendering 2D images. Such images may be stored for viewing later or displayed in real-time.

3D computer graphics rely on many of the same algorithms as 2D computer vector graphics in the wire-frame model and 2D computer raster graphics in the final rendered display. In computer graphics software, the distinction between 2D and 3D is occasionally blurred; 2D applications may use 3D techniques to achieve effects such as lighting, and 3D may use 2D rendering techniques.

3D computer graphics are often referred to as 3D models. Apart from the rendered graphic, the model is contained within the graphical data file. However, there are differences: a 3D model is the mathematical representation of any three-dimensional object. A model is not technically a graphic until it is displayed. A model can be displayed visually as a two-dimensional image through a process called 3D rendering or used in non-graphical computer simulations and calculations. With 3D printing, 3D models are similarly rendered into a 3D physical representation of the model, with limitations to how accurate the rendering can match the virtual model.

History

William Fetter was credited with coining the term *computer graphics* in 1961 to describe his work at Boeing. One of the first displays of computer animation was *Futureworld* (1976), which included an animation of a human face and a hand that had originally appeared in the 1972 experimental short *A Computer Animated Hand*, created by University of Utah students Edwin Catmull and Fred Parke.

3D computer graphics software began appearing for home computers in the late 1970s. The earliest known example is *3D Art Graphics*, a set of 3D computer graphics effects, written by Kazumasa Mitazawa and released in June 1978 for the Apple II.

Overview

3D computer graphics creation falls into three basic phases:

- 3D modeling – the process of forming a computer model of an object's shape
- Layout and animation – the placement and movement of objects within a scene
- 3D rendering – the computer calculations that, based on light placement, surface types, and other qualities, generate the image

Modeling

The model describes the process of forming the shape of an object. The two most common sources of 3D models are those that an artist or engineer originates on the computer with some kind of 3D modeling tool, and models scanned into a computer from real-world objects. Models can also be produced procedurally or via physical simulation. Basically, a 3D model is formed from points called vertices (or vertexes) that define the shape and form polygons. A polygon is an area formed from at least three vertexes (a triangle). A polygon of n points is an n-gon. The overall integrity of the model and its suitability to use in animation depend on the structure of the polygons.

Layout and Animation

Before rendering into an image, objects must be laid out (place) in a scene. This defines spatial relationships between objects, including location and size. Animation refers to the temporal description of an object (i.e., how it moves and deforms over time. Popular methods include keyframing, inverse kinematics, and motion capture). These techniques are often used in combination. As with animation, physical simulation also specifies motion.

Rendering

Rendering converts a model into an image either by simulating light transport to get photo-realistic images, or by applying an art style as in non-photorealistic rendering. The two basic operations in realistic rendering are transport (how much light gets from one place to another) and scattering (how surfaces interact with light). This step is usually performed using 3D computer graphics software or a 3D graphics API. Altering the scene into a suitable form for rendering also involves 3D projection, which displays a three-dimensional image in two dimensions. Although 3D modeling and CAD software may perform 3D rendering as well (e.g. Autodesk 3ds Max or Blender), exclusive 3D rendering software also exists.

Examples of 3D Rendering

Left: A 3D rendering with ray tracing and ambient occlusion using Blender and YafaRay.
Center: A 3d model of a Dunkerque-class battleship rendered with flat shading.
2-nd Center: During the 3D rendering step, the number of reflections "light rays" can take, as well as various other attributes, can be tailored to achieve a desired visual effect. Rendered with Cobalt.
Right: Experience Curiosity, a real-time web application which leverages 3D rendering capabilities of browsers (WebGL).

Software

3D computer graphics software produces computer-generated imagery (CGI) through 3D modeling and 3D rendering or produces 3D models for analytic, scientific and industrial purposes.

Modeling

3D modeling software is a class of 3D computer graphics software used to produce 3D models. Individual programs of this class are called modeling applications or modelers.

3D modelers allow users to create and alter models via their 3D mesh. Users can add, subtract, stretch and otherwise change the mesh to their desire. Models can be viewed from a variety of angles, usually simultaneously. Models can be rotated and the view can be zoomed in and out.

3D modelers can export their models to files, which can then be imported into other applications as long as the metadata are compatible. Many modelers allow importers and exporters to be plugged-in, so they can read and write data in the native formats of other applications.

Most 3D modelers contain a number of related features, such as ray tracers and other rendering alternatives and texture mapping facilities. Some also contain features that support or allow animation of models. Some may be able to generate full-motion video of a series of rendered scenes (i.e. animation).

Computer-aided Design

Computer aided design software may employ the same fundamental 3D modeling techniques that 3D modeling software use but their goal differs. They are used in computer-aided engineering, computer-aided manufacturing, Finite element analysis, product lifecycle management, 3D printing and Computer-aided architectural design.

Complementary Tools

After producing video, studios then edit or composite the video using programs such as Adobe Premiere Pro or Final Cut Pro at the mid-level, or Autodesk Combustion, Digital Fusion, Shake at the high-end. Match moving software is commonly used to match live video with computer-generated video, keeping the two in sync as the camera moves.

Use of real-time computer graphics engines to create a cinematic production is called machinima.

Communities

There are a multitude of websites designed to help, educate and support 3D graphic artists. Some are managed by software developers and content providers, but there are standalone sites as well. These communities allow for members to seek advice, post tutorials, provide product reviews or post examples of their own work.

Differences with other types of Computer Graphics

Distinction from Photorealistic 2D Graphics

Not all computer graphics that appear 3D are based on a wireframe model. 2D computer graphics with 3D photorealistic effects are often achieved without wireframe modeling and are sometimes indistinguishable in the final form. Some graphic art software includes filters that can be applied to 2D vector graphics or 2D raster graphics on transparent layers. Visual artists may also copy or visualize 3D effects and manually render photorealistic effects without the use of filters.

Pseudo-3D and *True 3D*

Some video games use restricted projections of three-dimensional environments, such as isometric graphics or virtual cameras with fixed angles, either as a way to improve performance of the game engine, or for stylistic and gameplay concerns. Such games are said to use pseudo-3D graphics. By contrast, games using 3D computer graphics without such restrictions are said to use true 3D.

3D Modeling

In 3D computer graphics, 3D modeling (or three-dimensional modeling) is the process of developing a mathematical representation of any *surface* of an object (either inanimate or living) in three dimensions via specialized software. The product is called a 3D model. Someone who works with 3D models may be referred to as a 3D artist. It can be displayed as a two-dimensional image through a process called *3D rendering* or used in a computer simulation of physical phenomena. The model can also be physically created using 3D printing devices.

Models may be created automatically or manually. The manual modeling process of preparing geometric data for 3D computer graphics is similar to plastic arts such as sculpting.

Models

Three-dimensional (3D) models represent a physical body using a collection of points in 3D space, connected by various geometric entities such as triangles, lines, curved surfaces, etc. Being a collection of data (points and other information), 3D models can be created by hand, algorithmically (procedural modeling), or scanned. Their surfaces may be further defined with texture mapping.

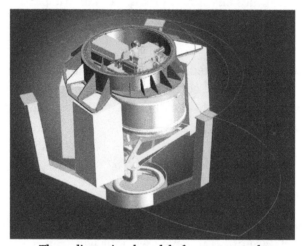

Three-dimensional model of a spectrograph

3D models are widely used anywhere in 3D graphics and CAD. Their use predates the widespread use of 3D graphics on personal computers. Many computer games used pre-rendered images of 3D models as sprites before computers could render them in real-time.

Today, 3D models are used in a wide variety of fields. The medical industry uses detailed models of organs; these may be created with multiple 2-D image slices from an MRI or CT scan. The movie industry uses them as characters and objects for animated and real-life motion pictures. The video game industry uses them as assets for computer and video games. The science sector uses them as highly detailed models of chemical compounds. The architecture industry uses them to demonstrate proposed buildings and landscapes in lieu of traditional, physical architectural models. The engineering community uses them as designs of new devices, vehicles and structures as well as a host of other uses. In recent decades the earth science community has started to construct 3D geological models as a standard practice. 3D models can also be the basis for physical devices that are built with 3D printers or CNC machines.

Representation

Almost all 3D models can be divided into two categories.

- Solid - These models define the volume of the object they represent (like a rock). Solid models are mostly used for engineering and medical simulations, and are usually built with constructive solid geometry

- Shell/boundary - these models represent the surface, e.g. the boundary of the object, not its volume (like an infinitesimally thin eggshell). Almost all visual models used in games and film are shell models.

A modern render of the iconic Utah teapot model developed by Martin Newell (1975).
The Utah teapot is one of the most common models used in 3D graphics education.

Solid and shell modeling can create functionally identical objects. Differences between them are mostly variations in the way they are created and edited and conventions of use in various fields and differences in types of approximations between the model and reality.

Shell models must be manifold (having no holes or cracks in the shell) to be meaningful as a real object. Polygonal meshes (and to a lesser extent subdivision surfaces) are by far the most common representation. Level sets are a useful representation for deforming surfaces which undergo many topological changes such as fluids.

The process of transforming representations of objects, such as the middle point coordinate of a sphere and a point on its circumference into a polygon representation of a sphere, is called tessellation. This step is used in polygon-based rendering, where objects are broken down from abstract representations ("primitives") such as spheres, cones etc., to so-called *meshes*, which are nets of interconnected triangles. Meshes of triangles (instead of e.g. squares) are popular as they have proven to be easy to rasterise (the surface described by each triangle is planar, so the projection is always convex); . Polygon representations are not used in all rendering techniques, and in these cases the tessellation step is not included in the transition from abstract representation to rendered scene.

Modeling Process

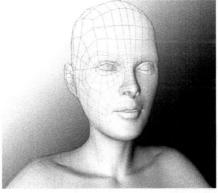

3D polygonal modelling of a human face.

There are three popular ways to represent a model:

1. Polygonal modeling - Points in 3D space, called vertices, are connected by line segments to form a polygon mesh. The vast majority of 3D models today are built as textured polygonal models, because they are flexible and because computers can render them so quickly. However, polygons are planar and can only approximate curved surfaces using many polygons.

2. Curve modeling - Surfaces are defined by curves, which are influenced by weighted control points. The curve follows (but does not necessarily interpolate) the points. Increasing the weight for a point will pull the curve closer to that point. Curve types include nonuniform rational B-spline (NURBS), splines, patches, and geometric primitives

3. Digital sculpting - Still a fairly new method of modeling, 3D sculpting has become very popular in the few years it has been around. There are currently three types of digital sculpting: Displacement, which is the most widely used among applications at this moment, uses a dense model (often generated by subdivision surfaces of a polygon control mesh) and stores new locations for the vertex positions through use of a 32bit image map that stores the adjusted locations. Volumetric, loosely based on voxels, has similar capabilities as displacement but does not suffer from polygon stretching when there are not enough polygons in a region to achieve a deformation. Dynamic tessellation is similar to voxel but divides the surface using triangulation to maintain a smooth surface and allow finer details. These methods allow for very artistic exploration as the model will have a new topology created over it once the models form and possibly details have been sculpted. The new mesh will usually have the original high resolution mesh information transferred into displacement data or normal map data if for a game engine.

A 3D fantasy fish composed of organic surfaces generated using LAI4D.

The modeling stage consists of shaping individual objects that are later used in the scene. There are a number of modeling techniques, including:

*   Constructive solid geometry

*   Implicit surfaces

*   Subdivision surfaces

Modeling can be performed by means of a dedicated program (e.g., Cinema 4D, Maya, 3ds Max, Blender, LightWave, Modo) or an application component (Shaper, Lofter in 3ds Max) or some scene description language (as in POV-Ray). In some cases, there is no strict distinction between these phases; in such cases modeling is just part of the scene creation process (this is the case, for example, with Caligari trueSpace and Realsoft 3D).

Complex materials such as blowing sand, clouds, and liquid sprays are modeled with particle systems, and are a mass of 3D coordinates which have either points, polygons, texture splats, or sprites assigned to them.

Human Models

The first widely available commercial application of human virtual models appeared in 1998 on the Lands' End web site. The human virtual models were created by the company My Virtual Mode Inc. and enabled users to create a model of themselves and try on 3D clothing. There are several modern programs that allow for the creation of virtual human models (Poser being one example).

3D Clothing

Dynamic 3D Clothing Model made in Marvelous Designer

The development of cloth simulation software such as Marvelous Designer, CLO3D and Optitex, has enabled artists and fashion designers to model dynamic 3D clothing on the computer. Dynamic 3D clothing is used for virtual fashion catalogs, as well as for dressing 3D characters for video games, 3D animation movies, for digital doubles in movies as well as for making clothes for avatars in virtual worlds such as SecondLife.

Compared to 2D Methods

3D photorealistic effects are often achieved without wireframe modeling and are sometimes indistinguishable in the final form. Some graphic art software includes filters that can be applied to 2D vector graphics or 2D raster graphics on transparent layers.

Advantages of wireframe 3D modeling over exclusively 2D methods include:

- *Flexibility,* ability to change angles or animate images with quicker rendering of the changes;

- *Ease of rendering,* automatic calculation and rendering photorealistic effects rather than mentally visualizing or estimating;

- *Accurate photorealism,* less chance of human error in misplacing, overdoing, or forgetting to include a visual effect.

A fully textured and lit rendering of a 3D model.

Disadvantages compare to 2D photorealistic rendering may include a software learning curve and difficulty achieving certain photorealistic effects. Some photorealistic effects may be achieved with special rendering filters included in the 3D modeling software. For the best of both worlds, some artists use a combination of 3D modeling followed by editing the 2D computer-rendered images from the 3D model.

3D Model Market

A large market for 3D models (as well as 3D-related content, such as textures, scripts, etc.) still exists - either for individual models or large collections. Several online marketplaces for 3D content allow individual artists to sell content that they have created, including TurboSquid, CGStudio, CreativeMarket and CGTrader. Often, the artists' goal is to get additional value out of assets they have previously created for projects. By doing so, artists can earn more money out of their old content, and companies can save money by buying pre-made models instead of paying an employee to create one from scratch. These marketplaces typically split the sale between themselves and the artist that created the asset, artists get 40% to 95% of the sales according to the marketplace. In most cases, the artist retains ownership of the 3d model; the customer only buys the right to use and present the model. Some artists sell their products directly in its own stores offering their products at a lower price by not using intermediaries.

Over the last several years numerous marketplaces specialized in 3D printing models have emerged. Some of the 3D printing marketplaces are combination of models sharing sites, with or without a built in e-com capability. Some of those platforms also offer 3D printing services on demand, software for model rendering and dynamic viewing of items, etc. 3D printing file sharing platforms include Shapeways, Pinshape, Thingiverse, TurboSquid, CGTrader, Threeding, MyMiniFactory, and GrabCAD.

3D Printing

3D printing is a form of additive manufacturing technology where a three dimensional object is created by laying down or build from successive layers of material.

In recent years, there has been an upsurge in the number of companies offering personalized 3D printed models of objects that have been scanned, designed in CAD software, and then printed to the customer's requirements. As previously mentioned, 3D models can be purchased from online marketplaces and printed by individuals or companies using commercially available 3D printers, enabling the home-production of objects such as spare parts, mathematical models, and even medical equipment.

Uses

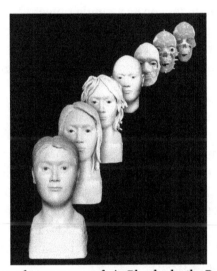

Step of Forensic facial reconstruction of a mummy made in Blender by the Brazilian 3D designer Cícero Moraes.

3D modeling is used in various industries like films, animation and gaming, interior designing and architecture. They are also used in the medical industry for the interactive representations of anatomy. A wide number of 3D software are also used in constructing digital representation of mechanical models or parts before they are actually manufactured. CAD/CAM related software are used in such fields, and with these software, not only can you construct the parts, but also assemble them, and observe their functionality.

3D modelling is also used in the field of Industrial Design, wherein products are 3D modeled before representing them to the clients. In Media and Event industries, 3D modelling is used in Stage/Set Design.

The OWL 2 translation of the vocabulary of X3D can be used to provide semantic descriptions for 3D models, which is suitable for indexing and retrieval of 3D models by features such as geometry, dimensions, material, texture, diffuse reflection, transmission spectra, transparency, reflectivity, opalescence, glazes, varnishes, and enamels (as opposed to unstructured textual descriptions or 2.5D virtual museums and exhibitions using Google Street View on Google Arts & Culture, for example). The RDF representation of 3D models can be used in reasoning, which enables intelligent 3D applications which, for example, can automatically compare two 3D models by volume.

Polygonal Modeling

In 3D computer graphics, Polygonal modeling is an approach for modeling objects by representing or approximating their surfaces using polygons. Polygonal modeling is well suited to scanline rendering and is therefore the method of choice for real-time computer graphics. Alternate methods of representing 3D objects include NURBS surfaces, subdivision surfaces, and equation-based representations used in ray tracers.

Geometric Theory and Polygons

The basic object used in mesh modeling is a vertex, a point in three-dimensional space. Two vertices connected by a straight line become an edge. Three vertices, connected to each other by three edges, define a triangle, which is the simplest polygon in Euclidean space. More complex polygons can be created out of multiple triangles, or as a single object with more than 3 vertices. Four sided polygons (generally referred to as quads) and triangles are the most common shapes used in polygonal modeling. A group of polygons, connected to each other by shared vertices, is generally referred to as an element. Each of the polygons making up an element is called a face.

In Euclidean geometry, any three non-collinear points determine a plane. For this reason, triangles always inhabit a single plane. This is not necessarily true of more complex polygons, however. The flat nature of triangles makes it simple to determine their surface normal, a three-dimensional vector perpendicular to the triangle's surface. Surface normals are useful for determining light transport in ray tracing, and are a key component of the popular Phong shading model. Some rendering systems use vertex normals instead of face normals to create a better-looking lighting system at the cost of more processing. Note that every triangle has two face normals, which point to opposite directions from each other. In many systems only one of these normals is considered valid – the other side of the polygon is referred to as a backface, and can be made visible or invisible depending on the programmer's desires.

Many modeling programs do not strictly enforce geometric theory; for example, it is possible for two vertices to have two distinct edges connecting them, occupying exactly the same spatial location. It is also possible for two vertices to exist at the same spatial coordinates, or two faces to exist at the same location. Situations such as these are usually not desired and many packages support an auto-cleanup function. If auto-cleanup is not present, however, they must be deleted manually.

A group of polygons which are connected by shared vertices is referred to as a mesh. In order for a mesh to appear attractive when rendered, it is desirable that it be non-self-intersecting, meaning that no edge passes through a polygon. Another way of looking at this is that the mesh cannot pierce itself. It is also desirable that the mesh not contain any errors such as doubled vertices, edges, or faces. For some purposes it is important that the mesh be a manifold – that is, that it does not contain holes or singularities (locations where two distinct sections of the mesh are connected by a single vertex).

Construction of Polygonal Meshes

Although it is possible to construct a mesh by manually specifying vertices and faces, it is much more common to build meshes using a variety of tools. A wide variety of 3D graphics software packages are available for use in constructing polygon meshes.

One of the more popular methods of constructing meshes is box modeling, which uses two simple tools:

- The subdivide tool splits faces and edges into smaller pieces by adding new vertices. For example, a square would be subdivided by adding one vertex in the center and one on each edge, creating four smaller squares.

- The extrude tool is applied to a face or a group of faces. It creates a new face of the same size and shape which is connected to each of the existing edges by a face. Thus, performing the extrude operation on a square face would create a cube connected to the surface at the location of the face.

A second common modeling method is sometimes referred to as inflation modeling or extrusion modeling. In this method, the user creates a 2D shape which traces the outline of an object from a photograph or a drawing. The user then uses a second image of the subject from a different angle and extrudes the 2D shape into 3D, again following the shape's outline. This method is especially common for creating faces and heads. In general, the artist will model half of the head and then duplicate the vertices, invert their location relative to some plane, and connect the two pieces together. This ensures that the model will be symmetrical.

Another common method of creating a polygonal mesh is by connecting together various primitives, which are predefined polygonal meshes created by the modeling environment. Common primitives include:

- Cubes

- Pyramids

- Cylinders

- 2D primitives, such as squares, triangles, and disks

- Specialized or esoteric primitives, such as the Utah Teapot or Suzanne, Blender's monkey mascot.

- Spheres - Spheres are commonly represented in one of two ways:

    o Icospheres are icosahedrons which possess a sufficient number of triangles to resemble a sphere.

    o UV spheres are composed of quads, and resemble the grid seen on some globes - quads are larger near the "equator" of the sphere and smaller near the "poles," eventually terminating in a single vertex.

Finally, some specialized methods of constructing high or low detail meshes exist. Sketch based modeling is a user-friendly interface for constructing low-detail models quickly, while 3D scanners can be used to create high detail meshes based on existing real-world objects in almost automatic way. These devices are very expensive, and are generally only used by researchers and industry professionals but can generate high accuracy sub-millimetric digital representations.

Operations

There is a very large number of operations which may be performed on polygonal meshes. Some of these roughly correspond to real-world manipulations of 3D objects, while others do not.

Polygonal mesh operations:

Creations - Create new geometry from some other mathematical object

- *Loft* - generate a mesh by sweeping a shape along a path
- Extrude - similar to loft, except the path is always a straight or linear line
- Revolve - generate a mesh by revolving (rotating) a shape around an axis
- Marching cubes - algorithm to construct a mesh from an implicit function

Binary Creations - Create a new mesh from a binary operation of two other meshes

- Add - boolean addition of two or more meshes
- Subtract - boolean subtraction of two or more meshes
- Intersect - boolean intersection
- Union - boolean union of two or more meshes
- Attach - attach one mesh to another (removing the interior surfaces)
- Chamfer - create a beveled surface which smoothly connects two surfaces

Deformations - Move only the vertices of a mesh

- Deform - systematically move vertices (according to certain functions or rules)
- Weighted Deform - move vertices based on localized weights per vertex
- Morph - move vertices smoothly between a source and target mesh
- Bend - move vertices to "bend" the object
- Twist - move vertices to "twist" the object

Manipulations - Modify the geometry of the mesh, but not necessarily topology

- Displace - introduce additional geometry based on a "displacement map" from the surface
- Simplify - systematically remove and average vertices
- Subdivide - smooth a course mesh by subdividing the mesh (Catmull-Clark, etc.)
- Convex Hull - generate another mesh which minimally encloses a given mesh (think shrink-wrap)
- Cut - create a hole in a mesh surface
- Stitch - close a hole in a mesh surface

Measurements - Compute some value of the mesh

- Volume - compute the 3D volume of a mesh (discrete volumetric integral)

- Surface Area - compute the surface area of a mesh (discrete surface integral)

- Collision Detection - determine if two complex meshes in motion have collided

- Fitting - construct a parametric surface (NURBS, bicubic spline) by fitting it to a given mesh

- Point-Surface Distance - compute distance from a point to the mesh

- Line-Surface Distance - compute distance from a line to the mesh

- Line-Surface Intersection - compute intersection of line and the mesh

- Cross Section - compute the curves created by a cross-section of a plane through a mesh

- Centroid - compute the centroid, geometric center, of the mesh

- Center-of-Mass - compute the center of mass, balance point, of the mesh

- Circumcenter - compute the center of a circle or sphere enclosing an element of the mesh

- Incenter - compute the center of a circle or sphere enclosed by an element of the mesh

Extensions

Once a polygonal mesh has been constructed, further steps must be taken before it is useful for games, animation, etc. The model must be texture mapped to add colors and texture to the surface and it must be given a skeleton for animation. Meshes can also be assigned weights and centers of gravity for use in physical simulation.

To display a model on a computer screen outside of the modeling environment, it is necessary to store that model in one of the file formats listed below, and then use or write a program capable of loading from that format. The two main methods of displaying 3D polygon models are OpenGL and Direct3D. Both of these methods can be used with or without a 3D accelerated graphics card.

Advantages and Disadvantages

There are many disadvantages to representing an object using polygons. Polygons are incapable of accurately representing curved surfaces, so a large number of them must be used to approximate curves in a visually appealing manner. The use of complex models has a cost in lowered speed. In scanline conversion, each polygon must be converted and displayed, regardless of size, and there are frequently a large number of models on the screen at any given time. Often, programmers must use multiple models at varying levels of detail to represent the same object in order to cut down on the number of polygons being rendered.

The main advantage of polygons is that they are faster than other representations. While a modern graphics card can show a highly detailed scene at a frame rate of 60 frames per second or higher, raytracers, the main way of displaying non-polygonal models, are incapable of achieving an interactive frame rate (10 frame/s or higher) with a similar amount of detail.

File Formats

A variety of formats are available for storing 3D polygon data. The most popular are:

- .3ds, .max, which is associated with 3D Studio Max

- .blend, which is associated with Blender

- .c4d associated with Cinema 4D

- .dae (COLLADA)

- .dxf, .dwg, .dwf, associated with AutoCAD

- .fbx (Autodesk former. Kaydara Filmbox)

- .jt originally developed by Siemens PLM Software; now an ISO standard.

- .lwo, which is associated with Lightwave

- .lxo, which is associated with MODO

- .mb and .ma, which are associated with Maya

- .md2, .md3, associated with the Quake series of games

- .mdl used with Valve Corporation's Source Engine

- .nif (NetImmerse/gamebryo)

- .obj (Wavefront's "The Advanced Visualizer")

- .ply used to store data from 3D scanners

- .rwx (Renderware)

- .stl used in rapid prototyping

- .u3d (Universal 3D)

- .wrl (VRML 2.0)

Digital Sculpting

Digital sculpting, also known as Sculpt Modeling or 3D Sculpting, is the use of software that offers tools to push, pull, smooth, grab, pinch or otherwise manipulate a digital object as if it were made of a real-life substance such as clay.

Sculpting Technology

The geometry used in digital sculpting programs to represent the model can vary; each offers different benefits and limitations. The majority of digital sculpting tools on the market use mesh-based geometry, in which an object is represented by an interconnected surface mesh of polygons that can be pushed and pulled around. This is somewhat similar to the physical process of beating copper plates to sculpt a scene in relief. Other digital sculpting tools use voxel-based geometry, in which the volume of the object is the basic element. Material can be added and removed, much like sculpting in clay. Still other tools make use of more than one basic geometry representation.

A benefit of mesh-based programs is that they support sculpting at multiple resolutions on a single model. Areas of the model that are finely detailed can have very small polygons while other areas can have larger polygons. In many mesh-based programs, the mesh can be edited at different levels of detail, and the changes at one level will propagate to higher and lower levels of model detail. A limitation of mesh-based sculpting is the fixed topology of the mesh; the specific arrangement of the polygons can limit the ways in which detail can be added or manipulated.

A benefit of voxel based sculpting is that voxels allow complete freedom over form. The topology of a model can be altered continually during the sculpting process as material is added and subtracted, which frees the sculptor from considering the layout of polygons on the model's surface. Voxels, however, are more limited in handling multiple levels of detail. Unlike mesh-based modeling, broad changes made to voxels at a low level of detail may completely destroy finer details.

Uses

It is used by auto manufacturers in their design of new cars.

Sculpting can often introduce details to meshes that would otherwise have been difficult or impossible to create using traditional 3D modeling techniques. This makes it preferable for achieving photorealistic and hyperrealistic results, though, many stylized results are achieved as well.

Sculpting is primarily used in high poly organic modeling (the creation of 3D models which consist mainly of curves or irregular surfaces, as opposed to hard surface modeling).

This rendering of two alien creatures shows the amount of photorealism achievable through digital sculpting in conjunction with other modeling, texturing, and rendering techniques.

It can create the source meshes for low poly game models used in video games. In conjunction with other 3D modeling and texturing techniques and Displacement and Normal mapping, it can greatly enhance the appearance of game meshes often to the point of photorealism. Some sculpting programs like 3D-Coat, Zbrush, and Mudbox offer ways to integrate their workflows with traditional 3D modeling and rendering programs. Conversely, 3D modeling applications like 3ds Max and

MODO are now incorporating sculpting capability as well, though these are usually less advanced than tools found in sculpting-specific applications.

High poly sculpts are also extensively used in CG artwork for movies, industrial design, art, photo-realistic illustrations, and for prototyping in 3D printing.

Sculpting Programs

There are a number of digital sculpting tools available. Some popular tools for creating are:

- Autodesk Alias
- 3D-Coat
- CB model pro
- Geomagic Freeform
- Geomagic Sculpt
- Mudbox
- Cinema 4D
- Sculptris
- SharpConstruct
- ZBrush

Traditional 3D modeling suites are also beginning to include sculpting capability. 3D modeling programs which currently feature some form of sculpting include the following:

- Softimage XSI
- Blender
- 3ds Max
- Bryce
- Cinema4D
- Form-Z
- Houdini
- Lightwave 3D
- Maya
- MODO
- Poser
- Silo

- Rhinoceros 3D

- SketchUp

- Strata 3D

- TrueSpace

Virtual Actor

A virtual human or digital clone is the creation or re-creation of a human being in image and voice using computer-generated imagery and sound, that is often indistinguishable from the real actor. This idea was first portrayed in the 1981 film *Looker*, wherein models had their bodies scanned digitally to create 3D computer generated images of the models, and then animating said images for use in TV commercials. Two 1992 books used this concept: "Fools" by Pat Cadigan, and *Et Tu, Babe* by Mark Leyner.

In general, virtual humans employed in movies are known as synthespians, virtual actors, vactors, cyberstars, or "silicentric" actors. There are several legal ramifications for the digital cloning of human actors, relating to copyright and personality rights. People who have already been digitally cloned as simulations include Bill Clinton, Marilyn Monroe, Fred Astaire, Ed Sullivan, Elvis Presley, Bruce Lee, Audrey Hepburn, Anna Marie Goddard, and George Burns. Ironically, data sets of Arnold Schwarzenegger for the creation of a virtual Arnold (head, at least) have already been made.

The name "Schwarzeneggerization" comes from the 1992 book *Et Tu, Babe* by Mark Leyner. In one scene, on pages 50–51, a character asks the shop assistant at a video store to have Arnold Schwarzenegger digitally substituted for existing actors into various works, including (amongst others) *Rain Man* (to replace both Tom Cruise and Dustin Hoffman), *My Fair Lady* (to replace Rex Harrison), *Amadeus* (to replace F. Murray Abraham), *The Diary of Anne Frank* (as Anne Frank), *Gandhi* (to replace Ben Kingsley), and *It's a Wonderful Life* (to replace James Stewart). Schwarzeneggerization is the name that Leyner gives to this process. Only 10 years later, Schwarzeneggerization was close to being reality.

By 2002, Schwarzenegger, Jim Carrey, Kate Mulgrew, Michelle Pfeiffer, Denzel Washington, Gillian Anderson, and David Duchovny had all had their heads laser scanned to create digital computer models thereof.

Early History

Early computer-generated animated faces include the 1985 film *Tony de Peltrie* and the music video for Mick Jagger's song "Hard Woman" (from *She's the Boss*). The first actual human beings to be digitally duplicated were Marilyn Monroe and Humphrey Bogart in a March 1987 film "Rendez-vous in Montreal" created by Nadia Magnenat Thalmann and Daniel Thalmann for the 100th anniversary of the Engineering Institute of Canada. The film was created by six people over a year, and had Monroe and Bogart meeting in a café in Montreal. The characters were rendered in three dimensions, and were capable of speaking, showing emotion, and shaking hands.

In 1987, the Kleiser-Walczak Construction Company (now Synthespian Studios), founded by Jeff Kleiser and Diana Walczak coined the term "synthespian" and began its Synthespian ("synthetic thespian") Project, with the aim of creating "life-like figures based on the digital animation of clay models".

In 1988, *Tin Toy* was the first entirely computer-generated movie to win an Academy Award (Best Animated Short Film). In the same year, Mike the Talking Head, an animated head whose facial expression and head posture were controlled in real time by a puppeteer using a custom-built controller, was developed by Silicon Graphics, and performed live at SIGGRAPH. In 1989, *The Abyss*, directed by James Cameron included a computer-generated face placed onto a watery pseudopod.

In 1991, *Terminator 2: Judgment Day*, also directed by Cameron, confident in the abilities of computer-generated effects from his experience with *The Abyss*, included a mixture of synthetic actors with live animation, including computer models of Robert Patrick's face. *The Abyss* contained just one scene with photo-realistic computer graphics. *Terminator 2: Judgment Day* contained over forty shots throughout the film.

In 1997, Industrial Light and Magic worked on creating a virtual actor that was a composite of the bodily parts of several real actors.

By the 21st century, virtual actors had become a reality. The face of Brandon Lee, who had died partway through the shooting of *The Crow* in 1994, had been digitally superimposed over the top of a body-double in order to complete those parts of the movie that had yet to be filmed. By 2001, three-dimensional computer-generated realistic humans had been used in *Final Fantasy: The Spirits Within*, and by 2004, a synthetic Laurence Olivier co-starred in *Sky Captain and the World of Tomorrow*.

Legal Issues

Critics such as Stuart Klawans in the *New York Times* expressed worry about the loss of "the very thing that art was supposedly preserving: our point of contact with the irreplaceable, finite person". And even more problematic are the issues of copyright and personality rights. Actors have little legal control over a digital clone of themselves. In the United States, for instance, they must resort to database protection laws in order to exercise what control they have (The proposed Database and Collections of Information Misappropriation Act would strengthen such laws). An actor does not own the copyright on his digital clones, unless they were created by him. Robert Patrick, for example, would not have any legal control over the liquid metal digital clone of himself that was created for *Terminator 2: Judgment Day*.

The use of digital clones in movie industry, to replicate the acting performances of a cloned person, represents a controversial aspect of these implications, as it may cause real actors to land in fewer roles, and put them in disadvantage at contract negotiations, since a clone could always be used by the producers at potentially lower costs. It is also a career difficulty, since a clone could be used in roles that a real actor would never accept for various reasons. Bad identifications of an actor's image with a certain type of roles could harm his career, and real actors, conscious of this, pick and choose what roles they play (Bela Lugosi and Margaret Hamilton became typecast with their roles as Count Dracula and the Wicked Witch of the West, whereas Anthony Hopkins and Dustin Hoffman have played a diverse range of parts). A digital clone could be used to play the parts of (for examples) an axe murderer or a prostitute, which would affect the actor's public image, and in turn affect what future casting opportunities were given to that actor. Both Tom Waits and Bette Midler have won actions for damages against people who employed their images in advertisements that they had refused to take part in themselves.

In the USA, the use of a digital clone in advertisements is required to be accurate and truthful (section 43(a) of the Lanham Act and which makes deliberate confusion unlawful). The use of a celebrity's image would be an implied endorsement. The New York District Court held that an advertisement employing a Woody Allen impersonator would violate the Act unless it contained a disclaimer stating that Allen did not endorse the product.

Other concerns include posthumous use of digital clones. Barbara Creed states that "Arnold's famous threat, 'I'll be back', may take on a new meaning". Even before Brandon Lee was digitally reanimated, the California Senate drew up the Astaire Bill, in response to lobbying from Fred Astaire's widow and the Screen Actors Guild, who were seeking to restrict the use of digital clones of Astaire. Movie studios opposed the legislation, and as of 2002 it had yet to be finalized and enacted. Several companies, including Virtual Celebrity Productions, have purchased the rights to create and use digital clones of various dead celebrities, such as Marlene Dietrich and Vincent Price.

In Fiction

- *Simone*, a 2002 science fiction drama film written, produced and directed by Andrew Niccol, starring Al Pacino.

- *The Congress (2013 Film)* a 2013 science fiction drama film written, produced and directed by Ari Folman, starring Robin Wright deals with this issue extensively.

Constructive Solid Geometry

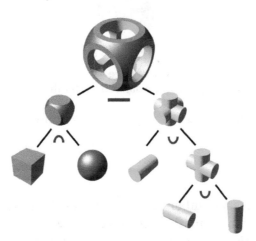

CSG objects can be represented by binary trees, where leaves represent primitives, and nodes represent operations. In this figure, the nodes are labeled ∩ for intersection, ∪ for union, and − for difference.

Constructive solid geometry (CSG) (formerly called computational binary solid geometry) is a technique used in solid modeling. Constructive solid geometry allows a modeler to create a complex surface or object by using Boolean operators to combine simpler objects. Often CSG presents a model or surface that appears visually complex, but is actually little more than cleverly combined or decombined objects.

In 3D computer graphics and CAD, CSG is often used in procedural modeling. CSG can also be performed on polygonal meshes, and may or may not be procedural and/or parametric.

Contrast CSG with polygon mesh modeling and box modeling.

Workings of CSG

The simplest solid objects used for the representation are called primitives. Typically they are the objects of simple shape: cuboids, cylinders, prisms, pyramids, spheres, cones. The set of allowable primitives is limited by each software package. Some software packages allow CSG on curved objects while other packages do not.

It is said that an object is constructed from primitives by means of allowable operations, which are typically Boolean operations on sets: union, intersection and difference, as well as geometric transformations of those sets.

A primitive can typically be described by a procedure which accepts some number of parameters; for example, a sphere may be described by the coordinates of its center point, along with a radius value. These primitives can be combined into compound objects using operations like these:

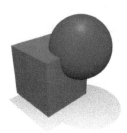

Union	**Difference**	**Intersection**
Merger of two objects into one	Subtraction of one object from another	Portion common to both objects

Combining these elementary operations, it is possible to build up objects with high complexity starting from simple ones.

Applications of CSG

Constructive solid geometry has a number of practical uses. It is used in cases where simple geometric objects are desired, or where mathematical accuracy is important. Nearly all engineering CAD packages use CSG (where it may be useful for representing tool cuts, and features where parts must fit together).

The Quake engine and Unreal engine both use this system, as does Hammer (the native Source engine level editor), and Torque Game Engine/Torque Game Engine Advanced. CSG is popular because a modeler can use a set of relatively simple objects to create very complicated geometry.

When CSG is procedural or parametric, the user can revise their complex geometry by changing the position of objects or by changing the Boolean operation used to combine those objects.

One of the advantages of CSG is that it can easily assure that objects are "solid" or water-tight if all of the primitive shapes are water-tight. This can be important for some manufacturing or engineering computation applications. By comparison, when creating geometry based upon boundary representations, additional topological data is required, or consistency checks must be performed to assure that the given boundary description specifies a valid solid object.

A convenient property of CSG shapes is that it is easy to classify arbitrary points as being either inside or outside the shape created by CSG. The point is simply classified against all the underlying primitives and the resulting boolean expression is evaluated. This is a desirable quality for some applications such as ray tracing.

Applications with CSG Support

Generic Modelling Languages and Software

- HyperFun
- PLaSM - Programming Language of Solid Modeling

Ray-tracing and Particle Transport

- PhotoRealistic RenderMan
- POV-Ray

CAD

- BRL-CAD
- SelfCAD
- FreeCAD
- OpenSCAD
- Antimony
- Pro/Engineer
- SolidWorks mechanical CAD suite
- Vectorworks
- AutoCAD
- Rhino
- Realsoft 3D

Gaming

- GtkRadiant
- Roblox Studio - Since 2014
- UnrealEd
- Valve Hammer Editor
- Unity (Edit mode and Real-time, requires using Asset Store Purchased plugins)

Others

- 3Delight
- Blender (Blender is a surface mesh editor, but can do simple CSG using meta objects)
- Clara.io
- Feature Manipulation Engine
- MCNP
- SketchUp

Subdivision Surface

A subdivision surface, in the field of 3D computer graphics, is a method of representing a smooth surface via the specification of a coarser piecewise linear polygon mesh. The smooth surface can be calculated from the coarse mesh as the limit of recursive subdivision of each polygonal face into smaller faces that better approximate the smooth surface.

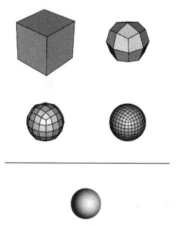

First three steps of Catmull–Clark subdivision of a cube with subdivision surface below

Overview

Subdivision surfaces are defined recursively. The process starts with a given polygonal mesh. A refinement scheme is then applied to this mesh. This process takes that mesh and subdivides it, creating new vertices and new faces. The positions of the new vertices in the mesh are computed based on the positions of nearby old vertices. In some refinement schemes, the positions of old vertices might also be altered (possibly based on the positions of new vertices).

This process produces a finer mesh than the original one, containing more polygonal faces. This resulting mesh can be passed through the same refinement scheme again and so on.

The limit subdivision surface is the surface produced from this process being iteratively applied infinitely many times. In practical use however, this algorithm is only applied a limited number of times. The limit surface can also be calculated directly for most subdivision surfaces using the technique of Jos Stam, which eliminates the need for recursive refinement. Subdivision surfaces and T-Splines are competing technologies. Mathematically, subdivision surfaces are spline surfaces with singularities.

Refinement Schemes

Subdivision surface refinement schemes can be broadly classified into two categories: interpolating and approximating. Interpolating schemes are required to match the original position of vertices in the original mesh. Approximating schemes are not; they can and will adjust these positions as needed. In general, approximating schemes have greater smoothness, but editing applications that allow users to set exact surface constraints require an optimization step.

There is another division in subdivision surface schemes as well, the type of polygon that they operate on. Some function for quadrilaterals (quads), while others operate on triangles.

Approximating Schemes

Approximating means that the limit surfaces approximate the initial meshes and that after subdivision, the newly generated control points are not in the limit surfaces. Examples of approximating subdivision schemes are:

- Catmull–Clark (1978) generalized bi-cubic uniform B-spline to produce their subdivision scheme. For arbitrary initial meshes, this scheme generates limit surfaces that are C^2 continuous everywhere except at extraordinary vertices where they are C^1 continuous (Peters and Reif 1998).

- Doo–Sabin - The second subdivision scheme was developed by Doo and Sabin (1978) who successfully extended Chaikin's corner-cutting method for curves to surfaces. They used the analytical expression of bi-quadratic uniform B-spline surface to generate their subdivision procedure to produce C^1 limit surfaces with arbitrary topology for arbitrary initial meshes.

- Loop, Triangles - Loop (1987) proposed his subdivision scheme based on a quartic box spline of six direction vectors to provide a rule to generate C^2 continuous limit surfaces everywhere except at extraordinary vertices where they are C^1 continuous.

- Mid-Edge subdivision scheme - The mid-edge subdivision scheme was proposed independently by Peters–Reif (1997) and Habib–Warren (1999). The former used the midpoint of each edge to build the new mesh. The latter used a four-directional box spline to build the scheme. This scheme generates C^1 continuous limit surfaces on initial meshes with arbitrary topology.

- $\sqrt{3}$ subdivision scheme - This scheme has been developed by Kobbelt (2000): it handles arbitrary triangular meshes, it is C^2 continuous everywhere except at extraordinary vertices where it is C^1 continuous and it offers a natural adaptive refinement when required. It exhibits at least two specificities: it is a *Dual* scheme for triangle meshes and it has a slower refinement rate than primal ones.

Interpolating Schemes

After subdivision, the control points of the original mesh and the new generated control points are interpolated on the limit surface. The earliest work was the butterfly scheme by Dyn, Levin and Gregory (1990), who extended the four-point interpolatory subdivision scheme for curves to a subdivision scheme for surface. Zorin, Schröder and Sweldens (1996) noticed that the butterfly scheme cannot generate smooth surfaces for irregular triangle meshes and thus modified this scheme. Kobbelt (1996) further generalized the four-point interpolatory subdivision scheme for curves to the tensor product subdivision scheme for surfaces. Deng and Ma (2013) further generalized the four-point interpolatory subdivision scheme to arbitrary degree.

- Butterfly, Triangles - named after the scheme's shape

- Midedge, Quads

- Kobbelt, Quads - a variational subdivision method that tries to overcome uniform subdivision drawbacks

- Deng-Ma, Quads - 2n point subdivision generalized to arbitrary odd degree

Editing a Subdivision Surface

Subdivision surfaces can be naturally edited at different levels of subdivision. Starting with basic shapes you can use binary operators to create the correct topology. Then edit the coarse mesh to create the basic shape, then edit the offsets for the next subdivision step, then repeat this at finer and finer levels. You can always see how your edits affect the limit surface via GPU evaluation of the surface.

A surface designer may also start with a scanned in object or one created from a NURBS surface. The same basic optimization algorithms are used to create a coarse base mesh with the correct topology and then add details at each level so that the object may be edited at different levels. These types of surfaces may be difficult to work with because the base mesh does not have control points in the locations that a human designer would place them. With a scanned object this surface is easier to work with than a raw triangle mesh, but a NURBS object probably had well laid out control points which behave less intuitively after the conversion than before.

3D Rendering

3D rendering is the 3D computer graphics process of automatically converting 3D wire frame models into 2D images with 3D photorealistic effects or non-photorealistic rendering on a computer.

Rendering Methods

Rendering is the final process of creating the actual 2D image or animation from the prepared scene. This can be compared to taking a photo or filming the scene after the setup is finished in real life. Several different, and often specialized, rendering methods have been developed. These range from the distinctly non-realistic wireframe rendering through polygon-based rendering, to more advanced techniques such as: scanline rendering, ray tracing, or radiosity. Rendering may take from fractions of a second to days for a single image/frame. In general, different methods are better suited for either photo-realistic rendering, or real-time rendering.

A photo realistic 3D render of 6 computer fans using radiosity rendering, DOF and procedural materials

Real-time

A screenshot from *Second Life*, an example of an old online game which renders frames in real time.

Rendering for interactive media, such as games and simulations, is calculated and displayed in real time, at rates of approximately 20 to 120 frames per second. In real-time rendering, the goal is to show as much information as possible as the eye can process in a fraction of a second (a.k.a. in one frame. In the case of 30 frame-per-second animation a frame encompasses one 30th of a second). The primary goal is to achieve an as high as possible degree of photorealism at an acceptable minimum rendering speed (usually 24 frames per second, as that is the minimum the human eye needs to see to successfully create the illusion of movement). In fact, exploitations can be applied in the way the eye 'perceives' the world, and as a result the final image presented is not necessarily that of the real-world, but one close enough for the human eye to tolerate. Rendering software may simulate such visual effects as lens flares, depth of field or motion blur. These are attempts to simulate visual phenomena resulting from the optical characteristics of cameras and of the human eye. These effects can lend an element of realism to a scene, even if the effect is merely a simulated artifact of a camera. This is the basic method employed in games, interactive worlds and VRML. The rapid increase in computer processing power has allowed a progressively higher degree of realism even for real-time rendering, including techniques such as HDR rendering. Real-time rendering is often polygonal and aided by the computer's GPU.

Non Real-time

Animations for non-interactive media, such as feature films and video, are rendered much more slowly. Non-real time rendering enables the leveraging of limited processing power in order to obtain higher image quality. Rendering times for individual frames may vary from a few seconds to several days for complex scenes. Rendered frames are stored on a hard disk then can be transferred to other media such as motion picture film or optical disk. These frames are then displayed sequentially at high frame rates, typically 24, 25, or 30 frames per second, to achieve the illusion of movement.

An example of a ray-traced image that typically takes seconds or minutes to render.

Computer-generated image created by Gilles Tran.

When the goal is photo-realism, techniques such as ray tracing or radiosity are employed. This is the basic method employed in digital media and artistic works. Techniques have been developed for the purpose of simulating other naturally occurring effects, such as the interaction of light with various forms of matter. Examples of such techniques include particle systems (which can simulate rain, smoke, or fire), volumetric sampling (to simulate fog, dust and other spatial atmospheric effects), caustics (to simulate light focusing by uneven light-refracting surfaces, such as the light ripples seen on the bottom of a swimming pool), and subsurface scattering (to simulate light reflecting inside the volumes of solid objects such as human skin).

The rendering process is computationally expensive, given the complex variety of physical processes being simulated. Computer processing power has increased rapidly over the years, allowing for a progressively higher degree of realistic rendering. Film studios that produce computer-generated animations typically make use of a render farm to generate images in a timely manner. However, falling hardware costs mean that it is entirely possible to create small amounts of 3D animation on a home computer system. The output of the renderer is often used as only one small part of a completed motion-picture scene. Many layers of material may be rendered separately and integrated into the final shot using compositing software.

Reflection and Shading Models

Models of reflection/scattering and shading are used to describe the appearance of a surface. Although these issues may seem like problems all on their own, they are studied almost exclusively within the context of rendering. Modern 3D computer graphics rely heavily on a simplified reflection model called Phong reflection model. In refraction of light, an important concept is the refractive index. In most 3D programming implementations, the term for this value is "index of refraction" (usually short for IOR). Shading can be broken down into two different techniques, which are often studied independently:

- Surface shading - How light spreads across a surface (mostly used for scanline rendering for real-time 3D rendering in video games)

- Reflection/Scattering - How light interacts with a surface *at a given point* (mostly used for ray tracing rendering for non real-time photo-realistic and artistic 3D rendering in both CGI still 3D images and CGI non-interactive 3D animations)

Surface Shading Algorithms

Popular surface shading algorithms in 3D computer graphics include:

- Flat shading: A technique that shades each polygon of an object based on the polygon's "normal" and the position and intensity of a light source.

- Gouraud shading: Invented by H. Gouraud in 1971, a fast and resource-conscious vertex shading technique used to simulate smoothly shaded surfaces.

- Phong shading: Invented by Bui Tuong Phong, used to simulate specular highlights and smooth shaded surfaces.

Reflection

The Utah teapot

Reflection or scattering is the relationship between the incoming and outgoing illumination at a given point. Descriptions of scattering are usually given in terms of a bidirectional scattering distribution function or BSDF.

Shading

Shading addresses how different types of scattering are distributed across the surface (i.e., which scattering function applies where). Descriptions of this kind are typically expressed with a program called a shader. (Note that there is some confusion since the word "shader" is sometimes used for programs that describe local *geometric* variation.) A simple example of shading is texture mapping, which uses an image to specify the diffuse color at each point on a surface, giving it more apparent detail.

Some shading techniques include:

- Bump mapping: Invented by Jim Blinn, a normal-perturbation technique used to simulate wrinkled surfaces.

- Cel shading: A technique used to imitate the look of hand-drawn animation.

Transport

Transport describes how illumination in a scene gets from one place to another. Visibility is a major component of light transport.

Projection

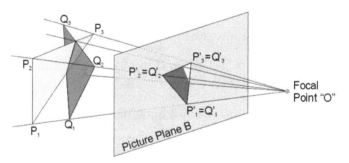

Perspective Projection

The shaded three-dimensional objects must be flattened so that the display device - namely a monitor - can display it in only two dimensions, this process is called 3D projection. This is done using projection and, for most applications, perspective projection. The basic idea behind perspective projection is that objects that are further away are made smaller in relation to those that are closer to the eye. Programs produce perspective by multiplying a dilation constant raised to the power of the negative of the distance from the observer. A dilation constant of one means that there is no perspective. High dilation constants can cause a "fish-eye" effect in which image distortion begins to occur. Orthographic projection is used mainly in CAD or CAM applications where scientific modeling requires precise measurements and preservation of the third dimension.

Photorealism

Photorealism is a genre of art that encompasses painting, drawing and other graphic media, in which an artist studies a photograph and then attempts to reproduce the image as realistically as possible in another medium. Although the term can be used broadly to describe artworks in many different media, it is also used to refer specifically to a group of paintings and painters of the American art movement that began in the late 1960s and early 1970s.

John's Diner with John's Chevelle, 2007
John Baeder, oil on canvas, 30×48 inches.

History

As a full-fledged art movement, Photorealism evolved from Pop Art and as a counter to Abstract Expressionism as well as Minimalist art movements in the late 1960s and early 1970s in the United States. Photorealists use a photograph or several photographs to gather the information to create their paintings and it can be argued that the use of a camera and photographs is an acceptance of Modernism. However, the admittance to the use of photographs in Photorealism was met with intense criticism when the movement began to gain momentum in the late 1960s, despite the fact that visual devices had been used since the fifteenth century to aid artists with their work.

Ralph's Diner (1981–1982), oil on canvas. Example of photorealist Ralph Goings' work

The invention of photography in the nineteenth century had three effects on art: portrait and scenic artists were deemed inferior to the photograph and many turned to photography as careers; within nineteenth- and twentieth-century art movements it is well documented that artists used the photograph as source material and as an aid—however, they went to great lengths to deny the fact fearing that their work would be misunderstood as imitations; and through the photograph's invention artists were open to a great deal of new experimentation. Thus, the culmination of the invention of the photograph was a break in art's history towards the challenge facing the artist—since the earliest known cave drawings—trying to replicate the scenes they viewed.

By the time the Photorealists began producing their bodies of work the photograph had become the leading means of reproducing reality and abstraction was the focus of the art world. Realism continued as an ongoing art movement, even experiencing a reemergence in the 1930s, but by the 1950s modernist critics and Abstract Expressionism had minimalized realism as a serious art undertaking. Though Photorealists share some aspects of American realists, such as Edward Hopper, they tried to set themselves as much apart from traditional realists as they did Abstract Expressionists. Photorealists were much more influenced by the work of Pop artists and were reacting against Abstract Expressionism.

Pop Art and Photorealism were both reactionary movements stemming from the ever increasing and overwhelming abundance of photographic media, which by the mid 20th century had grown into such a massive phenomenon that it was threatening to lessen the value of imagery in art. However, whereas the Pop artists were primarily pointing out the absurdity of much of the imagery (especially in commercial usage), the Photorealists were trying to reclaim and exalt the value of an image.

The association of Photorealism to *Trompe L'oeil* is a wrongly attributed comparison, an error in observation or interpretation made by many critics of the 1970s and 1980s. Trompe L'oeil paintings attempt to "fool the eye" and make the viewer think he is seeing an actual object, not a painted one. When observing a Photorealist painting, the viewer is always aware that they are looking at a painting.

Definition

The word *Photorealism* was coined by Louis K. Meisel in 1969 and appeared in print for the first time in 1970 in a Whitney Museum catalogue for the show "Twenty-two Realists." It is also sometimes labeled as Super-Realism, New Realism, Sharp Focus Realism, or Hyper-Realism.

Louis K. Meisel, two years later, developed a five-point definition at the request of Stuart M. Speiser, who had commissioned a large collection of works by the Photorealists, which later developed into a traveling show known as 'Photo-Realism 1973: The Stuart M. Speiser Collection', which was donated to the Smithsonian in 1978 and is shown in several of its museums as well as traveling under the auspices of SITE. The definition for the ORIGINATORS was as follows:

1. The Photo-Realist uses the camera and photograph to gather information.

2. The Photo-Realist uses a mechanical or semimechanical means to transfer the information to the canvas.

3. The Photo-Realist must have the technical ability to make the finished work appear photographic.

4. The artist must have exhibited work as a Photo-Realist by 1972 to be considered one of the central Photo-Realists.

5. The artist must have devoted at least five years to the development and exhibition of Photo-Realist work.

Styles

Photorealist painting cannot exist without the photograph. In Photorealism, change and movement must be frozen in time which must then be accurately represented by the artist. Photorealists gather their imagery and information with the camera and photograph. Once the photograph is developed (usually onto a photographic slide) the artist will systematically transfer the image from the photographic slide onto canvases. Usually this is done either by projecting the slide onto the canvas or by using traditional grid techniques. The resulting images are often direct copies of the original photograph but are usually larger than the original photograph or slide. This results in the photorealist style being tight and precise, often with an emphasis on imagery that requires a high level of technical prowess and virtuosity to simulate, such as reflections in specular surfaces and the geometric rigor of man-made environs.

Artists

The first generation of American photorealists includes such painters as John Baeder, Richard Estes, Ralph Goings, Chuck Close, Charles Bell, Audrey Flack, Don Eddy, Robert Bechtle, and Tom Blackwell. Often working independently of each other and with widely different starting points, these original photorealists routinely tackled mundane or familiar subjects in traditional art genres--landscapes (mostly urban rather than naturalistic), portraits, and still lifes. In the UK, photorealist approaches were favoured by many artists including Mike Gorman and Eric Scott. The introduction of these European painters to a wider US audience was brought about through the 1982 'Superhumanism' exhibition at the Arnold Katzen Gallery, New York.

Though the movement is primarily associated with painting, Duane Hanson and John DeAndrea are sculptors associated with photorealism for their painted, lifelike sculptures of average people that were complete with simulated hair and real clothes. They are called *Verists*.

Since 2000

Though the height of Photorealism was in the 1970s the movement continues and includes several of the original photorealists as well as many of their contemporaries. According to Meisel and Chase's *Photorealism at the Millennium*, only eight of the original photorealists were still creating photorealist work in 2002; ten including John Baeder and Howard Kanovitz.

Artists Charles Bell, John Kacere, and Howard Kanovitz have died; Audrey Flack, Chuck Close, and Don Eddy have moved in different directions other than photorealism; and Robert Cottingham no longer considers himself a photorealist.

Newer Photorealists are building upon the foundations set by the original photorealists. Examples would be the influence of Richard Estes in works by Anthony Brunelli or the influence of Ralph Goings and Charles Bell in works by Glennray Tutor. However, this has led many to move on from the strict definition of photorealism as the emulation of the photograph. Photorealism is also no longer simply an American art movement. Starting with Franz Gertsch in the 1980s Clive Head, Raphaella Spence, Bertrand Meniel, and Roberto Bernardi are several European artists associated with photorealism that have emerged since the mid-1990s. This internationalization of photorealism is also seen in photorealist events, such as The Prague Project, in which American and non-American photorealist painters have traveled together to locations including Prague, Zurich, Monaco and New York, to work alongside each other in producing work.

Dream of Love (2005), Oil on canvas. Example of Photorealist Glennray Tutor's work

The evolution of technology has brought forth photorealistic paintings that exceed what was thought possible with paintings; these newer paintings by the photorealists are sometimes referred to as "Hyperrealism." With new technology in cameras and digital equipment, artists are able to be far more precision-oriented.

Photorealism's influence and popularity continues to grow, with new books such as Juxtapoz's 2014 book entitled *Hyperreal* detailing current trends within the artistic genre.

List of Photorealists

Original Photorealists

Significant artists whose work helped define Photorealism:

- John Baeder
- Robert Bechtle
- Charles Bell
- Tom Blackwell
- Chuck Close
- Robert Cottingham
- Don Eddy
- Richard Estes
- Audrey Flack
- Ralph Goings
- Ian Hornak
- Howard Kanovitz
- John Kacere
- Ron Kleemann
- Malcolm Morley
- John Salt
- Ben Schonzeit

Photorealists

Significant artists whose work meets the criteria of Photorealism:

- Linda Bacon
- Mike Bayne
- Arne Besser
- Hilo Chen
- Davis Cone
- Randy Dudley
- Franz Gertsch
- Robert Gniewek
- Gus Heinze

- Gottfried Helnwein
- Don Jacot
- Noel Mahaffey
- Dennis James Martin
- Jack Mendenhall
- Kim Mendenhall
- Betrand Meniel
- Reynard Milici

- Robert Neffson
- Jerry Ott
- Denis Peterson
- Tjalf Sparnaay
- Paul Staiger
- Glennray Tutor
- Idelle Weber

Other Photorealists

- Roberto Bernardi
- Doug Bloodworth
- Anthony Brunelli
- Helmut Ditsch
- Clive Head
- Cheryl Kelley
- Rod Penner
- Raphaella Spence
- Robert Standish

Non-photorealistic Rendering

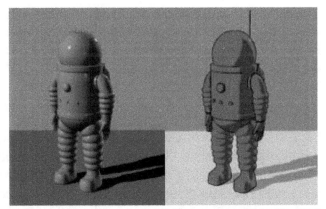

A normal shader (left) and a NPR shader using cel-shading (right)

Non-photorealistic rendering (NPR) is an area of computer graphics that focuses on enabling a wide variety of expressive styles for digital art. In contrast to traditional computer graphics, which has focused on photorealism, NPR is inspired by artistic styles such as painting, drawing, technical illustration, and animated cartoons. NPR has appeared in movies and video games in the form of "toon shading", as well as in scientific visualization, architectural illustration and experimental animation. An example of a modern use of this method is that of cel-shaded animation.

History

The term "non-photorealistic rendering" was probably coined by David Salesin and Georges Winkenbach in a 1994 paper. Many researchers find the terminology to be unsatisfying; some of the criticisms are as follows:

- The term "photorealism" has different meanings for graphics researchers and artists. For artists, who are the target consumers of NPR techniques, it refers to a school of painting that focuses on reproducing the effect of a camera lens, with all the distortion and hyper-reflections that it involves. For graphics researchers, it refers to an image that is visually indistinguishable from reality. In fact, graphics researchers lump the kinds of visual distortions that are used by photorealist painters into non-photorealism.

- Describing something by what it is not is problematic. Equivalent comparisons might be "non-elephant biology", or "non-geometric mathematics". NPR researchers have stated that they expect the term will disappear eventually, and be replaced by the more general term "computer graphics", with "photorealistic graphics" being used to describe traditional computer graphics.

- Many techniques that are used to create 'non-photorealistic' images are not rendering techniques. They are modelling techniques, or post-processing techniques. While the latter are coming to be known as 'image-based rendering', sketch-based modelling techniques, cannot technically be included under this heading, which is very inconvenient for conference organisers.

The first conference on Non-Photorealistic Animation and Rendering included a discussion of possible alternative names. Among those suggested were "expressive graphics", "artistic rendering", "non-realistic graphics", "art-based rendering", and "psychographics". All of these terms have been used in various research papers on the topic, but the term NPR seems to have nonetheless taken hold.

The first technical meeting dedicated to NPR was the ACM sponsored Symposium on Non-Photorealistic Rendering and Animation (NPAR) in 2000. NPAR is traditionally co-located with the Annecy Animated Film Festival, running on even numbered years. From 2007 NPAR began to also run on odd-numbered years, co-located with ACM SIGGRAPH.

3D

Three-dimensional NPR is the style that is most commonly seen in video games and movies. The output from this technique is almost always a 3D model that has been modified from the original input model to portray a new artistic style. In many cases, the geometry of the model is identical to the original geometry, and only the material applied to the surface is modified. With increased availability of programmable GPU's, shaders have allowed NPR effects to be applied to the rasterised image that is to be displayed to the screen. The majority of NPR techniques applied to 3D geometry are intended to make the scene appear two-dimensional.

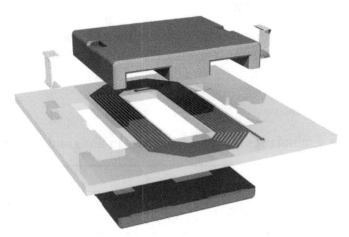

An example of NPR used for technical illustrations

NPR techniques for 3D images include cel shading and Gooch shading.

For enhanced legibility, the most useful technical illustrations for technical communication are not necessarily photorealistic. Non-photorealistic renderings, such as exploded view diagrams, greatly assist in showing placement of parts in a complex system.

2D

An example of a non-photoreal rendering of an existing 2D image.

The input to a two-dimensional NPR system is most commonly an image; however, there are systems that take 3D geometry information as input and produce a 2D image or video as output. Again, many of the systems are intended to mimic a desired artistic style, such as watercolor, impressionism, or pen and ink drawing. Sketchy style is a rendering form that mimic hand-drawn graph primitive.

Users who are interested in having much more control in the NPR process may be more interested in interactive techniques. Many of these NPR systems provide the user with a canvas that they can "paint" on using the cursor — as the user paints, a stylized version of the image is revealed on the canvas. This is especially useful for people who want to simulate different sizes of brush strokes according to different areas of the image.

In contrast to the methods mentioned previously, another technique in NPR is simulating the painter's medium. Methods include simulating the diffusion of ink through different kinds of paper, and also of pigments through water for simulation of watercolor.

Notable Films and Software

Here is a list of some seminal uses of NPR techniques in films and software.

Short films		
Technological Threat	1988	Early use of toon shading together with Tex Avery-style cartoon characters.
Gas Planet	1992	Pencil-sketching 3D rendering by Eric Darnell.
Fishing	2000	Watercolor-style 3D rendering David Gainey.
RoadHead Snack and Drink	1998 1999	Short films created with Rotoshop by Bob Sabiston.
Ryan	2004	Nonlinear projection and other distortions of 3D geometry.
The Girl Who Cried Flowers	2008	Watercolor-style rendering by Auryn.
Feature films		
What Dreams May Come	1998	Painterly rendering in the "painted world" sequence.
Tarzan	1999	First use of Disney's "Deep Canvas" system.
Waking Life	2001	First use of rotoshop in a feature film.
A Scanner Darkly	2006	"a 15-month animation process"
Video games and other software		
Jet Set Radio	2000	Early use of toon-shading in video games.
SketchUp	2000	Sketch-like modelling software with toon rendering.
The Legend of Zelda: The Wind Waker	2002	One of the most well-known cel-shaded games
XIII	2003	done as "comic"-like as possible
Ōkami	2006	A game whose visuals emulate the style of sumi-e (Japanese Ink Wash Painting)

Computer Animation

Computer animation is the process used for generating animated images. The more general term computer-generated imagery (CGI) encompasses both static scenes and dynamic images, while computer animation *only* refers to the moving images. Modern computer animation usually uses 3D computer graphics, although 2D computer graphics are still used for stylistic, low bandwidth, and faster real-time renderings. Sometimes, the target of the animation is the computer itself, but sometimes film as well.

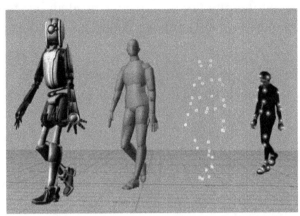

An example of computer animation which is produced in the "motion capture" technique

Computer animation is essentially a digital successor to the stop motion techniques using 3D models, and traditional animation techniques using frame-by-frame animation of 2D illustrations. Computer-generated animations are more controllable than other more physically based processes, constructing miniatures for effects shots or hiring extras for crowd scenes, and because it allows the creation of images that would not be feasible using any other technology. It can also allow a single graphic artist to produce such content without the use of actors, expensive set pieces, or props. To create the illusion of movement, an image is displayed on the computer monitor and repeatedly replaced by a new image that is similar to it, but advanced slightly in time (usually at a rate of 24 or 30 frames/second). This technique is identical to how the illusion of movement is achieved with television and motion pictures.

For 3D animations, objects (models) are built on the computer monitor (modeled) and 3D figures are rigged with a virtual skeleton. For 2D figure animations, separate objects (illustrations) and separate transparent layers are used with or without that virtual skeleton. Then the limbs, eyes, mouth, clothes, etc. of the figure are moved by the animator on key frames. The differences in appearance between key frames are automatically calculated by the computer in a process known as tweening or morphing. Finally, the animation is rendered.

For 3D animations, all frames must be rendered after the modeling is complete. For 2D vector animations, the rendering process is the key frame illustration process, while tweened frames are rendered as needed. For pre-recorded presentations, the rendered frames are transferred to a different format or medium, like digital video. The frames may also be rendered in real time as they are presented to the end-user audience. Low bandwidth animations transmitted via the internet (e.g. Adobe Flash, X3D) often use software on the end-users computer to render in real time as an alternative to streaming or pre-loaded high bandwidth animations.

Explanation

To trick the eye and the brain into thinking they are seeing a smoothly moving object, the pictures should be drawn at around 12 frames per second or faster. (A frame is one complete image.) With rates above 75-120 frames per second, no improvement in realism or smoothness is perceivable due to the way the eye and the brain both process images. At rates below 12 frames per second, most people can detect jerkiness associated with the drawing of new images that detracts from the illusion of realistic movement. Conventional hand-drawn cartoon animation often uses 15 frames per second in order to save on the number of drawings needed, but this is usually accepted because of the stylized nature of cartoons. To produce more realistic imagery, computer animation demands higher frame rates.

Films seen in theaters in the United States run at 24 frames per second, which is sufficient to create the illusion of continuous movement. For high resolution, adapters are used.

History

Early digital computer animation was developed at Bell Telephone Laboratories in the 1960s by Edward E. Zajac, Frank W. Sinden, Kenneth C. Knowlton, and A. Michael Noll. Other digital animation was also practiced at the Lawrence Livermore National Laboratory.

An early step in the history of computer animation was the sequel to the 1973 film *Westworld*, a science-fiction film about a society in which robots live and work among humans. The sequel, *Futureworld* (1976), used the 3D wire-frame imagery, which featured a computer-animated hand and face both created by University of Utah graduates Edwin Catmull and Fred Parke. This imagery originally appeared in their student film *A Computer Animated Hand*, which they completed in 1972.

Developments in CGI technologies are reported each year at SIGGRAPH, an annual conference on computer graphics and interactive techniques that is attended by thousands of computer professionals each year. Developers of computer games and 3D video cards strive to achieve the same visual quality on personal computers in real-time as is possible for CGI films and animation. With the rapid advancement of real-time rendering quality, artists began to use game engines to render non-interactive movies, which led to the art form Machinima.

The very first full length computer animated television series was *ReBoot*, which debuted in September 1994; the series followed the adventures of characters who lived inside a computer. The first feature-length computer animated film was *Toy Story* (1995), which was made by Pixar. It followed an adventure centered around toys and their owners. This groundbreaking film was also the first of many fully computer-animated movies.

Animation Methods

In most 3D computer animation systems, an animator creates a simplified representation of a character's anatomy, which is analogous to a skeleton or stick figure. The position of each segment of the skeletal model is defined by animation variables, or Avars for short. In human and animal characters, many parts of the skeletal model correspond to the actual bones, but skeletal animation is also used to animate other things, with facial features (though other methods for facial animation exist). The character "Woody" in *Toy Story*, for example, uses 700 Avars (100 in the face alone). The computer doesn't usually render the skeletal model directly (it is invisible), but it does use the skeletal model to compute the exact position and orientation of that certain character, which is eventually rendered into an image. Thus by changing the values of Avars over time, the animator creates motion by making the character move from frame to frame.

There are several methods for generating the Avar values to obtain realistic motion. Traditionally, animators manipulate the Avars directly. Rather than set Avars for every frame, they usually set Avars at strategic points (frames) in time and let the computer interpolate or tween between them in a process called keyframing. Keyframing puts control in the hands of the animator and has roots in hand-drawn traditional animation.

In contrast, a newer method called motion capture makes use of live action footage. When computer animation is driven by motion capture, a real performer acts out the scene as if they were the character to be animated. His/her motion is recorded to a computer using video cameras and markers and that performance is then applied to the animated character.

Each method has its advantages and as of 2007, games and films are using either or both of these methods in productions. Keyframe animation can produce motions that would be difficult or impossible to act out, while motion capture can reproduce the subtleties of a particular actor. For example, in the 2006 film *Pirates of the Caribbean: Dead Man's Chest*, Bill Nighy provided the performance for the character Davy Jones. Even though Nighy doesn't appear in the movie himself, the movie benefited from his performance by recording the nuances of his body language, posture, facial expressions, etc. Thus motion capture is appropriate in situations where believable, realistic behavior and action is required, but the types of characters required exceed what can be done throughout the conventional costuming.

Modeling

3D computer animation combines 3D models of objects and programmed or hand "keyframed" movement. These models are constructed out of geometrical vertices, faces, and edges in a 3D coordinate system. Objects are sculpted much like real clay or plaster, working from general forms to specific details with various sculpting tools. Unless a 3D model is intended to be a solid color, it must be painted with "textures" for realism. A bone/joint animation system is set up to deform the CGI model (e.g., to make a humanoid model walk). In a process known as rigging, the virtual marionette is given various controllers and handles for controlling movement. Animation data can be created using motion capture, or keyframing by a human animator, or a combination of the two.

3D models rigged for animation may contain thousands of control points — for example, "Woody" from *Toy Story* uses 700 specialized animation controllers. Rhythm and Hues Studios labored for two years to create Aslan in the movie *The Chronicles of Narnia: The Lion, the Witch and the Wardrobe*, which had about 1,851 controllers (742 in the face alone). In the 2004 film *The Day After Tomorrow*, designers had to design forces of extreme weather with the help of video references and accurate meteorological facts. For the 2005 remake of *King Kong*, actor Andy Serkis was used to help designers pinpoint the gorilla's prime location in the shots and used his expressions to model "human" characteristics onto the creature. Serkis had earlier provided the voice and performance for Gollum in J. R. R. Tolkien's *The Lord of the Rings* trilogy.

Equipment

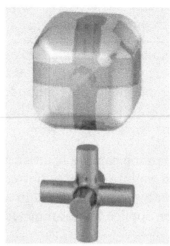

A ray-traced 3-D model of a jack inside a cube, and the jack alone below.

Computer animation can be created with a computer and an animation software. Some impressive animation can be achieved even with basic programs; however, the rendering can take a lot of time on an ordinary home computer. Professional animators of movies, television and video games could make photorealistic animation with high detail. This level of quality for movie animation would take hundreds of years to create on a home computer. Instead, many powerful workstation computers are used. Graphics workstation computers use two to four processors, and they are a lot more powerful than an actual home computer and are specialized for rendering. A large number of workstations (known as a "render farm") are networked together to effectively act as a giant computer. The result is a computer-animated movie that can be completed in about one to five years (however, this process is not composed solely of rendering). A workstation typically costs $2,000-16,000 with the more expensive stations being able to render much faster due to the more technologically-advanced hardware that they contain. Professionals also use digital movie cameras, motion/performance capture, bluescreens, film editing software, props, and other tools used for movie animation.

Facial Animation

The realistic modeling of human facial features is both one of the most challenging and sought after elements in computer-generated imagery. Computer facial animation is a highly complex field where models typically include a very large number of animation variables. Historically speaking, the first SIGGRAPH tutorials on *State of the art in Facial Animation* in 1989 and 1990 proved to be a turning point in the field by bringing together and consolidating multiple research elements and sparked interest among a number of researchers.

The Facial Action Coding System (with 46 "action units", "lip bite" or "squint"), which had been developed in 1976, became a popular basis for many systems. As early as 2001, MPEG-4 included 68 Face Animation Parameters (FAPs) for lips, jaws, etc., and the field has made significant progress since then and the use of facial microexpression has increased.

In some cases, an affective space, the PAD emotional state model, can be used to assign specific emotions to the faces of avatars. In this approach, the PAD model is used as a high level emotional space and the lower level space is the MPEG-4 Facial Animation Parameters (FAP). A mid-level Partial Expression Parameters (PEP) space is then used to in a two-level structure – the PAD-PEP mapping and the PEP-FAP translation model.

Realism

Realism in computer animation can mean making each frame look photorealistic, in the sense that the scene is rendered to resemble a photograph or make the characters' animation believable and lifelike. Computer animation can also be realistic with or without the photorealistic rendering.

One of the greatest challenges in computer animation has been creating human characters that look and move with the highest degree of realism. Part of the difficulty in making pleasing, realistic human characters is the uncanny valley, the concept where the human audience (up to a point) tends to have an increasingly negative, emotional response as a human replica looks and acts more and more human. Films that have attempted photorealistic human characters, such as *The Polar Express*, *Beowulf*, and *A Christmas Carol* have been criticized as "creepy" and "disconcerting".

The goal of computer animation is not always to emulate live action as closely as possible, so many animated films instead feature characters who are anthropomorphic animals, fantasy creatures and characters, superheroes, or otherwise have non-realistic, cartoon-like proportions. Computer animation can also be tailored to mimic or substitute for other kinds of animation, traditional stop-motion animation (as shown in *Flushed Away* or *The Lego Movie*). Some of the long-standing basic principles of animation, like squash & stretch, call for movement that is not strictly realistic, and such principles still see widespread application in computer animation.

Notable Examples

- *Final Fantasy: The Spirits Within*: often cited as the first computer-generated movie to attempt to show realistic-looking humans

- *The Polar Express*

- *Mars Needs Moms*

- *L.A. Noire*: received attention for its use of MotionScan technology

- *The Adventures of Tintin: The Secret of the Unicorn*

- *Heavy Rain*

- *Beyond: Two Souls*

- *Beowulf*

Films

CGI short films have been produced as independent animation since 1976, although the popularity of computer animation (especially in the field of special effects) skyrocketed during the modern era of U.S. animation. The first completely computer-animated movie was *Toy Story* (1995), but

VeggieTales is the first American fully 3D computer animated series sold directly(made in 1993), that started animation series such as "ReBoot" in 1994.

Animation Studios

Some notable producers of computer-animated feature films include:

- Animal Logic - Films include *Happy Feet* (2006), *Walking with Dinosaurs* (2013) and *The Lego Movie* (2014)

- Blue Sky Studios - Films include *Ice Age* (2002), *Rio* (2011), *The Peanuts Movie* (2015)

- DreamWorks Animation - Films include *Shrek* (2001), *Kung Fu Panda* (2008), *How to Train Your Dragon* (2010)

- Illumination Entertainment — Films include *Despicable Me* (2010), *Minions* (2015), *The Secret Life of Pets* (2016)

- Industrial Light & Magic - Films include *Rango* (2011) and *Strange Magic* (2015)

- Pixar - Films include *Toy Story* (1995), *Finding Nemo* (2003), *Cars* (2006)

- Reel FX Animation Studios - Films include *Free Birds* (2013) and *The Book of Life* (2014)

- Sony Pictures Animation - Films include *Cloudy with a Chance of Meatballs* (2009), *The Smurfs* (2011), *Hotel Transylvania* (2012)

- Sony Pictures Imageworks - Films include *The Angry Birds Movie* (2016)

- Walt Disney Animation Studios - Films include *Tangled* (2010), *Wreck-It Ralph* (2012), *Frozen* (2013)

- Warner Animation Group - Films include *The Lego Movie* (2014), and *Storks* (2016)

Web Animations

The popularity of websites that allow members to upload their own movies for others to view has created a growing community of amateur computer animators. With utilities and programs often included free with modern operating systems, many users can make their own animated movies and shorts. Several free and open source animation software applications exist as well. The ease at which these animations can be distributed has attracted professional animation talent also. Companies such as PowToon and GoAnimate attempt to bridged the gap by giving amateurs access to professional animations as clip art.

The oldest (most backward compatible) web-based animations are in the animated GIF format, which can be uploaded and seen on the web easily . However, the raster graphics format of GIF animations slows the download and frame rate, especially with larger screen sizes. The growing demand for higher quality web-based animations was met by a vector graphics alternative that relied on the use of a plugin. For decades, Flash animations were the most popular format, until the web development community abandoned support for the Flash player plugin. Web browsers on mobile devices and mobile operating systems never fully supported the Flash plugin.

By this time, internet bandwidth and download speeds increased, making raster graphic animations more convenient. Some of the more complex vector graphic animations had a slower frame rate due to complex rendering than some of the raster graphic alternatives. Many of the GIF and Flash animations were already converted to digital video formats, which were compatible with mobile devices and reduced file sizes via video compression technology. However, compatibility was still problematic as some of the popular video formats such as Apple's QuickTime and Microsoft Silverlight required plugins. YouTube, the most popular video viewing website, was also relying on the Flash plugin to deliver digital video in the Flash Video format.

The latest alternatives are HTML5 compatible animations. Technologies such as JavaScript and CSS animations made sequencing the movement of images in HTML5 web pages more convenient. SVG animations offered a vector graphic alternative to the original Flash graphic format, SmartSketch. YouTube offers an HTML5 alternative for digital video. APNG (Animated PNG) offered a raster graphic alternative to animated GIF files that enables multi-level transparency not available in GIFs.

Detailed Examples and Pseudocode

In 2D computer animation, moving objects are often referred to as "sprites." A sprite is an image that has a location associated with it. The location of the sprite is changed slightly, between each displayed frame, to make the sprite appear to move. The following pseudocode makes a sprite move from left to right:

```
var int x := 0, y := screenHeight / 2;

while x < screenWidth

drawBackground()

drawSpriteAtXY (x, y) // draw on top of the background

x := x + 5 // move to the right
```

Computer animation uses different techniques to produce animations. Most frequently, sophisticated mathematics is used to manipulate complex three-dimensional polygons, apply "textures", lighting and other effects to the polygons and finally rendering the complete image. A sophisticated graphical user interface may be used to create the animation and arrange its choreography. Another technique called constructive solid geometry defines objects by conducting boolean operations on regular shapes, and has the advantage that animations may be accurately produced at any resolution.

Computer-assisted vs Computer-generated

To animate means, figuratively, to "give life to". There are two basic methods that animators commonly use to accomplish this.

Computer-assisted animation is usually classed as two-dimensional (2D) animation. Creators drawings either hand drawn (pencil to paper) or interactively drawn(drawn on the computer) using different assisting appliances and are positioned into specific software packages. Within the software package the creator will place drawings into different key frames which fundamentally create an outline of the most important movements. The computer will then fill in all the "in-between frames", commonly known as Tweening. Computer-assisted animation is basically using new technologies to cut down the time scale that traditional animation could take, but still having the elements of traditional drawings of characters or objects.

Three examples of films using computer-assisted animation are *Beauty and the Beast*, *The Road to El Dorado* and *Tarzan*.

Computer-generated animation is known as 3-dimensional (3D) animation. Creators will design an object or character with an X,Y and Z axis. Unlike the traditional way of animation no pencil to paper drawings create the way computer generated animation works. The object or character created will then be taken into a software, key framing and tweening are also carried out in computer generated animation but are also a lot of techniques used that do not relate to traditional animation. Animators can break physical laws by using mathematical algorithms to cheat, mass, force and gravity rulings. Fundamentally, time scale and quality could be said to be a preferred way to produce animation as they are two major things that are enhanced by using computer generated animation. Another positive aspect of CGA is the fact one can create a flock of creatures to act independently when created as a group. An animal's fur can be programmed to wave in the wind and lie flat when it rains instead of programming each strand of hair separately.

A few examples of computer-generated animation movies are *Tangled*, *Toy Story*, *Frozen*, *Inside Out*, *Shrek*, *Finding Nemo*, *Ice Age*, *Despicable Me* and *Zootopia*.

Real-time Computer Graphics

Real-time computer graphics or real-time rendering is the subfield of computer graphics focused on producing and analyzing images in real time. The term is most often used in reference to interactive 3D computer graphics, typically using a GPU, with video games the most noticeable users. The term can also refer to anything from rendering an application's GUI to real-time image processing and image analysis.

Although computers have been known from the beginning to be capable of generating 2D images involving simple lines, images and polygons in real-time (e.g. Bresenham's line drawing algorithm), the creation of 3D computer graphics and the speed necessary for generating fast, good quality 3D images onto a display screen has always been a daunting task for traditional Von Neumann architecture-based systems. The rest of this lesson concentrates on this widely accepted aspect of real-time graphics rather than expanding on the principles of real-time 2D computer graphics.

Overview

This lesson refers to doing the *rendering*-computation fast enough, so that the series of rendered images induce the illusion of movement in the human brain of the user. This illusion allows for the interaction with the software doing the calculations taking into account user input. The unit used for measuring the frame rate in a series of images is frames per second (fps). Different techniques for rendering exist, e.g. ray-tracing and rasterizing.

Principles of Real-time 3D Computer Graphics

The goal of computer graphics is to generate a computer generated image using certain desired metrics. This image is often called a frame. How fast these images or frames are generated in a given second determines the method's real-timeliness.

One interesting aspect of real-time computer graphics is the way in which it differs from traditional off-line rendering systems (and hence, these are the non-real-time graphics systems); non-real-time graphics typically rely on ray-tracing where the expensive operation of tracing rays from the camera to the world is allowed and can take as much as hours or even days for a single frame. On the other hand, in the case of real-time graphics, the system has less than 1/30th of a second per image. In order to do that, the current systems cannot afford shooting millions or even billions of rays; instead, they rely on the technique of z-buffer triangle rasterization. In this technique, every object is decomposed into individual primitives—the most popular and common one is the triangle. These triangles are then 'drawn' or rendered onto the screen one by one. Each of these triangles get positioned, rotated and scaled on the screen and a special hardware (or in the case of an emulator, the software rasterizer) called rasterizer generates the pixels inside each of these triangles. These triangles are then decomposed into further smaller atomic units called pixels (or in computer graphics terminology, aptly called fragments) that are suitable for displaying on a display screen. The pixels are then drawn on the screen using a certain color; current systems are capable of deciding the color that results in these triangles—for e.g. a texture can be used to 'paint' onto a triangle, which is simply deciding what color to output at each pixel based on a stored picture; or in a more complex case, at each pixel, one can compute if a certain light is being seen or not resulting in very good shadows (using a technique called shadow mapping).

Thus, real-time graphics is oriented toward providing as much quality as possible for the lowest performance cost possible for a given class of hardware. Most video-games and simulators fall in this category of real-time graphics. As mentioned above, real-time graphics is currently possible due to the significant recent advancements in these special hardware components called graphics processing units (GPUs). These GPUs are capable of handling millions of triangles *per frame* and within each such triangle capable of handling millions or even billions of pixels (i.e. generating these pixel colors). Current DirectX 11/OpenGL 4.x class hardware is capable of generating complex effects on the fly (i.e. in real-time) such as shadow volumes, motion blurring, real-time triangle generation among many others. Although the gap in quality between real-time graphics and traditional off-line graphics is narrowing, the accuracy is still far below the accuracy of offline rendering.

Advantages

Another interesting difference between real-time and non-real-time graphics is the interactivity desired in real-time graphics. Feedback is typically the main motivation for pushing real-time graphics to its furore. In cases like films, the director has the complete control and determinism of what has to be drawn on each frame, typically involving weeks or even years of decision-making involving a number of people.

In the case of real-time interactive computer graphics, usually a user is in control of what is *about to be* drawn on the display screen; the user typically uses an input device to provide feedback to the system—for example, wanting to move a character on the screen—and the system decides the next frame based on this particular instance of action. Usually the display is far slower (in terms of the number of frames per second) in responsiveness than the input device (in terms of the input device's response time measured in *ms*). In a way this is justified due to the immense difference between the infinitesimal response time generated by a human-being's motion and the very slow perspective speed of the human-visual system; this results in significant advancements in computer graphics, whereas the advancements in input devices typically take a much longer time to achieve the same state of fundamental advancement (e.g., the current Wii Remote), as these input devices have to be extremely fast in order to be usable.

Another important factor controlling real-time computer graphics is the combination of physics and animation. These techniques largely dictate what is to be drawn on the screen—or more precisely, *where* to draw certain objects (deciding their position) on the screen. These techniques imitate the behavior (the temporal dimension, not the spatial dimensions) seen in real-world to a degree that is far more realistic than and compensating computer-graphics' degree of realism.

The Graphics Rendering Pipeline

Graphics rendering pipeline is known as the rendering pipeline or simply the pipeline. It is the foundation of real-time graphics. Its main function is to generate, or render, a two-dimensional image, given a virtual camera, three-dimensional objects (an object that has width, length, and depth), light sources, lighting models, textures, and more.

Architecture

The architecture of the real-time rendering pipeline can be divided into three conceptual stages as shown as in the figure below. These stages include application, geometry, and rasterizer. This structure is the core which is used in real-time computer graphics applications.

Application Stage

The application stage is driven by the application where "it begins the image generation process that results in the final scene of frame of animation. Therefore creating a base filled with simple images, that then later on build up into a bigger, more clear image". The application is implemented in the software thus giving the developers total control over the implementation in order to change the performance. This stage may, for example, contain collision detection, speed-up techniques, animations, force feedback, etc. One of the processes that is usually implemented in this stage is collision detection. Collision detection is usually includes algorithms that detects whether two objects collide. After a collision is detected between two objects, a response may be generated and sent back to the colliding objects as well as to a force feedback device. Other processes implemented in this stage included texture animation, animations via transforms, geometry morphing, or any kind of calculations that are not performed in any other stages. At the end of the application stage, which is also the most important part of this stage, the geometry to be rendered is fed to the next stage in the rendering pipeline. These are the rendering primitives that might eventually end up on the output device, such as points, lines, and triangles, etc.

Geometry Stage

The geometry stage is responsible for the majority of the per-polygon operations or per-vertex operation; it means that this stage computes what is to be drawn, how it should be drawn, and where it should be drawn. In some case, this stage might be defined as one pipeline stage or several different stages, mainly due to the different implementation of this stage. However, in this case, this stage is further divided into different functional group.

Model and View Transform

Before the final model is shown on the output device, the model is transformed into several different spaces or coordinate systems. That is, when an object is being moved or manipulated, the object's vertices are what are being transformed.

Lighting

In order to give the model a more realistic appearance, one or more light sources are usually equipped during the scene of transforming the model. However, this stage cannot be reached without completing the 3D scene being transformed into the view space; the view space is where the camera is placed at the origin and aimed in a way that the camera is looking in the direction of the negative z-axis, with the y-axis pointing upwards and the x-axis pointing to the right.

Projection

There are two types of projection, orthographic (also called parallel) and perspective projection. Orthographic projection is used to represent a 3D model in a two dimensional (2D) space. The main characteristic of orthographic projection is that the parallel lines remain parallel even after the transformation without distorting them. Perspective projection is when a camera is farther away from the model, the smaller the model it appears. Essentially, perspective projection is the way that we see things from our eyes.

Clipping

Clipping is the process of removing primitives that are outside of the view box in order to continue on to the rasterizer stage. Primitives that are outside of the view box are removed or "clipped" away. Once the primitives that are outside of the view box are removed, the primitives that are still inside of the view box will be drawn into new triangles to be proceeded to the next stage.

Screen Mapping

The purpose of screen mapping, as the name implies, is to find out the coordinates of the primitives that were determined to be on the inside of the view box in the clipping stage.

Rasterizer Stage

Once all of the necessary steps are completed from the two previous stages, all the elements, including the lines that have been drawn and the models that have been transformed, are ready to enter the rasterizer stages. Rasterizer stage means turning all of those elements into pixels, or picture elements, and adding color onto them.

Skeletal Animation

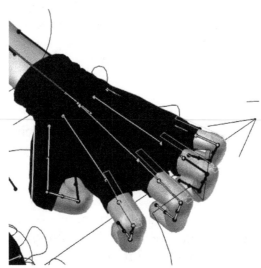

'Bones' (in green) used to pose a hand. In practice, the 'bones' themselves are often hidden and replaced by more user-friendly objects. In this example from the open source project Blender, these 'handles' (in blue) have been scaled down to bend the fingers. The bones are still controlling the deformation, but the animator only sees the 'handles'.

Skeletal animation is a technique in computer animation in which a character (or other articulated object) is represented in two parts: a surface representation used to draw the character (called *skin* or *mesh*) and a hierarchical set of interconnected bones (called the *skeleton* or *rig*) used to animate (*pose* and *keyframe*) the mesh. While this technique is often used to animate humans or more generally for organic modeling, it only serves to make the animation process more intuitive and the same technique can be used to control the deformation of any object — a door, a spoon, a building, or a galaxy. When the animated object is more general than, for example, a humanoid character the set of bones may not be hierarchical or interconnected, but it just represents a higher level description of the motion of the part of mesh or skin it is influencing.

The technique was introduced in 1988 by Nadia Magnenat Thalmann, Richard Laperrière, and Daniel Thalmann. This technique is used in virtually all animation systems where simplified user interfaces allows animators to control often complex algorithms and a huge amount of geometry; most notably through inverse kinematics and other "goal-oriented" techniques. In principle, however, the intention of the technique is never to imitate real anatomy or physical processes, but only to control the deformation of the mesh data.

Technique

"Rigging is making our characters able to move. The process of rigging is we take that digital sculpture, and we start building the skeleton, the muscles, and we attach the skin to the character, and we also create a set of animation controls, which our animators use to push and pull the body around."

This technique is used by constructing a series of 'bones,' sometimes referred to as *rigging*. Each bone has a three-dimensional transformation (which includes its position, scale and orientation), and an optional parent bone. The bones therefore form a hierarchy. The full transform of a child node is the product of its parent transform and its own transform. So moving a thigh-bone will move the lower leg too. As the character is animated, the bones change their transformation over time, under the influence of some animation controller. A rig is generally composed of both forward kinematics and inverse kinematics parts that may interact with each other. Skeletal animation is referring to the forward kinematics part of the rig, where a complete set of bones configurations identifies a unique pose.

Each bone in the skeleton is associated with some portion of the character's visual representation. *Skinning* is the process of creating this association. In the most common case of a polygonal mesh character, the bone is associated with a group of vertices; for example, in a model of a human being, the 'thigh' bone would be associated with the vertices making up the polygons in the model's thigh. Portions of the character's skin can normally be associated with multiple bones, each one having a scaling factors called vertex weights, or blend weights. The movement of skin near the joints of two bones, can therefore be influenced by both bones. In most state-of-the-art graphical engines, the skinning process is done on the GPU thanks to a shader program.

For a polygonal mesh, each vertex can have a blend weight for each bone. To calculate the final position of the vertex, a transformation matrix is created for each bone which, when applied to the vertex, first puts the vertex in bone space then puts it back into mesh space, the vertex. After applying a matrix to the vertex, it is scaled by its corresponding weight. This algorithm is called matrix palette skinning, because the set of bone transformations (stored as transform matrices) form a palette for the skin vertex to choose from.

Benefits and Drawbacks

Strengths

- Bone represent set of vertices (or some other objects, which represent for example a leg).
    - o Animator controls fewer characteristics of the model
        - ☐ Animator can focus on the large scale motion.
    - o Bones are independently movable.

An animation can be defined by simple movements of the bones, instead of vertex by vertex (in the case of a polygonal mesh).

Weaknesses

- Bone represents set of vertices (or some other object).
    - o Does not provide realistic muscle movement and skin motion
    - o Possible solutions to this problem:
        - ☐ Special muscle controllers attached to the bones
        - ☐ Consultation with physiology experts (increase accuracy of musculoskeletal realism with more thorough virtual anatomy simulations)

Applications

Skeletal animation is the standard way to animate characters or mechanical objects for a prolonged period of time (usually over 100 frames). It is commonly used by video game artists and in the movie industry, and can also be applied to mechanical objects and any other object made up of rigid elements and joints.

Performance capture (or motion capture) can speed up development time of skeletal animation, as well as increasing the level of realism.

For motion that is too dangerous for performance capture, there are computer simulations that automatically calculate physics of motion and resistance with skeletal frames. Virtual anatomy properties such as weight of limbs, muscle reaction, bone strength and joint constraints may be added for realistic bouncing, buckling, fracture and tumbling effects known as virtual stunts. However, there are other applications of virtual anatomy simulations such as military and emergency response. Virtual soldiers, rescue workers, patients, passengers and pedestrians can be used for training, virtual engineering and virtual testing of equipment. Virtual anatomy technology may be combined with artificial intelligence for further enhancement of animation and simulation technology.

Computer Facial Animation

Computer facial animation is primarily an area of computer graphics that encapsulates methods and techniques for generating and animating images or models of a character face. The character can be a human, a humanoid, an animal, a fantasy creature or character, etc. Due to its subject and output type, it is also related to many other scientific and artistic fields from psychology to traditional animation. The importance of human faces in verbal and non-verbal communication and advances in computer graphics hardware and software have caused considerable scientific, technological, and artistic interests in computer facial animation.

Although development of computer graphics methods for facial animation started in the early-1970s, major achievements in this field are more recent and happened since the late 1980s.

The body of work around computer facial animation can be divided in two main areas. Techniques to generate animation data and methods to apply such data to a character. Techniques such as motion capture and keyframing belong to the first group, while morph targets animation (more commonly known as blendshape animation) and skeletal animation belong to the second. Facial animation has become well-known and popular through animated feature films and computer games but its applications include many more areas such as communication, education, scientific simulation, and agent-based systems (for example online customer service representatives). With the recent advancements in computational power in personal and mobile devices, facial animation has transitioned from appearing in pre-rendered content to being created at runtime.

History

Human facial expression has been the subject of scientific investigation for more than one hundred years. Study of facial movements and expressions started from a biological point of view. After some older investigations, for example by John Bulwer in the late 1640s, Charles Darwin's book *The Expression of the Emotions in Men and Animals* can be considered a major departure for modern research in behavioural biology.

Computer based facial expression modelling and animation is not a new endeavour. The earliest work with computer based facial representation was done in the early-1970s. The first three-dimensional facial animation was created by Parke in 1972. In 1973, Gillenson developed an interactive system to assemble and edit line drawn facial images. in 1974, Parke developed a parameterized three-dimensional facial model.

One of the most important attempts to describe facial movements was Facial Action Coding System (FACS). Originally developed by Carl-Herman Hjortsjö in the 1960s and updated by Ekman and Friesen in 1978, FACS defines 46 basic facial Action Units (AUs). A major group of these Action Units represent primitive movements of facial muscles in actions such as raising brows, winking, and talking. Eight AU's are for rigid three-dimensional head movements, (i.e. turning and tilting left and right and going up, down, forward and backward). FACS has been successfully used for describing desired movements of synthetic faces and also in tracking facial activities.

The early-1980s saw the development of the first physically based muscle-controlled face model by Platt and the development of techniques for facial caricatures by Brennan. In 1985, the animated short film *Tony de Peltrie* was a landmark for facial animation. This marked the first time computer facial expression and speech animation were a fundamental part of telling the story.

The late-1980s saw the development of a new muscle-based model by Waters, the development of an abstract muscle action model by Magnenat-Thalmann and colleagues, and approaches to automatic speech synchronization by Lewis and Hill. The 1990s have seen increasing activity in the development of facial animation techniques and the use of computer facial animation as a key storytelling component as illustrated in animated films such as *Toy Story* (1995), *Antz* (1998), *Shrek*, and *Monsters, Inc.* (both 2001), and computer games such as *Sims. Casper* (1995), a milestone in this decade, was the first movie in which a lead actor was produced exclusively using digital facial animation.

The sophistication of the films increased after 2000. In *The Matrix Reloaded* and *Matrix Revolutions*, dense optical flow from several high-definition cameras was used to capture realistic facial movement at every point on the face. *Polar Express (film)* used a large Vicon system to capture upward of 150 points. Although these systems are automated, a large amount of manual clean-up effort is still needed to make the data usable. Another milestone in facial animation was reached by *The Lord of the Rings*, where a character specific shape base system was developed. Mark Sagar pioneered the use of FACS in entertainment facial animation, and FACS based systems developed by Sagar were used on *Monster House*, *King Kong*, and other films.

Techniques

Generating Facial Animation Data

The generation of facial animation data can be approached in different ways: 1.) marker-based motion capture on points or marks on the face of a performer, 2.) markerless motion capture techniques using different type of cameras, 3.) audio-driven techniques, and 4.) keyframe animation.

- Motion capture uses cameras placed around a subject. The subject is generally fitted either with reflectors (passive motion capture) or sources (active motion capture) that precisely determine the subject's position in space. The data recorded by the cameras is then digitized and converted into a three-dimensional computer model of the subject. Until recently, the size of the detectors/sources used by motion capture systems made the technology inappropriate for facial capture. However, miniaturization and other advancements have made motion capture a viable tool for computer facial animation. Facial motion capture was used extensively in Polar Express by Imageworks where hundreds of motion points were captured. This film was very accomplished and while it attempted to recreate realism, it was criticized for having fallen in the 'uncanny valley', the realm where animation realism is sufficient for human recognition and to convey the emotional message but where the characters fail to be perceived as realistic. The main difficulties of motion capture are the quality of the data which may include vibration as well as the retargeting of the geometry of the points.

- Markerless motion capture aims at simplifying the motion capture process by avoiding encumbering the performer with markers. Several techniques came out recently leveraging different sensors, among which standard video cameras, Kinect and depth sensors or other structured-light based devices. Systems based on structured light may achieve real-time performance without the use of any markers using a high speed structured light scanner. The system is based on a robust offline face tracking stage which trains the system with different facial expressions. The matched sequences are used to build a person-specific linear face model that is subsequently used for online face tracking and expression transfer.

- Audio-driven techniques are particularly well fitted for speech animation. Speech is usually treated in a different way to the animation of facial expressions, this is because simple keyframe-based approaches to animation typically provide a poor approximation to real speech dynamics. Often visemes are used to represent the key poses in observed speech (i.e. the position of the lips, jaw and tongue when producing a particular phoneme), however there is a great deal of variation in the realisation of visemes during the production of natural speech. The source of this variation is termed coarticulation which is the influence of surrounding visemes upon the current viseme (i.e. the effect of context). To account for coarticulation current systems either explicitly take into account context when blending viseme keyframes or use longer units such as diphone, triphone, syllable or even word and sentence-length units. One of the most common approaches to speech animation is the use of dominance functions introduced by Cohen and Massaro. Each dominance function represents the influence over time that a viseme has on a speech utterance. Typically the influence will be greatest at the center of the viseme and will degrade with distance from the viseme center. Dominance functions are blended together to generate a speech trajectory in much the same way that spline basis functions are blended together to generate a curve. The shape of each dominance function will be different according to both which viseme it represents and what aspect of the face is being controlled (e.g. lip width, jaw rotation etc.). This approach to computer-generated speech animation can be seen in the Baldi talking head. Other models of speech use basis units which include context (e.g. diphones, triphones etc.) instead of visemes. As the basis units already incorporate the variation of each viseme according to context and to some degree the dynamics of each viseme, no model of coarticulation is required. Speech is simply generated by selecting appropriate units from a database and blending the units together. This is similar to concatenative techniques in audio speech synthesis. The disadvantage to these models is that a large amount of captured data is required to produce natural results, and whilst longer units produce more natural results the size of database required expands with the average length of each unit. Finally, some models directly generate speech animations from audio. These systems typically use hidden markov models or neural nets to transform audio parameters into a stream of control parameters for a facial model. The advantage of this method is the capability of voice context handling, the natural rhythm, tempo, emotional and dynamics handling without complex approximation algorithms. The training database is not needed to be labeled since there are no phonemes or visemes needed; the only needed data is the voice and the animation parameters.

- Keyframe animation is the least automated of the processes to create animation data although it delivers the maximum amount of control over the animation. It is often used in combination with other techniques to deliver the final polish to the animation. The keyframe data can be made of scalar values defining the morph targets coefficients or rotation and translation values of the bones in models with a bone based rig. Often to speed up the keyframe animation process a control rig is used by the animation. The control rig represents a higher level of abstraction that can act on multiple morph targets coefficients or bones at the same time. For example, a "smile" control can act simultaneously on the mouth shape curving up and the eyes squinting.

Applying Facial Animation to a Character

The main techniques used to apply facial animation to a character are: 1.) morph targets animation, 2.) bone driven animation, 3.) texture-based animation (2D or 3D), and 4.) physiological models.

- Morph targets (also called "blendshapes") based systems offer a fast playback as well as a high degree of fidelity of expressions. The technique involves modeling portions of the face mesh to approximate expressions and visemes and then blending the different sub meshes, known as morph targets or blendshapes. Perhaps the most accomplished character using this technique was Gollum, from *The Lord of the Rings*. Drawbacks of this technique are that they involve intensive manual labor and are specific to each character. Recently, new concepts in 3D modeling have started to emerge. Recently, a new technology departing from the traditional techniques starts to emerge, such as *Curve Controlled Modeling* that emphasizes the modeling of the movement of a 3D object instead of the traditional modeling of the static shape.

- Bone driven animation is very broadly used in games. The bones setup can vary between few bones to close to a hundred to allow all subtle facial expressions. The main advantages of bone driven animation is that the same animation can be used for different characters as long as the morphology of their faces is similar, and secondly they do not require loading in memory all the Morph targetsdata. Bone driven animation is most widely supported by 3D game engines. Bone driven animation can be used both 2D and 3D animation. For example, it is possible to rig and animated using bones a 2D character using Adobe Flash.

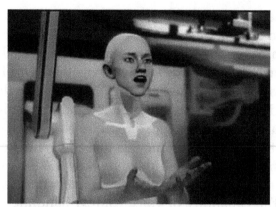

Screenshot from "Kara" animated short by Quantic Dream

- Texture-based animation uses pixel color to create the animation on the character face. 2D facial animation is commonly based upon the transformation of images, including both images from still photography and sequences of video. Image morphing is a technique which allows in-between transitional images to be generated between a pair of target still images or between frames from sequences of video. These morphing techniques usually consist of a combination of a geometric deformation technique, which aligns the target images, and a cross-fade which creates the smooth transition in the image texture. An early example of image morphing can be seen in Michael Jackson's video for "Black Or White". In 3D animation texture based animation can be achieved by animating the texture itself or the UV mapping. In the latter case a texture map of all the facial expression is created and the UV map animation is used to transition from one expression to the next.

- Physiological models, such as skeletal muscle systems and physically based head models, form another approach in modeling the head and face. Here, the physical and anatomical characteristics of bones, tissues, and skin are simulated to provide a realistic appearance (e.g. spring-like elasticity). Such methods can be very powerful for creating realism but the complexity of facial structures make them computationally expensive, and difficult to create. Considering the effectiveness of parameterized models for communicative purposes, it may be argued that physically based models are not a very efficient choice in many applications. This does not deny the advantages of physically based models and the fact that they can even be used within the context of parameterized models to provide local details when needed.

Face Animation Languages

Many face animation languages are used to describe the content of facial animation. They can be input to a compatible "player" software which then creates the requested actions. Face animation languages are closely related to other multimedia presentation languages such as SMIL and VRML. Due to the popularity and effectiveness of XML as a data representation mechanism, most face animation languages are XML-based. For instance, this is a sample from Virtual Human Markup Language (VHML):

```
<vhml>

  <person disposition="angry">

    First I speak with an angry voice and look very angry,
```

```
  <surprised intensity="50">
    but suddenly I change to look more surprised.
  </surprised>
 </person>
</vhml>
```

More advanced languages allow decision-making, event handling, and parallel and sequential actions. Following is an example from Face Modeling Language (FML):

```
<fml>
  <act>
    <par>
      <hdmv type="yaw" value="15" begin="0" end="2000" />
      <expr type="joy" value="-60" begin="0" end="2000" />
    </par>
    <excl event_name="kbd" event_value="" repeat="kbd;F3_up" >
      <hdmv type="yaw" value="40" begin="0" end="2000" event_value="F1_up" />
      <hdmv type="yaw" value="-40" begin="0" end="2000" event_value="F2_up" />
    </excl>
  </act>
</fml>
```

Key Frame

A key frame in animation and filmmaking is a drawing that defines the starting and ending points of any smooth transition. The drawings are called "frames" because their position in time is measured in frames on a strip of film. A sequence of key frames defines which movement the viewer will see, whereas the position of the key frames on the film, video, or animation defines the timing of the movement. Because only two or three key frames over the span of a second do not create the illusion of movement, the remaining frames are filled with inbetweens.

Use of Key Frames as a Means to Change Parameters

In software packages that support animation, especially 3D graphics, there are many parameters that can be changed for any one object. One example of such an object is a light (In 3D graphics, lights function similarly to real-world lights. They cause illumination, cast shadows, and create specular highlights). Lights have many parameters including light intensity, beam size, light color, and the texture cast by the light. Supposing that an animator wants the beam size of the light to change smoothly from one value to another within a predefined period of time, that could be achieved by using key frames. At the start of the animation, a beam size value is set. Another value is set for the end of the animation. Thus, the software program automatically interpolates the two values, creating a smooth transition.

Video Editing

In non-linear digital video editing, as well as in video compositing software, a key frame is a frame used to indicate the beginning or end of a change made to the gsignal. For example, a key frame could be set to indicate the point at which audio will have faded up or down to a certain level.

Video Compression

In video compression, a key frame, also known as an "intra-frame", is a frame in which a complete image is stored in the data stream. In video compression, only changes that occur from one frame to the next are stored in the data stream, in order to greatly reduce the amount of information that must be stored. This technique capitalizes on the fact that most video sources (such as a typical movie) have only small changes in the image from one frame to the next. Whenever a drastic change to the image occurs, such as when switching from one camera shot to another, or at a scene change, a key frame must be created. The entire image for the frame must be output when the visual difference between the two frames is so great that representing the new image incrementally from the previous frame would require more data than recreating the whole image.

Because video compression only stores incremental changes between frames (except for key frames), it is not possible to fast forward or rewind to any arbitrary spot in the video stream. That is because the data for a given frame only represents how that frame was different from the preceding one. For that reason, it is beneficial to include key frames at arbitrary intervals while encoding video. For example, a key frame may be output once for each 10 seconds of video, even though the video image does not change enough visually to warrant the automatic creation of the key frame. That would allow seeking within the video stream at a minimum of 10-second intervals. The down side is that the resulting video stream will be larger in size because many key frames are added when they are not necessary for the frame's visual representation. This drawback, however, does not produce significant compression loss when the bitrate is already set at a high value for better quality (as in the DVD MPEG-2 format).

References

- OpenGL Programming Guide: The Official Guide to Learning OpenGL, Version 1.4, Fourth Edition by OpenGL Architecture Review Board ISBN 0-321-17348-1

- Sikos, L. F. (2016). Rich Semantics for Interactive 3D Models of Cultural Artifacts. Communications in Computer and Information Science. 672. Springer International Publishing. pp. 169–180. doi:10.1007/978-3-319-49157-8_14

- "Pixar founder's Utah-made Hand added to National Film Registry". The Salt Lake Tribune. December 28, 2011. Retrieved January 8, 2012

- OpenGL(R) Reference Manual : The Official Reference Document to OpenGL, Version 1.4 (4th Edition) by OpenGL Architecture Review Board ISBN 0-321-17383-X

- Stam, J. (1998). "Exact evaluation of Catmull-Clark subdivision surfaces at arbitrary parameter values". Proceedings of the 25th annual conference on Computer graphics and interactive techniques - SIGGRAPH '98 (PDF). pp. 395–404. ISBN 0-89791-999-8. doi:10.1145/280814.280945

- Yu, D.; Hunter, J. (2014). "X3D Fragment Identifiers—Extending the Open Annotation Model to Support Semantic Annotation of 3D Cultural Heritage Objects over the Web". International Journal of Heritage in the Digital Era. 3 (3): 579–596. doi:10.1260/2047-4970.3.3.579

- Nadia Magnenat-Thalmann and Daniel Thalmann (2004). Handbook of Virtual Humans. John Wiley and Sons. pp. 6–7. ISBN 0-470-02316-3

- Peters, J. R.; Reif, U. (2008). "Subdivision Surfaces". Geometry and Computing. 3. ISBN 978-3-540-76405-2. doi:10.1007/978-3-540-76406-9

- Laikwan Pang (2006). "Expressions, originality, and fixation". Cultural Control And Globalization in Asia: Copyright, Piracy, and Cinema. Routledge. p. 20. ISBN 0-415-35201-0

- Bloomenthal, Jules; Bajaj, Chandrajit (1997), "5.2.5 Intersection with CSG Trees", Introduction to Implicit Surfaces, Morgan Kaufmann, pp. 178–180, ISBN 9781558602335

- Reif, U. (1995). "A unified approach to subdivision algorithms near extraordinary vertices". Computer Aided Geometric Design. 12 (2): 153–201. doi:10.1016/0167-8396(94)00007-F

- Lucero, J.C.; Munhall, K.G. (1999). "A model of facial biomechanics for speech production". Journal of the Acoustical Society of America. 106: 2834–2842. PMID 10573899. doi:10.1121/1.428108

- Fleming, John and Honour, Hugh (1991), The Visual Arts: A History, 3rd Edition. New York: Abrams. p. 709. ISBN 0810939134

- Soriano, Marc. "Skeletal Animation". Bourns College of Engineering. Retrieved January 2011. Check date values in: |access-date= (help)

4

Applications of Computer-Aided Design

The method used to map three-dimensional points on a two-dimensional plane is termed as 3D projection. 3D reconstruction, anaglyph 3D, game engine and medical animation are important applications of computer-aided design. Applications of computer-aided design are best understood in confluence with the major topics listed in the following chapter. The topics discussed in the chapter are of great importance to broaden the existing knowledge on computer-aided design.

3D Projection

3D projection is any method of mapping three-dimensional points to a two-dimensional plane. As most current methods for displaying graphical data are based on planar (pixel information from several bitplanes) two-dimensional media, the use of this type of projection is widespread, especially in computer graphics, engineering and drafting.

Orthographic Projection

When the human eye looks at a scene, objects in the distance appear smaller than objects close by. Orthographic projection ignores this effect to allow the creation of to-scale drawings for construction and engineering.

Orthographic projections are a small set of transforms often used to show profile, detail or precise measurements of a three dimensional object. Common names for orthographic projections include plane, cross-section, bird's-eye, and elevation.

If the normal of the viewing plane (the camera direction) is parallel to one of the primary axes (which is the x, y, or z axis), the mathematical transformation is as follows; To project the 3D point a_x, a_y, a_z onto the 2D point b_x, b_y using an orthographic projection parallel to the y axis (profile view), the following equations can be used:

$$b_x = s_x a_x + c_x$$

$$b_y = s_z a_z + c_z$$

where the vector s is an arbitrary scale factor, and c is an arbitrary offset. These constants are optional, and can be used to properly align the viewport. Using matrix multiplication, the equations become:

$$\begin{bmatrix} b_x \\ b_y \end{bmatrix} = \begin{bmatrix} s_x & 0 & 0 \\ 0 & 0 & s_z \end{bmatrix} \begin{bmatrix} a_x \\ a_y \\ a_z \end{bmatrix} + \begin{bmatrix} c_x \\ c_z \end{bmatrix}.$$

While orthographically projected images represent the three dimensional nature of the object projected, they do not represent the object as it would be recorded photographically or perceived by a viewer observing it directly. In particular, parallel lengths at all points in an orthographically projected image are of the same scale regardless of whether they are far away or near to the virtual viewer. As a result, lengths near to the viewer are not foreshortened as they would be in a perspective projection.

Weak Perspective Projection

A "weak" perspective projection uses the same principles of an orthographic projection, but requires the scaling factor to be specified, thus ensuring that closer objects appear bigger in the projection, and vice versa. It can be seen as a hybrid between an orthographic and a perspective projection, and described either as a perspective projection with individual point depths Z_i replaced by an average constant depth Z_{ave}, or simply as an orthographic projection plus a scaling.

The weak-perspective model thus approximates perspective projection while using a simpler model, similar to the pure (unscaled) orthographic perspective. It is a reasonable approximation when the depth of the object along the line of sight is small compared to the distance from the camera, and the field of view is small. With these conditions, it can be assumed that all points on a 3D object are at the same distance Z_{ave} from the camera without significant errors in the projection (compared to the full perspective model).

Equation

$$P_x = \frac{X}{Z_{ave}}$$

$$P_y = \frac{Y}{Z_{ave}}$$

assuming focal length $f = 1$.

Perspective Projection

When the human eye views a scene, objects in the distance appear smaller than objects close by - this is known as perspective. While orthographic projection ignores this effect to allow accurate measurements, perspective projection shows distant objects as smaller to provide additional realism.

The perspective projection requires a more involved definition as compared to orthographic projections. A conceptual aid to understanding the mechanics of this projection is to imagine the 2D projection as though the object(s) are being viewed through a camera viewfinder. The camera's position, orientation, and field of view control the behavior of the projection transformation. The following variables are defined to describe this transformation:

- $a_{x,y,z}$ - the 3D position of a point A that is to be projected.

- $c_{x,y,z}$ - the 3D position of a point C representing the camera.

- $\theta_{x,y,z}$ - The orientation of the camera (represented by Tait–Bryan angles).

- $e_{x,y,z}$ - the viewer's position relative to the display surface which goes through point C representing the camera.

Which results in:

- $b_{x,y}$ - the 2D projection of a.

When $c_{x,y,z} = \langle 0,0,0 \rangle$, and $\theta_{x,y,z} = \langle 0,0,0 \rangle$, the 3D vector $\langle 1,2,0 \rangle$ is projected to the 2D vector $\langle 1,2 \rangle$.

Otherwise, to compute $b_{x,y}$ we first define a vector $d_{x,y,z}$ as the position of point A with respect to a coordinate system defined by the camera, with origin in C and rotated by θ with respect to the initial coordinate system. This is achieved by subtracting c from a and then applying a rotation by $-\theta$ to the result. This transformation is often called a camera transform, and can be expressed as follows, expressing the rotation in terms of rotations about the x, y, and z axes (these calculations assume that the axes are ordered as a left-handed system of axes):

$$\begin{bmatrix} d_x \\ d_y \\ d_z \end{bmatrix} = \begin{bmatrix} 1 & 0 & 0 \\ 0 & \cos(\theta_x) & \sin(\theta_x) \\ 0 & -\sin(\theta_x) & \cos(\theta_x) \end{bmatrix} \begin{bmatrix} \cos(\theta_y) & 0 & -\sin(\theta_y) \\ 0 & 1 & 0 \\ \sin(\theta_y) & 0 & \cos(\theta_y) \end{bmatrix} \begin{bmatrix} \cos(\theta_z) & \sin(\theta_z) & 0 \\ -\sin(\theta_z) & \cos(\theta_z) & 0 \\ 0 & 0 & 1 \end{bmatrix} \left(\begin{bmatrix} a_x \\ a_y \\ a_z \end{bmatrix} - \begin{bmatrix} c_x \\ c_y \\ c_z \end{bmatrix} \right)$$

This representation corresponds to rotating by three Euler angles (more properly, Tait–Bryan angles), using the xyz convention, which can be interpreted either as "rotate about the *extrinsic* axes (axes of the *scene*) in the order z, y, x (reading right-to-left)" or "rotate about the *intrinsic* axes (axes of the *camera*) in the order x, y, z (reading left-to-right)". Note that if the camera is not rotated ($\theta_{x,y,z} = \langle 0,0,0 \rangle$), then the matrices drop out (as identities), and this reduces to simply a shift: $d = a - c$.

Alternatively, without using matrices (let's replace $(a_x - c_x)$ with x and so on, and abbreviate $\cos\theta$ to c and $\sin\theta$ to s):

$$d_x = c_y(s_z y + c_z x) - s_y z$$
$$d_y = s_x(c_y z + s_y(s_z y + c_z x)) + c_x(c_z y - s_z x)$$
$$d_z = c_x(c_y z + s_y(s_z y + c_z x)) - s_x(c_z y - s_z x)$$

This transformed point can then be projected onto the 2D plane using the formula (here, x/y is used as the projection plane; literature also may use x/z):

$$b_x = \frac{e_z}{d_z} d_x - e_x$$

$$b_y = \frac{e_z}{d_z} d_y - e_y$$

Or, in matrix form using homogeneous coordinates, the system

$$
\begin{bmatrix} f_x \\ f_y \\ f_z \\ f_w \end{bmatrix} = \begin{bmatrix} 1 & 0 & -\dfrac{e_x}{e_z} & 0 \\ 0 & 1 & -\dfrac{e_y}{e_z} & 0 \\ 0 & 0 & 1 & 0 \\ 0 & 0 & 1/e_z & 0 \end{bmatrix} \begin{bmatrix} d_x \\ d_y \\ d_z \\ 1 \end{bmatrix}
$$

in conjunction with an argument using similar triangles, leads to division by the homogeneous coordinate, giving

$$
\begin{aligned}
b_x &= f_x/f_w \\
b_y &= f_y/f_w
\end{aligned}
$$

The distance of the viewer from the display surface, e_z, directly relates to the field of view, where $\alpha = 2 \cdot \tan^{-1}(1/e_z)$ is the viewed angle. (Note: This assumes that you map the points (-1,-1) and (1,1) to the corners of your viewing surface)

The above equations can also be rewritten as:

$$
\begin{aligned}
b_x &= (d_x s_x)/(d_z r_x)r_z \\
b_y &= (d_y s_y)/(d_z r_y)r_z
\end{aligned}
$$

In which $s_{x,y}$ is the display size, $r_{x,y}$ is the recording surface size (CCD or film), r_z is the distance from the recording surface to the entrance pupil (camera center), and d_z is the distance, from the 3D point being projected, to the entrance pupil.

Subsequent clipping and scaling operations may be necessary to map the 2D plane onto any particular display media.

Diagram

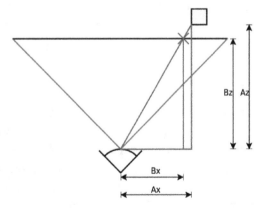

To determine which screen x-coordinate corresponds to a point at A_x, A_z multiply the point coordinates by:

$$B_x = A_x \frac{B_z}{A_z}$$

where

B_x is the screen x coordinate

A_x is the model x coordinate

B_z is the focal length—the axial distance from the camera center to the image plane

A_z is the subject distance.

Because the camera is in 3D, the same works for the screen y-coordinate, substituting y for x in the above diagram and equation.

3D Reconstruction

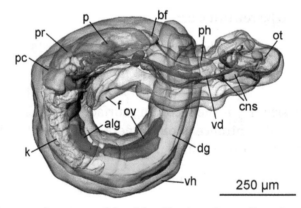

3D reconstruction of the general anatomy of the right side view of a small marine slug *Pseudunela viatoris*.

In computer vision and computer graphics, 3D reconstruction is the process of capturing the shape and appearance of real objects. This process can be accomplished either by active or passive methods. If the model is allowed to change its shape in time, this is referred to as non-rigid or spatio-temporal reconstruction.

Motivation and Applications

The research of 3D reconstruction has always been a difficult goal. Using 3D reconstruction one can determine any object's 3D profile, as well as knowing the 3D coordinate of any point on the profile.The 3D reconstruction of objects is a generally scientific problem and core technology of a wide variety of fields, such as Computer Aided Geometric Design (CAGD), Computer Graphics, Computer Animation, Computer Vision, medical imaging, computational science, Virtual Reality, digital media, etc. For instance, the lesion information of the patients can be presented in 3D on the computer, which offers a new and accurate approach in diagnosis and thus has vital clinical value.

Active Methods

Active methods, i.e. range data methods, given the depth map, reconstruct the 3D profile by numerical approximation approach and build the object in scenario based on model. These methods actively interfere with the reconstructed object, either mechanically or radiometrically using rangefinders, in order to acquire the depth map, e.g. structured light, laser range finder and other active sensing techniques. A simple example of a mechanical method would use a depth gauge to measure a distance to a rotating object put on a turntable. More applicable radiometric methods emit radiance towards the object and then measure its reflected part. Examples range from moving light sources, colored visible light, time-of-flight lasers to microwaves or ultrasound.

Passive Methods

Passive methods of 3D reconstruction do not interfere with the reconstructed object; they only use a sensor to measure the radiance reflected or emitted by the object's surface to infer its 3D structure through image understanding. Typically, the sensor is an image sensor in a camera sensitive to visible light and the input to the method is a set of digital images (one, two or more) or video. In this case we talk about image-based reconstruction and the output is a 3D model. By comparison to active methods, passive methods can be applied to a wider range of situations.

Monocular Cues Methods

Monocular cues methods refer to use image (one, two or more) from one viewpoint (camera) to proceed 3D construction. It makes use of 2D characteristics(e.g. Silhouettes, shading and texture) to measure 3D shape, and that's why it is also named Shape-From-X, where X can be silhouettes, shading, texture etc. 3D reconstruction through monocular cues is simple and quick, and only one appropriate digital image is needed thus only one camera is adequate. Technically, it avoids stereo correspondence, which is fairly complex.

Shape-from-shading Due to the analysis of the shade information in the image, by using Lambertian reflectance, the depth of normal information of the object surface is restored to reconstruct.

Photometric Stereo This approach is more sophisticated than the shape-of-shading method. Images taken in different lighting conditions are used to solve the depth information. It is worth mentioning that more than one image is required by this approach.

Shape-from-texture Suppose such an object with smooth surface covered by replicated texture units, and its projection from 3D to 2D causes distortion and perspective. Distortion and perspective measured in 2D images provide the hint for inversely solving depth of normal information of the object surface.

Binocular Stereo Vision

Binocular Stereo Vision obtains the 3-dimensional geometric information of an object from multiple images based on the research of human visual system. The results are presented in form of depth maps. Images of an object acquired by two cameras simultaneously in different viewing angles, or by one single camera at different time in different viewing angles, are used to restore its 3D geometric information and reconstruct its 3D profile and location. This is more direct than Monocular methods such as shape-from-shading.

Binocular stereo vision method requires two identical cameras with parallel optical axis to observe one same object, acquiring two images from different points of view. In terms of trigonometry relations, depth information can be calculated from disparity. Binocular stereo vision method is well developed and stably contributes to favorable 3D reconstruction, leading to a better performance when compared to other 3D construction. Unfortunately, it is computationally intensive, besides it performs rather poorly when baseline distance is large.

Problem Statement and Basics

The approach of using Binocular Stereo Vision to acquire object's 3D geometric information is on the basis of visual disparity. The following picture provides a simple schematic diagram of horizontally sighted Binocular Stereo Vision, where b is the baseline between projective centers of two cameras.

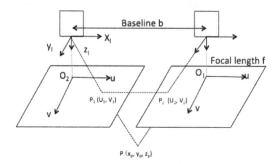

Geometry of a stereoscopic system

The origin of the camera's coordinate system is at the optical center of the camera's lens as shown in the figure. Actually, the camera's image plane is behind the optical center of the camera's lens. However, to simplify the calculation, images are drawn in front of the optical center of the lens by f. The u-axis and v-axis of the image's coordinate system O_1uv are in the same direction with x-axis and y-axis of the camera's coordinate system respectively. The origin of the image's coordinate system is located on the intersection of imaging plane and the optical axis. Suppose such world point P whose corresponding image points are $P_1(u_1,v_1)$ and $P_2(u_2,v_2)$ respectively on the left and right image plane. Assume two cameras are in the same plane, then y-coordinates of P_1 and P_2 are identical, i.e.,$v_1=v_2$. According to trigonometry relations,

$$u_1 = f\frac{x_p}{z_p}$$

$$u_2 = f\frac{x_p - b}{z_p}$$

$$v_1 = v_2 = f\frac{y_p}{z_p}$$

where(x_p, y_p, z_p) are coordinates of P in the left camera's coordinate system, f is focal length of the camera. Visual disparity is defined as the difference in image point location of a certain world point acquired by two cameras,

$$d = u_1 - u_2 = f \frac{b}{z_p}$$

based on which the coordinates of P can be worked out.

Therefore, once the coordinates of image points is known, besides the parameters of two cameras, the 3D coordinate of the point can be determined.

$$x_p = \frac{bu_1}{d}$$

$$y_p = \frac{bv_1}{d}$$

$$z_p = \frac{bf}{d}$$

The 3D reconstruction consists of the following sections:

Image Acquisition

2D digital image acquisition is the information source of 3D reconstruction. Commonly used 3D reconstruction is based on two or more images, although it may employ only one image in some cases. There are various types of methods for image acquisition that depends on the occasions and purposes of the specific application. Not only the requirements of the application must be met, but also the visual disparity, illumination, performance of camera and the feature of scenario should be considered.

Camera Calibration

Camera calibration in Binocular Stereo Vision refers to the determination of the mapping relationship between the image points $P_1(u_1,v_1)$ and $P_2(u_2,v_2)$, and space coordinate $P(x_p, y_p, z_p)$ in the 3D scenario. Camera calibration is a basic and essential part in 3D reconstruction via Binocular Stereo Vision.

Feature Extraction

The aim of feature extraction is to gain the characteristics of the images, through which the stereo correspondence processes. As a result, the characteristics of the images closely link to the choice of matching methods. There is no such universally applicable theory for features extraction, leading to a great diversity of stereo correspondence in Binocular Stereo Vision research.

Stereo Correspondence

Stereo correspondence is to establish the correspondence between primitive factors in images, i.e. to match $P_1(u_1,v_1)$ and $P_2(u_2,v_2)$ from two images. Certain interference factors in the scenario should be noticed, e.g. illumination, noise, surface physical characteristic and etc.

Restoration

According to precise correspondence, combined with camera location parameters, 3D geometric information can be recovered without difficulties. Due to the fact that accuracy of 3D reconstruction depends on the precision of correspondence, error of camera location parameters and so on, the previous procedures must be done carefully to achieve relatively accurate 3D reconstruction.

3D Reconstruction of Medical Images

Clinical routine of diagnosis, patient follow-up, computer assisted surgery, surgical planning etc. are facilitated by accurate 3D models of the desired part of human anatomy. Main motivation behind 3D reconstruction includes

- Improved accuracy due to multi view aggregation.

- Detailed surface estimates.

- Can be used to plan, simulate, guide, or otherwise assist a surgeon in performing a medical procedure.

- The precise position and orientation of the patient's anatomy can be determined.

- Helps in a number of clinical areas, such as radiotherapy planning and treatment verification, spinal surgery, hip replacement, neurointerventions and aortic stenting.

Applications

3D reconstruction system finds its application in a variety of field they are

- Medicine
- Film industry
- Robotics
- City planning
- Gaming
- Virtual environment
- Earth observation
- Archaeology
- Augmented reality
- Reverse engineering
- Animation
- Human computer interaction

Problem Statement

Mostly algorithms available for 3D reconstruction are extremely slow and cannot be used in re-al-time. Though the algorithms presented are still in infancy but they have the potential for fast computation.

Existing Approaches

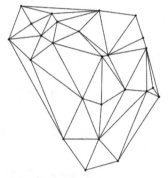

Delaunay Triangulation (25 Points)

Delaunay and Alpha-shapes

- Delaunay method involves extraction of tetrahedron surfaces from initial point cloud. The idea of 'shape' for a set of points in space is given by concept of alpha-shapes. Given a finite point set S, and the real parameter alpha, the alpha-shape of S is a polytope (the generalization to any dimension of a two dimensional polygon and a three-dimensional polyhedron) which is neither convex nor necessarily connected. For a large value, the alpha-shape is identical to the convex-hull of S. The algorithm proposed by Edelsbrunner and Mucke eliminates all tetrahedrons which are delimited by a surrounding sphere smaller than α. The surface is then obtained with the external triangles from the resulting tetrahedron.

- Another algorithm called Tight Cocone labels the initial tetrahedrons as interior and exterior. The triangles found in and out generate the resulting surface.

Both methods have been recently extended for reconstructing point clouds with noise. In this method the quality of points determines the feasibility of the method. For precise triangulation since we are using the whole point cloud set, the points on the surface with the error above the threshold will be explicitly represented on reconstructed geometry.

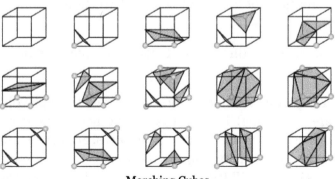

Marching Cubes

Zero Set Methods

Reconstruction of the surface is performed using a distance function which assigns to each point in the space a signed distance to the surface S. A contour algorithm is used to extracting a zero-set which is used to obtain polygonal representation of the object. Thus, the problem of reconstructing a surface from a disorganized point cloud is reduced to the definition of the appropriate function f with a zero value for the sampled points and different to zero value for the rest. An algorithm called Marching-Cubes established the use of such methods. There are different variants for given algorithm, some use a discrete function f, while other use a polyharmonic radial basis function is used to adjust the initial point set. Functions like Moving Least Squares, basic functions with local support, based on the Poisson equation have also been used. Loss of the geometry precision in areas with extreme curvature, i.e., corners, edges is one of the main issues encountered. Furthermore, pretreatment of information, by applying some kind of filtering technique, also affects the definition of the corners by softening them. There are several studies related to post-processing techniques used in the reconstruction for the detection and refinement of corners but these methods increase the complexity of the solution.

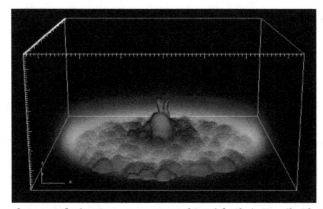

Solid geometry with volume rendering Image courtesy of Patrick Chris Fragile Ph.D., UC Santa Barbara

VR Technique

Entire volume transparence of the object is visualized using VR technique. Images will be performed by projecting rays through volume data. Along each ray, opacity and color need to be calculated at every voxel. Then information calculated along each ray will to be aggregated to a pixel on image plane. This technique helps us to see comprehensively an entire compact structure of the object. Since the technique needs enormous amount of calculations, which requires strong configuration computers is appropriate for low contrast data. Two main methods for rays projecting can be considered as follows:

- Object-order method: Projecting rays go through volume from back to front (from volume to image plane).

- Image-order or ray-casting method: Projecting rays go through volume from front to back (from image plane to volume).There exists some other methods to composite image, appropriate methods depending on the user's purposes. Some usual methods in medical image are MIP (maximum intensity projection), MinIP (minimum intensity projection), AC (alpha compositing) and NPVR (non-photorealistic volume rendering).

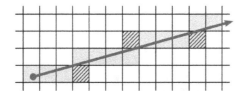

Tracing a ray through a voxel grid. The voxels which are traversed in addition to those
selected using an standard 8-connected algorithm are shown hatched.

Voxel Grid

In this filtering technique input space is sampled using a grid of 3D voxels to reduce the number
of points. For each voxel, a centroid is chosen as the representative of all points. There are two
approaches, the selection of the voxel centroid or select the centroid of the points lying within the
voxel. To obtain internal points average has a higher computational cost, but offers better results.
Thus, a subset of the input space is obtained that roughly represents the underlying surface. The
Voxel Grid method presents the same problems as other filtering techniques: impossibility of defining the final number of points that represent the surface, geometric information loss due to the
reduction of the points inside a voxel and sensitivity to noisy input spaces.

Anaglyph 3D

Anaglyph 3D is the name given to the stereoscopic 3D effect achieved by means of encoding each
eye's image using filters of different (usually chromatically opposite) colors, typically red and cyan.
Anaglyph 3D images contain two differently filtered colored images, one for each eye. When viewed
through the "color-coded" "anaglyph glasses", each of the two images reaches the eye it's intended
for, revealing an integrated stereoscopic image. The visual cortex of the brain fuses this into the
perception of a three-dimensional scene or composition.

Stereoscopic effect used in macro photography
3D red cyan glasses are recommended to view this image correctly.

Anaglyph images have seen a recent resurgence due to the presentation of images and video on the
Web, Blu-ray Discs, CDs, and even in print. Low cost paper frames or plastic-framed glasses hold
accurate color filters that typically, after 2002, make use of all 3 primary colors. The current norm
is red and cyan, with red being used for the left channel. The cheaper filter material used in the
monochromatic past dictated red and blue for convenience and cost. There is a material improvement of full color images, with the cyan filter, especially for accurate skin tones.

Anaglyph of Saguaro National Park at dusk
3D red cyan glasses are recommended to view this image correctly.

Anaglyph of a column head in Persepolis, Iran
3D red cyan glasses are recommended to view this image correctly.

Video games, theatrical films, and DVDs can be shown in the anaglyph 3D process. Practical images, for science or design, where depth perception is useful, include the presentation of full scale and microscopic stereographic images. Examples from NASA include Mars Rover imaging, and the solar investigation, called STEREO, which uses two orbital vehicles to obtain the 3D images of the sun. Other applications include geological illustrations by the United States Geological Survey, and various online museum objects. A recent application is for stereo imaging of the heart using 3D ultra-sound with plastic red/cyan glasses.

Anaglyph images are much easier to view than either parallel (diverging) or crossed-view pairs stereograms. However, these side-by-side types offer bright and accurate color rendering, not easily achieved with anaglyphs. Recently, cross-view prismatic glasses with adjustable masking have appeared, that offer a wider image on the new HD video and computer monitors. Template:3D Glasses

History

The oldest known description of anaglyph images was written in August 1853 by W. Rollmann in Stargard about his "Farbenstereoscope" (color stereoscope). He had the best results viewing a yellow/blue drawing with red/blue glasses. Rollmann found that with a red/blue drawing the red lines were not as distinct as yellow lines through the blue glass.

In 1858 Joseph D'Almeida began projecting three-dimensional magic lantern slide shows using red and green filters with the audience wearing red and green goggles.

Louis Ducos du Hauron produced the first printed anaglyphs in 1891. This process consisted of printing the two negatives which form a stereoscopic photograph on to the same paper, one in blue (or green), one in red. The viewer would then use coloured glasses with red (for the left eye) and blue or green (right eye). The left eye would see the blue image which would appear black, whilst it would not see the red; similarly the right eye would see the red image, this registering as black. Thus a three dimensional image would result.

William Friese-Green created the first three-dimensional anaglyphic motion pictures in 1889, which had public exhibition in 1893. 3-D films enjoyed something of a boom in the 1920s. The term "3-D" was coined in the 1950s. As late as 1954 films such as *The Creature from the Black Lagoon* were very successful. Originally shot and exhibited using the Polaroid system, "The Creature from the Black Lagoon" was successfully reissued much later in an anaglyph format so it could be shown in cinemas without the need special equipment. In 1953, the anaglyph had begun appearing in newspapers, magazines and comic books. The 3-D comic books were one of the most interesting applications of anaglyph to printing.

Over the years, anaglyphic pictures have sporadically appeared in comics and magazine ads. Although not anaglyphic, *Jaws 3*-D was a box-office success in 1983. At present the excellent quality of computer displays and user-friendly stereo-editing programs offer new and exciting possibilities for experimenting with anaglyph stereo.

Production

Stereo monochrome image anaglyphed for red (left eye) and cyan (right eye) filters.
3D red cyan glasses are recommended to view this image correctly.

Stereogram source image for the anaglyph above

Anaglyph from Stereo Pairs

A stereo pair is a pair of images from slightly different perspectives at the same time. Objects closer to the camera(s) have greater differences in appearance and position within the image frames than objects further from the camera.

Historically cameras captured two colour filtered images from the perspective of the left and right eyes which were projected or printed together as a single image, one side through a red filter and the other side through a contrasting colour such as blue or green or mixed cyan. As outlined below, one may now, typically, use an image processing computer program to simulate the effect of using color filters, using as a source image a pair of either color or monochrome images. This is called mosaicking or image stitching.

In the 1970s filmmaker Stephen Gibson filmed direct anaglyph blaxploitation and adult movies. His "Deep Vision" system replaced the original camera lens with two color-filtered lenses focused on the same film frame. In the 1980s, Gibson patented his mechanism.

Many computer graphics programs provide the basic tools (typically layering and adjustments to individual colour channels to filter colours) required to prepare anaglyphs from stereo pairs. In simple practice, the left eye image is filtered to remove blue & green. The right eye image is filtered to remove red. The two images are usually positioned in the compositing phase in close overlay registration (of the main subject). Plugins for some of these programs as well as programs dedicated to anaglyph preparation are available which automate the process and require the user to choose only a few basic settings.

Stereo Conversion (Single 2D Image to 3D)

There also exist methods for making anaglyphs using only one image, a process called stereo conversion. In one, individual elements of a picture are horizontally offset in one layer by differing amounts with elements offset further having greater apparent changes in depth (either forward or back depending on whether the offset is to the left or right). This produces images that tend to look like elements are flat standees arranged at various distances from the viewer similar to cartoon images in a View-Master.

A more sophisticated method involves use of a depth map (a false colour image where colour indicates distance, for example, a greyscale depth map could have lighter indicate an object closer to the viewer and darker indicate an object further away). As for preparing anaglyphs from stereo pairs, stand-alone software and plug-ins for some graphics apps exist which automate production of anaglyphs (and stereograms) from a single image or from an image and its corresponding depth map.

As well as fully automatic methods of calculating depth maps (which may be more or less successful), depth maps can be drawn entirely by hand. Also developed are methods of producing depth maps from sparse or less accurate depth maps. A sparse depth map is a depth map consisting of only a relatively few lines or areas which guides the production of the full depth map. Use of a sparse depth map can help overcome auto-generation limitations. For example, if a depth finding algorithm takes cues from image brightness an area of shadow in the foreground may be incorrectly assigned as background. This misassignment is overcome by assigning the shaded area a close value in the sparse depth map.

Mechanics

Viewing anaglyphs through spectrally opposed glasses or gel filters enables each eye to see independent left and right images from within a single anaglyphic image. Red-cyan filters can be employed because our vision processing systems use red and cyan comparisons, as well as blue and yellow, to determine the color and contours of objects. In a red-cyan anaglyph, the eye viewing through the red filter sees red within the anaglyph as "white", and the cyan within the anaglyph as "black". The eye viewing through the cyan filter perceives the opposite. Actual black or white in the anaglyph display, being void of color, are perceived the same by each eye. The brain blends together the red and cyan channelled images as in regular viewing but only green and blue are perceived. Red is not perceived because red equates with white through red gel and is black through cyan gel. However green and blue are perceived through cyan gel.

Types

Complementary Color

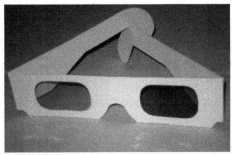

Paper anaglyph filters produce an acceptable image at low cost and are suitable for inclusion in magazines.

Complementary color anaglyphs employ one of a pair of complementary color filters for each eye. The most common color filters used are red and cyan. Employing tristimulus theory, the eye is sensitive to three primary colors, red, green, and blue. The red filter admits only red, while the cyan filter blocks red, passing blue and green (the combination of blue and green is perceived as cyan). If a paper viewer containing red and cyan filters is folded so that light passes through both, the image will appear black. Another recently introduced form employs blue and yellow filters. (Yellow is the color perceived when both red and green light passes through the filter.)

Piero della Francesca, Ideal City in an Anaglyph version
3D red cyan glasses are recommended to view this image correctly.

Anaglyph images have seen a recent resurgence because of the presentation of images on the Internet. Where traditionally, this has been a largely black & white format, recent digital camera and processing advances have brought very acceptable color images to the internet and DVD field. With the online availability of low cost paper glasses with improved red-cyan filters, and plastic framed glasses of increasing quality, the field of 3D imaging is growing quickly. Scientific images where depth perception is useful include, for instance, the presentation of complex multi-dimensional data sets and stereographic images of the surface of Mars. With the recent release of 3D DVDs, they are more commonly being used for entertainment. Anaglyph images are much easier to view than either parallel sighting or crossed eye stereograms, although these types do offer more bright and accurate color rendering, most particularly in the red component, which is commonly muted or desaturated with even the best color anaglyphs. A compensating technique, commonly known as Anachrome, uses a slightly more transparent cyan filter in the patented glasses associated with the technique. Processing reconfigures the typical anaglyph image to have less parallax to obtain a more useful image when viewed without filters.

Compensating Focus Diopter Glasses for Red-cyan Method

Simple sheet or uncorrected molded glasses do not compensate for the 250 nanometer difference in the wavelengths of the red-cyan filters. With simple glasses the red filter image can be blurry when viewing a close computer screen or printed image since the retinal focus differs from the cyan filtered image, which dominates the eyes' focusing. Better quality molded plastic glasses employ a compensating differential diopter power to equalize the red filter focus shift relative to the cyan. The direct view focus on computer monitors has been recently improved by manufacturers providing secondary paired lenses, fitted and attached inside the red-cyan primary filters of some high-end anaglyph glasses. They are used where very high resolution is required, including science, stereo macros, and animation studio applications. They use carefully balanced cyan (blue-green) acrylic lenses, which pass a minute percentage of red to improve skin tone perception. Simple red/blue glasses work well with black and white, but the blue filter is unsuitable for human skin in color. U.S. Patent No. 6,561,646 was issued to the inventor in 2003. In the trade, the label "www.anachrome" is used to label diopter corrected 3D glasses covered by this patent.

(ACB) 3-D

(ACB) 'Anaglyphic Contrast Balance' is a patented anaglyphic production method by Studio 555. Retinal Rivalry of color contrasts within the color channels of anaglyph images is addressed.

Contrasts and details from the stereo pair are maintained and re-presented for view within the anaglyph image. The (ACB) method of balancing the color contrasts within the stereo pair enables a stable view of contrast details, thus eliminating retinal rivalry. The process is available for red/cyan color channels but may use any of the opposing color channel combinations. As with all stereoscopic anaglyphic systems, screen or print, the display color should be RGB accurate and the viewing gels should match the color channels to prevent double imaging. The basic (ACB) method adjusts red, green and blue, however adjusting all six color primaries is preferred.

The effectiveness of the (ACB) process is proven with the inclusion of primary color charts within a stereo pair. A contrast balanced view of the stereo pair and color charts is evident in the resulting (ACB) processed anaglyph image. The (ACB) process also enables black and white (monochromatic) anaglyphs with contrast balance.

Where full color to each eye is enabled via alternating color channels and color alternating viewing filters, (ACB) prevents shimmer from pure colored objects within the modulating image. Vertical and diagonal parallax is enabled with concurrent use of a horizontally oriented lenticular or parallax barrier screen. This enables a Quadrascopic full color holographic effect from a monitor.

ColorCode 3-D

ColorCode 3-D was deployed in the 2000s and uses amber and blue filters. It is intended to provide the perception of nearly full color viewing (particularly within the RG color space) with existing television and paint mediums. One eye (left, amber filter) receives the cross-spectrum color information and one eye (right, blue filter) sees a monochrome image designed to give the depth effect. The human brain ties both images together.

Images viewed without filters will tend to exhibit light-blue and yellow horizontal fringing. The backwards compatible 2D viewing experience for viewers not wearing glasses is improved, generally being better than previous red and green anaglyph imaging systems, and further improved by the use of digital post-processing to minimize fringing. The displayed hues and intensity can be subtly adjusted to further improve the perceived 2D image, with problems only generally found in the case of extreme blue.

The blue filter is centered around 450 nm and the amber filter lets in light at wavelengths at above 500 nm. Wide spectrum color is possible because the amber filter lets through light across most wavelengths in spectrum and even has a small leakage of the blue color spectrum. When presented the original left and right images are run through the ColorCode 3-D encoding process to generate one single ColorCode 3-D encoded image.

In the United Kingdom, television station Channel 4 commenced broadcasting a series of programs encoded using the system during the week of 16 November 2009. Previously the system had been used in the United States for an "all 3-D advertisement" during the 2009 Super Bowl for SoBe, Monsters vs. Aliens animated movie and an advertisement for the Chuck television series in which the full episode the following night used the format.

Inficolor 3D

Developed by TriOviz, Inficolor 3D is a patent pending stereoscopic system, first demonstrated at the International Broadcasting Convention in 2007 and deployed in 2010. It works with traditional 2D flat panels and HDTV sets and uses expensive glasses with complex color filters and dedicated image processing that allow natural color perception with a 3D experience. This is achieved through having the left image using the green channel only and the right using the red and blue channels with some added post processing, which the brain then combines the two images to produce a nearly full color experience. When observed without glasses, some slight doubling can be noticed in the background of the action which allows watching the movie or the video game in 2D without the glasses. This is not possible with traditional brute force anaglyphic systems.

Inficolor 3D is a part of TriOviz for Games Technology, developed in partnership with TriOviz Labs and Darkworks Studio. It works with Sony PlayStation 3 (Official PlayStation 3 Tools & Middleware Licensee Program) and Microsoft Xbox 360 consoles as well as PC. TriOviz for Games Technology was showcased at Electronic Entertainment Expo 2010 by Mark Rein (vice president of Epic Games) as a 3D tech demo running on an Xbox 360 with Gears of War 2. In October 2010 this technology has been officially integrated in Unreal Engine 3, the computer game engine developed by Epic Games.

Video games equipped with TriOviz for Games Technology are: *Batman Arkham Asylum: Game of the Year Edition* for PS3 and Xbox 360 (March 2010), *Enslaved: Odyssey to the West + DLC Pigsy's Perfect 10* for PS3 and Xbox 360 (Nov. 2010), *Thor: God of Thunder* for PS3 and Xbox 360 (May 2011), *Green Lantern: Rise of the Manhunters* for PS3 and Xbox 360 (June 2011), *Captain America: Super Soldier* for PS3 and Xbox 360 (July 2011). *Gears of War 3* for Xbox 360 (September 2011), *Batman: Arkham City* for PS3 and Xbox 360 (October 2011), *Assassin's Creed: Revelations* for PS3 and Xbox 360 (November 2011), and *Assassin's Creed III* for Wii U (November 2012). The first DVD/Blu-ray including Inficolor 3D Tech is: *Battle for Terra 3D* (published in France by Pathé & Studio 37 - 2010).

Most other games can be played in this format with Tridef 3D with display settings set to Colored Glasses>Green/Purple, although this is not officially supported by Trioviz, but the results are nearly identical without limiting the game selection.

Anachrome RED/CYAN Filters

Anachrome optical diopter glasses

Full color Anachrome red (left eye) and cyan (right eye) filters
3D anachrome glasses are recommended to view this image correctly.

A variation on the anaglyph technique from the early 2000s is called "Anachrome method". This approach is an attempt to provide images that look nearly normal, without glasses, for small images, either 2D or 3D. With most of the negative qualities, being masked innately by the small display. Being "compatible" for small size posting in conventional websites or magazines. Usually a larger file can be selected that will fully present the 3D with the dramatic definition. The 3D,(Z axis) depth effect is generally more subtle than simple anaglyph images, which are usually made from wider spaced stereo pairs. Anachrome images are shot with a typically narrower stereo base, (the distance between the camera lenses). Pains are taken to adjust for a better overlay fit of the two images, which are layered one on top of another. Only a few pixels of non-registration give the depth cues. The range of color perceived, is noticeably wider in Anachrome image, when viewed with the intended filters. This is due to the deliberate passage of a small (1 to 2%) of the red information through the cyan filter. Warmer tones can be boosted, because each eye sees some color reference to red. The brain responds in the mental blending process and usual perception. It is claimed to provide warmer and more complex perceived skin tones and vividness.

Interference Filter Systems

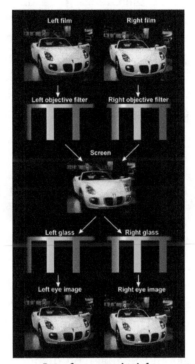

Interference principle

This technique uses specific wavelengths of red, green, and blue for the right eye, and different wavelengths of red, green, and blue for the left eye. Eyeglasses which filter out the very specific wavelengths allow the wearer to see a full color 3D image. Special interference filters (dichromatic filters) in the glasses and in the projector form the main item of technology and have given the system this name. It is also known as spectral comb filtering or wavelength multiplex visualization. Sometimes this technique is described as a "super-anaglyph" because it is an advanced form of spectral-multiplexing which is at the heart of the conventional anaglyph technique. This technology eliminates the expensive silver screens required for polarized systems such as RealD, which is the most common 3D display system in theaters. It does, however, require much more expensive glasses than the polarized systems.

Dolby 3D uses this principle. The filters divide the visible color spectrum into six narrow bands – two in the red region, two in the green region, and two in the blue region (called R1, R2, G1, G2, B1 and B2 for the purposes of this description). The R1, G1 and B1 bands are used for one eye image, and R2, G2, B2 for the other eye. The human eye is largely insensitive to such fine spectral differences so this technique is able to generate full-color 3D images with only slight color differences between the two eyes.

The Omega 3D/Panavision 3D system also used this technology, though with a wider spectrum and more "teeth" to the "comb" (5 for each eye in the Omega/Panavision system). The use of more spectral bands per eye eliminates the need to color process the image, required by the Dolby system. Evenly dividing the visible spectrum between the eyes gives the viewer a more relaxed "feel" as the light energy and color balance is nearly 50-50. Like the Dolby system, the Omega system can be used with white or silver screens. But it can be used with either film or digital projectors, unlike the Dolby filters that are only used on a digital system with a color correcting processor provided by Dolby. The Omega/Panavision system also claims that their glasses are cheaper to manufacture than those used by Dolby. In June 2012 the Omega 3D/Panavision 3D system was discontinued by DPVO Theatrical, who marketed it on behalf of Panavision, citing "challenging global economic and 3D market conditions". Although DPVO dissolved its business operations, Omega Optical continues promoting and selling 3D systems to non-theatrical markets. Omega Optical's 3D system contains projection filters and 3D glasses. In addition to the passive stereoscopic 3D system, Omega Optical has produced enhanced anaglyph 3D glasses. The Omega's red/cyan anaglyph glasses use complex metal oxide thin film coatings and high quality annealed glass optics.

Viewing

Red-green anaglyph glasses

A pair of glasses with filters of opposing colors, is worn to view an anaglyphic photo image. A red filter lens over the left eye allows graduations of red to cyan from within the anaglyph to be perceived as graduations of bright to dark. The cyan (blue/green) filter over the right eye conversely allows graduations of cyan to red from within the anaglyph to be perceived as graduations of bright to dark. Red and cyan colour fringes in the anaglyph display represent the red and cyan colour channels of the parallax displaced left and right images. The viewing filters each cancel out opposing colored areas, including graduations of less pure opposing colored areas, to each reveal an image from within its color channel. Thus the filters enable each eye to see only its intended view from color channels within the single anaglyphic image.

Red Sharpened Anaglyph glasses

Simple paper, uncorrected gel glasses, cannot compensate for the 250 nanometer difference in the wavelengths of the red-cyan filters. With simple glasses, the red filtered image is somewhat blurry, when viewing a close computer screen or printed image. The (RED) retinal focus differs from the image through the (CYAN) filter, which dominates the eyes' focusing. Better quality, molded acrylic glasses frequently employ a compensating differential diopter power (a spherical correction) to balance the red filter focus shift relative to the cyan, which reduces the innate softness, and diffraction of red filtered light. Low power reading glasses worn along with the paper glasses also sharpen the image noticeably.

The correction is only about 1/2 + diopter on the red lens. However, some people with corrective glasses are bothered by difference in lens diopters, as one image is a slightly larger magnification than the other. Though endorsed by many 3D websites, the diopter "fix" effect is still somewhat controversial. Some, especially the nearsighted, find it uncomfortable. There is about a 400% improvement in acuity with a molded diopter filter, and a noticeable improvement of contrast and blackness. The American Amblyopia Foundation uses this feature in their plastic glasses for school screening of children's vision, judging the greater clarity as a significant plus factor.

Anachrome Filters

Plastic anaglyph glasses can employ diopter correction for improved viewing.

Plastic glasses, developed in recent years, provide both the diopter "fix" noted above, and a change in the cyan filter. The formula provides intentional "leakage" of a minimal (2%) percentage of red light with the conventional range of the filter. This assigns two-eyed "redness cues" to objects and details, such as lip color and red clothing, that are fused in the brain. Care must be taken, however, to closely overlay the red areas into near-perfect registration, or "ghosting" can occur. Anachrome formula lenses work well with black and white, but can provide excellent results when the glasses are used with conforming, "anachrome friendly" images. The US Geological Survey has thousands of these "conforming", full-color images, which depict the geology and scenic features of the U.S. National Park system. By convention, anachrome images try to avoid excess separation of the cameras, and parallax, thereby reducing the ghosting that the extra color bandwidth introduces to the images.

Anaglyph from monochrome images 3D red cyan glasses are recommended to view this image correctly.

Traditional Anaglyph Processing Methods

One monochromatic method uses a stereo pair available as a digitized image, along with access to general-purpose image processing software. In this method, the images are run through a series of processes and saved in an appropriate transmission and viewing format such as JPEG.

B&W anaglyph of Zagreb taken using one camera. Images were taken about 2m (7ft) apart to get the 3D effect. 3D red cyan glasses are recommended to view this image correctly.

Color anaglyph taken using two cameras about 40cm (16in) apart for enhanced depth effect. 3D red cyan glasses are recommended to view this image correctly.

Several computer programs will create color anaglyphs without Adobe Photoshop, or a traditional, more complex compositing method can be used with Photoshop. Using color information, it is possible to obtain reasonable (but not accurate) blue sky, green vegetation, and appropriate skin tones. Color information appears disruptive when used for brightly colored and/ or high-contrast objects such as signs, toys, and patterned clothing when these contain colors that are close to red or cyan.

Only few color anaglyphic processes, e.g. interference filter systems used for Dolby 3D, can reconstruct full-color 3D images. However, other stereo display methods can easily reproduce full-color photos or movies, e.g. active shutter 3D or polarized 3D systems. Such processes allow better viewing comfort than most limited color anaglyphic methods. According to entertainment trade papers, 3D films had a revival in recent years and 3D is now also used in 3D Television.

Depth Adjustment

The adjustment suggested is applicable to any type of stereogram but is particularly appropriate when anaglyphed images are to be viewed on a computer screen or on printed matter.

Image as originally presented by NASA with foreground spilling from the frame. This is a two-color (red-cyan) ana-glyph from the Mars Pathfinder mission. To view, use a red filter for the left eye and a cyan filter for the right eye. Note that the distant mountain images are aligned, placing them at the screen, and the confusing appearance in the lower right corner. ▪▪ 3D red cyan glasses are recommended to view this image correctly.

Image adjusted so that most objects appear to be beyond the frame. Note that the mountain images are now separat-ed when viewed without the glasses. This follows the rule for a red left eye filter when distant objects are beyond the image plane: RRR-Red to Right Receding for dark objects on lighter background in the image as it appears without wearing the filters. ▪▪ 3D red cyan glasses are recommended to view this image correctly.

Those portions of the left and right images that are coincident will appear to be at the surface of the screen. Depending upon the subject matter and the composition of the image it may be appro-priate to make this align to something slightly behind the nearest point of the principal subject (as when imaging a portrait). This will cause the near points of the subject to "pop out" from the screen. For best effect, any portions of a figure to be imaged forward of the screen surface should not intercept the image boundary, as this can lead to a discomforting "amputated" appearance. It is of course possible to create a three-dimensional "pop out" frame surrounding the subject in order to avoid this condition.

Shelf edge at screen depth ▪▪ 3D red cyan glasses are recommended to view this image correctly.

If the subject matter is a landscape, you may consider putting the frontmost object at or slightly behind the surface of the screen. This will cause the subject to be framed by the window bound-ary and recede into the distance. Once the adjustment is made, trim the picture to contain only the portions containing both left and right images. In the example shown above, the upper image appears (in a visually disruptive manner) to spill out from the screen, with the distant mountains appearing at the surface of the screen. In the lower modification of this image the red channel has been translated horizontally to bring the images of the nearest rocks into coincidence (and thus appearing at the surface of the screen) and the distant mountains now appear to recede into the image. This latter adjusted image appears more natural, appearing as a view through a window onto the landscape.

Scene Composition

Monochrome version ▪▪▫ 3D red cyan glasses are recommended to view this image correctly.

In the toy images to the right, the shelf edge was selected as the point where images are to coincide and the toys were arranged so that only the central toy was projecting beyond the shelf. When the image is viewed the shelf edge appears to be at the screen, and the toy's feet and snout project toward the viewer, creating a "pop out" effect.

Dual Purpose, 2D or 3D "Compatible Anaglyph" Technique

Since the advent of the Internet, a variant technique has developed where the images are specially processed to minimize visible mis-registration of the two layers. This technique is known by various names, the most common, associated with diopter glasses, and warmer skin tones, is Anachrome. The technique allows most images to be used as large thumbnails, while the 3D information is encoded into the image with less parallax than conventional anaglyphs.

Anaglyphic Color Channels

Anaglyph images may use any combination of color channels. However, if a stereoscopic image is to be pursued, the colors should be diametrically opposed. Impurities of color channel display, or of the viewing filters, allow some of the image meant for the other channel to be seen. This results in stereoscopic double imaging, also called ghosting. Color channels may be left-right reversed. Red/Cyan is most common. Magenta/Green and Blue/Yellow are also popular. Red/Green and Red/Blue enable monochromatic images especially Red/Green. Many anaglyph makers purposely integrate impure color channels and viewing filters to enable better color perception, but this results in a corresponding degree of double imaging. Color Channel Brightness % of White: Red-30/Cyan-70, Magenta-41/Green-59 or especially Blue- 11/Yellow-89), the lighter display channel may be darkened or the brighter viewing filter may be darkened to allow both eyes a balanced view. However the Pulfrich effect can be obtained from a light/dark filter arrangement. The color channels of an anaglyphic image require pure color display fidelity and corresponding viewing filter gels. The choice of ideal viewing filters is dictated by the color channels of the anaglyph to be viewed. Ghosting can be eliminated by ensuring a pure color display and viewing filters that mach the display. Retinal rivalry can be eliminated by the (ACB) 3-D 'Anaglyphic Contrast Balance' method patented by that prepares the image pair prior to color channelling in any color.

scheme	left eye	L	R	right eye	color rendering	description
red-green	pure red			pure green	monochrome	the predecessor of red-cyan;. Used for printed materials, e.g. books and comics.
red-blue	pure red			pure blue	monochrome	Some green-blue color perception. Often used for printed materials.
red-cyan	pure red			pure cyan (green+blue)	color (poor reds, good greens)	good color perception of green and blue, no red. Currently the most common in use. Regular version (red channel has only the red third of the view) Half version (red channel is a red-tinted grayscale view. Less retinal rivalry)
anachrome	dark red			cyan (green+blue+some red)	color (poor reds)	a variant of red-cyan; left eye has dark red filter, right eye has a cyan filter leaking some red; better color perception, shows red hues with some ghosting.
mirachrome	dark red+lens			cyan (green+blue+some red)	color (poor reds)	same as anachrome, with addition of a weak positive correction lens on the red channel to compensate for the chromatic aberration soft focus of red.
Trioscopic	pure green			pure magenta (red+blue)	color (better reds, oranges and wider range of blues than red/cyan)	Same principle as red-cyan, somewhat newer. Less chromatic aberration, as the red and blue in magenta brightness balance well with green.
ColorCode 3-D	amber (red+green+- neutral grey)			pure dark blue (+optional lens)	color (almost full-color perception)	(also named yellow-blue, ochre-blue, or brown-blue) a newer system deployed in 2000s; better color rendering, but dark image, requires dark room or very bright image. Left filter darkened to equalize the brightness received by both eyes as the sensitivity to dark blue is poor. Older people may have problems perceiving the blue. Like in the mirachrome system, the chromatic aberration can be compensated with a weak negative correction lens (-0.7 diopter) over the right eye. Works best in the RG color space. The weak perception of the blue image may allow watching the movie without glasses and not seeing the disturbing double-image.

scheme	left eye	L	R	right eye	color rendering	description
magenta-cyan	pure magenta (red+blue)			pure cyan (green+blue)	color (better than red-cyan)	experimental; similar to red-cyan, better brightness balance of the color channels and the same retinal rivalry. Blue channel is blurred horizontally by the amount equal to the average parallax, and visible to both eyes; the blurring prevents eyes from using the blue channel to construct stereoscopic image and therefore prevents ghosting, while supplying both eyes with color information.
Infitec	white (Red 629 nm, Green 532 nm, Blue 446 nm)			white (Red 615 nm, Green 518 nm, Blue 432 nm)	color (full color)	uses narrow-band interference filters, requires corresponding interference filters for projectors, technical requirements comparable with polarization-based schemes. Not usable with standard CRT, LCD, etc. displays.

In theory, under trichromatic principles, it is possible to introduce a limited amount of multiple-perspective capability (a technology not possible with polarization schemes). This is done by overlapping three images instead of two, in the sequence of green, red, blue. Viewing such an image with red-green glasses would give one perspective, while switching to blue-red would give a slightly different one. In practice, this remains elusive as some blue is perceived through green gel and most green is perceived through blue gel. It is also theoretically possible to incorporate rod cells, which optimally perform at a dark cyan color, in well-optimized mesopic vision, to create a fourth filter color and yet another perspective; however, this has not yet been demonstrated, nor would most televisions be able to process such tetrachromatic filtering.

Applications

On April 1, 2010, Google launched a feature in Google Street View that shows anaglyphs rather than regular images, allowing users to see the streets in 3D.

Home Entertainment

Disney Studios released *Hannah Montana & Miley Cyrus: Best of Both Worlds Concert* in August 2008, its first anaglyph 3D Blu-ray Disc. This was shown on the Disney Channel with red-cyan paper glasses in July 2008.

However, on Blu-ray Disc anaglyph techniques have more recently been supplanted by the Blu-ray 3D format, which uses Multiview Video Coding (MVC) to encode full stereoscopic images. Though Blu-ray 3D does not require a specific display method, and some Blu-ray 3D software players (such as Arcsoft TotalMedia Theatre) are capable of anaglyphic playback, most Blu-ray 3D players are connected via HDMI 1.4 to 3D televisions and other 3D displays using more advanced stereoscopic display methods, such as alternate-frame sequencing (with active shutter glasses) or FPR polarization (with the same passive glasses as RealD theatrical 3D).

Comics

These techniques have been used to produce 3-dimensional comic books, mostly during the early 1950s, using carefully constructed line drawings printed in colors appropriate to the filter glasses provided. The material presented were from a wide variety of genres, including war, horror, crime, and superhero. Anaglyphed comics were far more difficult to produce than normal comics, requiring each panel to be drawn multiple times on layers of acetate. While the first 3D comic in 1953 sold over two million copies, by the end of the year sales had bottomed out, though 3D comics have continued to be released irregularly up until the present day.

Science and Mathematics

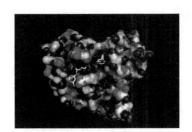 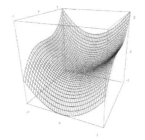 

Anaglyph image of the protein DHFR.

The single valued function of two variables z(x,y)=x²+y³ with the function value displayed as the height.

Anaglyph image of the Ribosome.

3D red cyan glasses are recommended to view this image correctly.

Three-dimensional display can also be used to display scientific data sets, or to illustrate mathematical functions. Anaglyph images are suitable both for paper presentation, and moving video display . They can easily be included in science books, and viewed with cheap anaglyph glasses. Anaglyphy (including, among others, aerial, telescopic, and microscopic images) is being applied to scientific research, popular science, and higher education.

Also, chemical structures, particularly for large systems, can be difficult to represent in two dimensions without omitting geometric information. Therefore, most chemistry computer software can output anaglyph images, and some chemistry textbooks include them.

Today, there are more advanced solutions for 3D imaging available, like shutter glasses together with fast monitors. These solutions are already extensively used in science. Still, anaglyph images provide a cheap and comfortable way to view scientific visualizations.

Game Engine

A game engine is a software framework designed for the creation and development of video games. Developers use them to create games for consoles, mobile devices and personal computers. The core functionality typically provided by a game engine includes a rendering engine ("renderer") for 2D or 3D graphics, a physics engine or collision detection (and collision response), sound, scripting, animation, artificial intelligence, networking, streaming, memory management, thread-ing, localization support, scene graph, and may include video support for cinematics. The process of game development is often economized, in large part, by reusing/adapting the same game engine to create different games, or to make it easier to "port" games to multiple platforms.

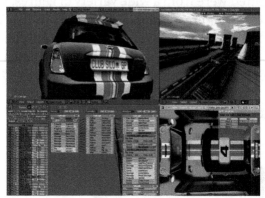

Creating a racing game in Blender Game Engine

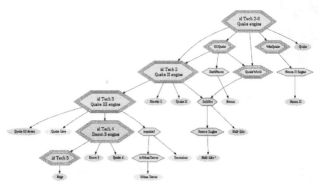

Some game engines experience an evolution over time and develop a family tree,
like for instance id's Quake engine which resulted in the id Tech family

Purpose

In many cases game engines provide a suite of visual development tools in addition to reusable software components. These tools are generally provided in an integrated development environ-ment to enable simplified, rapid development of games in a data-driven manner. Game engine developers attempt to "pre-invent the wheel" by developing robust software suites which include many elements a game developer may need to build a game. Most game engine suites provide facilities that ease development, such as graphics, sound, physics and AI functions. These game engines are sometimes called "middleware" because, as with the business sense of the term, they provide a flexible and reusable software platform which provides all the core functionality needed, right out of the box, to develop a game application while reducing costs, complexities, and time-to-market — all critical factors in the highly competitive video game industry. Gamebryo, JMonkey Engine and RenderWare are such widely used middleware programs.

Like other middleware solutions, game engines usually provide platform abstraction, allowing the same game to be run on various platforms including game consoles and personal computers with few, if any, changes made to the game source code. Often, game engines are designed with a com-ponent-based architecture that allows specific systems in the engine to be replaced or extended with more specialized (and often more expensive) game middleware components such as Havok for physics, Miles Sound System for sound, or Bink for video. Some game engines such as Render-Ware are even designed as a series of loosely connected game middleware components that can be selectively combined to create a custom engine, instead of the more common approach of extending or customizing a flexible integrated solution. However extensibility is achieved, it remains a high priority for game engines due to the wide variety of uses for which they are applied. Despite the specificity of the name, game engines are often used for other kinds of interactive applications with real-time graphical needs such as marketing demos, architectural visualizations, training simulations, and modeling environments.

Some game engines only provide real-time 3D rendering capabilities instead of the wide range of functionality needed by games. These engines rely upon the game developer to implement the rest of this functionality or assemble it from other game middleware components. These types of engines are generally referred to as a "graphics engine," "rendering engine," or "3D engine" instead of the more encompassing term "game engine." This terminology is inconsistently used as many full-featured 3D game engines are referred to simply as "3D engines." A few examples of graphics engines are: Crystal Space, Genesis3D, Irrlicht, OGRE, RealmForge, Truevision3D, and Vision Engine. Modern game or graphics engines generally provide a scene graph, which is an object-oriented representation of the 3D game world which often simplifies game design and can be used for more efficient rendering of vast virtual worlds.

As technology ages, the components of an engine may become outdated or insufficient for the requirements of a given project. Since the complexity of programming an entirely new engine may result in unwanted delays (or necessitate that the project be completely restarted), a development team may elect to update their existing engine with newer functionality or components.

Components

Such a framework is composed of a multitude of very different components.

Main Game Program

The actual game logic has to be implemented by some algorithms. It is distinct from any rendering, sound or input work.

Rendering Engine

The rendering engine generates 3D animated graphics by the chosen method (rasterization, ray-tracing or any different technique).

Instead of being programmed and compiled to be executed on the CPU or GPU directly, most often rendering engines are built upon one or multiple rendering application programming interfaces (APIs), such as Direct3D or OpenGL which provide a software abstraction of the graphics processing unit (GPU).

Low-level libraries such as DirectX, Simple DirectMedia Layer (SDL), and OpenGL are also commonly used in games as they provide hardware-independent access to other computer hardware such as input devices (mouse, keyboard, and joystick), network cards, and sound cards. Before hardware-accelerated 3D graphics, software renderers had been used. Software rendering is still used in some modeling tools or for still-rendered images when visual accuracy is valued over real-time performance (frames-per-second) or when the computer hardware does not meet needs such as shader support.

With the advent of hardware accelerated physics processing, various physics APIs such as PAL and the physics extensions of COLLADA became available to provide a software abstraction of the physics processing unit of different middleware providers and console platforms.

Game engines can be written in any programming language like C++, C or Java, though each language is structurally different and may provide different levels of access to specific functions.

Audio Engine

The audio engine is the component which consists of algorithms related to sound. It can calculate things on the CPU, or on a dedicated ASIC. Abstraction APIs, such as OpenAL, SDL audio, XAudio 2, Web Audio, etc. are available.

Physics Engine

The physics engine is responsible for emulating the laws of physics realistically within the application.

Artificial Intelligence

The AI is usually outsourced from the main game program into a special module to be designed and written by software engineers with specialist knowledge.

History

Before game engines, games were typically written as singular entities: a game for the Atari 2600, for example, had to be designed from the bottom up to make optimal use of the display hardware—this core display routine is today called the kernel by retro developers. Other platforms had more leeway, but even when the display was not a concern, memory constraints usually sabotaged attempts to create the data-heavy design that an engine needs. Even on more accommodating platforms, very little could be reused between games. The rapid advance of arcade hardware—which was the leading edge of the market at the time—meant that most of the code would have to be thrown out afterwards anyway, as later generations of games would use completely different game designs that took advantage of extra resources. Thus most game designs through the 1980s were designed through a hard-coded ruleset with a small number of levels and graphics data. Since the golden age of arcade video games, it became common for video game companies to develop in-house game engines for use with first party software.

While third-party game engines were not common up until the rise of 3D computer graphics in the 1990s, there were several 2D game creation systems produced in the 1980s for independent video game development. These include Pinball Construction Set (1983), ASCII's War Game Construction Kit (1983), Thunder Force Construction (1984), Adventure Construction Set (1984), Garry Kitchen's GameMaker (1985), Wargame Construction Set (1986), Shoot'Em-

Up Construction Kit (1987), Arcade Game Construction Kit (1988), and most popularly AS-CII's RPG Maker engines from 1988 onwards. Klik & Play (1994) is another legacy offering that's still available.

The term "game engine" arose in the mid-1990s, especially in connection with 3D games such as first-person shooters (FPS). Such was the popularity of Id Software's *Doom* and *Quake* games that, rather than work from scratch, other developers licensed the core portions of the software and designed their own graphics, characters, weapons and levels—the "game content" or "game assets." Separation of game-specific rules and data from basic concepts like collision detection and game entity meant that teams could grow and specialize.

Later games, such as id Software's *Quake III Arena* and Epic Games's 1998 *Unreal* were designed with this approach in mind, with the engine and content developed separately. The practice of licensing such technology has proved to be a useful auxiliary revenue stream for some game developers, as a one license for a high-end commercial game engine can range from US$10,000 to millions of dollars, and the number of licensees can reach several dozen companies, as seen with the Unreal Engine. At the very least, reusable engines make developing game sequels faster and easier, which is a valuable advantage in the competitive video game industry. While there was a strong rivalry between Epic and id around 2000, since then Epic's Unreal Engine has been far more popular than id Tech 4 and its successor id Tech 5.

Modern game engines are some of the most complex applications written, often featuring dozens of finely tuned systems interacting to ensure a precisely controlled user experience. The continued evolution of game engines has created a strong separation between rendering, scripting, artwork, and level design. It is now common, for example, for a typical game development team to have several times as many artists as actual programmers.

First-person shooter games remain the predominant users of third-party game engines, but they are now also being used in other genres. For example, the role-playing video game *The Elder Scrolls III: Morrowind* and the MMORPG *Dark Age of Camelot* are based on the Gamebryo engine, and the MMORPG *Lineage II* is based on the Unreal Engine. Game engines are used for games originally developed for home consoles as well; for example, the RenderWare engine is used in the *Grand Theft Auto* and *Burnout* franchises.

Threading is taking on more importance due to modern multi-core systems (e.g. Cell) and increased demands in realism. Typical threads involve rendering, streaming, audio, and physics. Racing games have typically been at the forefront of threading with the physics engine running in a separate thread long before other core subsystems were moved, partly because rendering and related tasks need updating at only 30–60 Hz. For example, on PlayStation 3, physics ran in *Need For Speed* at 100 Hz versus *Forza Motorsport 2* at 360 Hz.

Although the term was first used in the 1990s, there are a few earlier systems in the 1980s that are also considered to be game engines, such as Sierra's Adventure Game Interpreter (AGI) and SCI systems, LucasArts' SCUMM system and Incentive Software's Freescape engine. Unlike most modern game engines, these game engines were never used in any third-party products (except for the SCUMM system which was licensed to and used by Humongous Entertainment).

Recent Trends

As game engine technology matures and becomes more user-friendly, the application of game engines has broadened in scope. They are now being used for serious games: visualization, training, medical, and military simulation applications, with the CryEngine being one example. To facilitate this accessibility, new hardware platforms are now being targeted by game engines, including mobile phones (e.g. Android phones, iPhone) and web browsers (e.g. WebGL, Shockwave, Flash, Trinigy's WebVision, Silverlight, Unity Web Player, O3D and pure DHTML).

Additionally, more game engines are being built upon higher level languages such as Java and C#/.NET (e.g. TorqueX, and Visual3D.NET), Python (Panda3D), or Lua Script (Leadwerks). As most 3D rich games are now mostly GPU-limited (i.e. limited by the power of the graphics card), the potential slowdown due to translation overheads of higher level languages becomes negligible, while the productivity gains offered by these languages work to the game engine developers' benefit. These recent trends are being propelled by companies such as Microsoft to support Indie game development. Microsoft developed XNA as the SDK of choice for all video games released on Xbox and related products. This includes the Xbox Live Indie Games channel designed specifically for smaller developers who don't have the extensive resources necessary to box games for sale on retail shelves. It is becoming easier and cheaper than ever to develop game engines for platforms that support managed frameworks.

Game Middleware

In the broader sense of the term, game engines themselves can be described as middleware. In the context of video games, however, the term "middleware" is often used to refer to subsystems of functionality within a game engine. Some game middleware does only one thing but does it more convincingly or more efficiently than general purpose middleware. For example, *SpeedTree* was used to render the realistic trees and vegetation in the role-playing video game *The Elder Scrolls IV: Oblivion* and *Fork Particle* was used to simulate and render real time particle system visual effects or particle effects in Sid Meier's Civilization V.

The four most widely used middleware packages that provide subsystems of functionality include RAD Game Tools' Bink, Firelight FMOD, Havok, and Scaleform GFx. RAD Game Tools develops Bink for basic video rendering, along with Miles audio, and Granny 3D rendering. Firelight FMOD is a low cost robust audio library and toolset. Havok provides a robust physics simulation system, along with a suite of animation and behavior solutions. *Scaleform* provides GFx for high performance Flash UI, along with a high quality video playback solution, and an Input Method Editor (IME) add-on for in-game Asian chat support.

Other middleware is used for performance optimisation - for example 'Simplygon' helps to optimise and generate level of detail meshes, and 'Umbra' adds occlusion culling optimisations to 3d graphics.

Some middleware contains full source code, others just provide an API reference for a compiled binary library. Some middleware programs can be licensed either way, usually for a higher fee for full source code.

Massively Multiplayer Online Games

The Game Engine (or Middleware) for massively multiplayer online games (MMOs, MMOGs) is far more complex than for single-player video games. Technically every normal game engine can be used to implement an MMO game by combining it with MMO middleware. The increasing popularity of MMOGs is spurring development of MMO middleware packages. Some MMO middleware software packages already include a game engine, while others provide networking only and therefore must be combined with a game engine to create an MMO game.

First-person Shooter Engines

A well-known subset of game engines are 3D first-person shooter (FPS) game engines. Groundbreaking development in terms of visual quality is done in FPS games on the human scale. While flight and driving simulators and real-time strategy (RTS) games increasingly provide realism on a large scale, first-person shooters are at the forefront of computer graphics on these smaller scales.

The development of the FPS graphic engines that appear in games can be characterized by a steady increase in technologies, with some breakthroughs. Attempts at defining distinct generations lead to arbitrary choices of what constitutes a highly modified version of an "old engine" and what is a brand-new engine.

The classification is complicated as game engines blend old and new technologies. Features that were considered advanced in a new game one year become the expected standard the next year. Games with a mix of older generation and newer feature are the norm. For example, *Jurassic Park: Trespasser* (1998) introduced physics to the FPS games, but it did not become common until around 2002. *Red Faction* (2001) featured destructible walls and ground, something still not common in engines years later (for example in *Unreal Tournament 2004* there are still no destructible objects). *Battlezone* (1998) and *Battlezone II: Combat Commander* (1999) added vehicle based combat to the usual FPS mix, which did not hit the mainstream until later. *Tribes 2*, *Battlefield 1942*, *Halo: Combat Evolved*, and *Unreal Tournament 2004* fully realized the potential for vehicular-combat and first person shooter integration.

Medical Animation

A medical animation is a short educational film, usually based around a physiological or surgical topic, that is rendered using 3D computer graphics. While it may be intended for an array of audiences, the medical animation is most commonly utilized as an instructional tool for medical professionals or their patients.

Early medical animations were limited to basic wire-frame models because of low processor speed. However, rapid evolution in microprocessor design and computer memory has led to animations that are significantly more intricate.

The medical animation may be viewed as a standalone visualization, or in combination with other sensory input devices, such as head-mounted displays, stereoscopic lenses, haptic gloves, interactive workstations, or Cave Automatic Virtual Environments (CAVEs).

History

Though evolved from the field of realistic medical illustrations (such as those created by Flemish anatomist Andreas Vesalius in the 16th century), medical animations are also indebted to motion picture technology and computer-generated imagery.

The term *medical animation* predates the advent of computer-generated graphics by approximately three decades. Though the first computer animation was created at Bell Telephone Labs in 1963, the phrase "medical animation" appears in scholarly contexts as early as 1932 in the Journal of Biological Photography. As discussed by Clarke and Hoshall, the term referred to two-dimensional illustrated motion pictures produced for inclusion in films screened for medical students.

The creation of the computer-generated medical animation began in earnest in the early 1970s. The first description of the use of 3D computer graphics for a medical purpose can be found in an issue of the journal *Science*, dated 1975. Its authors, a team of researchers from the Departments of Chemistry and of Biochemistry and Biophysics at Texas A&M University, described the potential uses of medical animation for visualizing complex macromolecules.

By the late 1980s, the medical animation had become a distinct modality of physiological and surgical instruction. By that point, researchers had suggested that the 3D medical animations could illustrate physiological, molecular or anatomical concepts that might otherwise be infeasible.

Today's medical animation industry comprises one facet of the non-entertainment computer animation industry, which has annual revenues of $15 billion per year worldwide.

Applications

Patient Education

A growing trend among medical animation studios is the creation of clips that explain surgical procedures or pharmaceutical mechanisms of action in terms simple enough for a layperson to understand. These animations may be found on hospital websites, in doctor's office workstations or via medical studios themselves. Such animations may also appear on television shows and other popular entertainment venues as a way to educate an audience on a medical topic under discussion.

Occasionally, this form of animation is used in-hospital. In this context, clips may be used in order to get fully informed consent from patients facing surgery or medical treatment. Likewise, studies have suggested that patient-educating medical animations may be able to reduce the rate of accidental wrong-site surgeries.

Medical simulation

Due to both the relative scarcity of cadavers to be used for surgical instruction and to the dwindling use of animals and patients who have not given consent, institutes may utilize medical animations as a way to teach doctors-to-be anatomical and surgical concepts. Such simulations may be viewed passively (as in the case of 3D medical animations included via CD-ROM in medical textbook packages) or using interactive controls. The stimulation of hand-eye skills using haptics is another possible use of medical animation technology, one that stems from the replacement of cadavers in surgical classrooms with task trainers and mannequins.

The creation of proportionally accurate virtual bodies is often accomplished using medical scans, such as computed tomography (CT) or magnetic resonance imaging (MRI). Such techniques represent a cost- and time-saving move away from the creation of medical animations using sectioned cadavers. For instance, the National Library of Medicine's Visible Human Project created 3D medical animations of the male and female bodies by scanning cadavers using CT technology, after which they were frozen, shaved into millimeter-thick sections and recorded using high-resolution photographs.

By comparison, medical animations made using only scanned data can recreate the internal structures of live patients, often in the context of surgical planning.

Cellular and Molecular Animation

Medical animations are often employed as a method of visualizing the vast number of microscopic processes that occur in the human body. These may involve the interplay between organelles, the transcription of DNA, the molecular action of enzymes, the interactions between pathogens and white blood cells or virtually any other cellular or sub-cellular process.

Molecular animations are similar in that they depict structures that are too small for the human eye to see. However, this latter category is also capable of illustrating atomic structures, which are often too minute to be visualized with any clarity via microscopy.

Pharmaceutical Mechanism of Action

As a way to explain how medications work, pharmaceutical manufacturers may provide mechanism of action animations, often through websites dedicated to specific prescription drugs. These medical visualizations typically do not represent cellular structures in a fully accurate or proportional way. Instead, mechanism of action animations may visually simplify the interaction between drug molecules and cells. These medical animations may also explain the physiological origins of the disease itself.

Emergency Care Instruction

Several studies have suggested that 3D medical animations may be used to instruct novices on how to perform cardiopulmonary resuscitation in an emergency. These reports usually suggest the use of pre-prepared, voice-narrated motion-capture animations that are viewed by means of a cellphone or other portable electronic device.

Forensic Reconstruction

A number of applications for medical animations has been developed in the field of forensics. These include the so-called "virtutopsy," or MRI-assisted virtual autopsy, of remains that are too damaged to be otherwise inspected or reconstructed. Likewise, medical animations can appear in courtrooms, be used as forensic "reconstructions" of crime scenes or recreate the crimes themselves. The admissibility of such evidence is questionable.

Electronic Learning

Researchers have suggested that medical animations can be used to disseminate medical education materials electronically, allowing them to be accessed and utilized by professional and amateur health practitioners alike.

Surgical Training and Planning

Some institutes use animations both to teach medical students how to perform basic surgery, and to give seasoned surgeons the chance to expand their skill set. Multiple studies have been conducted on the effectiveness and feasibility of medical animation-based surgical pre-planning. Experimental animation tools have been created as integral technology in image-guided surgery as well.

References

- Riley, K F (2006). Mathematical Methods for Physics and Engineering. Cambridge University Press. pp. 931, 942. ISBN 0-521-67971-0. doi:10.2277/0521679710

- Jorke, Helmut; Fritz M. (2006). "Stereo projection using interference filters". Stereoscopic Displays and Applications. Proc. SPIE 6055. Retrieved 2008-11-19

- Hortolà, P. (2009). "Using digital anaglyph to improve the relief effect of SEM micrographs of bloodstains". Micron. 40 (3): 409–412. doi:10.1016/j.micron.2008.09.008

- Kass, Michael, Andrew Witkin, and Demetri Terzopoulos. "Snakes: Active contour models." International journal of computer vision 1.4 (1988): 321-331

- Goldstein, Herbert (1980). Classical Mechanics (2nd ed.). Reading, Mass.: Addison-Wesley Pub. Co. pp. 146–148. ISBN 0-201-02918-9

- "Gaming: Mobile and Wireless Trends for 2008". M-trends.org. Archived from the original on 2011-01-08. Retrieved 2011-01-17

- Ingrid Carlbom, Joseph Paciorek (1978). "Planar Geometric Projections and Viewing Transformations" (PDF). ACM Computing Surveys. 10 (4): 465–502. doi:10.1145/356744.356750

- Sonka, M; Hlavac, V; Boyle, R (1995). Image Processing, Analysis & Machine Vision (2nd ed.). Chapman and Hall. p. 14. ISBN 0-412-45570-6

- Rollmann, W. (1853), "Zwei neue stereoskopische Methoden", Annalen der Physik (in German), 90: 186–187, Bibcode:1853AnP...166..186R, doi:10.1002/andp.18531660914

Various Computer-Aided Design Softwares

The various computer-aided design software are Blender, BRL-CAD, Archimedes, FreeCAD, Open-SCAD, SolveSpace, LibreCAD and Magic. Blender is a software that is used to create visual effects and animation movies. Some of the features of Blender are texturing, ringing and skinning, fluid and smoke simulation, 3D modeling and video editing. The topics elaborated in this chapter will help in gaining a better perspective about the various computer-aided design softwares.

Blender (Software)

Blender is a professional free and open-source 3D computer graphics software product used for creating animated films, visual effects, art, 3D printed models, interactive 3D applications and video games. Blender's features include 3D modeling, UV unwrapping, texturing, raster graphics editing, rigging and skinning, fluid and smoke simulation, particle simulation, soft body simulation, sculpting, animating, match moving, camera tracking, rendering, video editing and compositing. It further features an integrated game engine.

History

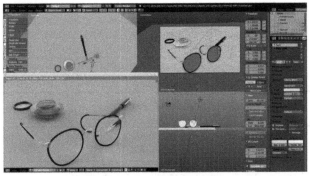

The desktop scene in version 2.77

The Dutch animation studio Neo Geo developed Blender as an in-house application in January 1995, with the primary author being software developer Ton Roosendaal. The name *Blender* was inspired by a song by Yello, from the album *Baby*. When Neo Geo was acquired by another company, Ton Roosendaal and Frank van Beek founded Not a Number Technologies (NaN) in June 1998 to further develop Blender, initially distributing it as shareware until NaN went bankrupt in 2002.

On July 18, 2002, Roosendaal started the *"Free Blender"* campaign, a crowdfunding precursor. The campaign aimed for open-sourcing Blender for a one-time payment of €100,000 (US$100,670 at the time) collected from the community. On September 7, 2002, it was announced that they had collected enough funds and would release the Blender source code. Today, Blender is free, open-source software that is—apart from the Blender Institute's two full-time and two part-time employees—developed by the community.

The Blender Foundation initially reserved the right to use dual licensing, so that, in addition to GPLv2, Blender would have been available also under the *Blender License* that did not require disclosing source code but required payments to the Blender Foundation. However, they never exercised this option and suspended it indefinitely in 2005. Blender is solely available under "GNU GPLv2 or any later" and was not updated to the GPLv3, as "no evident benefits" were seen.

The following program developed in each version:

Version	Release	Notes and key changes
2.03	around 2002	Handbook *The official Blender 2.0 guide*.
2.26	August 20, 2003	First ever free version.
2.30	November 22, 2003	New GUI; edits are now revertible.
2.32	February 3, 2004	Ray tracing in internal renderer; support for YafaRay.
2.34	August 5, 2004	LSCM-UV-Unwrapping, object-particle interaction.
2.37	May 31, 2005	Simulation of elastic surfaces; improved subdivision surface.
2.40	December 22, 2005	Greatly improved system and character animations (with a non-linear editing tool), and added fluid and hair simulator. New functionality was based on *Google Summer of Code* 2005.
2.41	January 25, 2006	Improvements of the game engine (programmable vertex and pixel shaders, using Blender materials, split-screen mode, improvements to the physics engine), improved UV mapping, recording of the Python scripts for sculpture or sculpture works with the help of grid or mesh (mesh sculpting) and set-chaining models.
2.42	July 14, 2006	The film *Elephants Dream* resulted in high development as a necessity. In particular the Node-System (Material- and Compositor) has been implemented.
2.43	February 16, 2007	*Sculpt-Modeling* as a result of *Google Summer of Code 2006*
2.46	May 19, 2008	With the production of *Big Buck Bunny* Blender set to produce grass quickly and efficiently.
2.48	October 14, 2008	Due to development of *Yo Frankie!*, the game engine was improved substantially.
2.49	June 13, 2009	First official stable release 2.5. New window and file manager, new interface, new Python API, and new animation system.
2.57	April 13, 2011	First official stable release of 2.5er branch: new interface, new window manager and rewritten event — and tool — file processing system, new animation system (each setting can be animated now), and new Python API.
2.58	June 22, 2011	New features, such as the addition of the warp modifier and render baking. Improvements in sculpting.
2.58a	July 4, 2011	Some bug fixes, along with small extensions in GUI and Python interface.

2.59	August 13, 2011	3D mouse support
2.60	October 19, 2011	Developer branches integrated into main developer branch: among other things, B-mesh, a new rendering/shading system, NURBS, to name a few, directly from Google Summer of Code
2.61	December 14, 2011	Render-Engine Cycles, Motion Tracking, Dynamic Paint, Ocean Simulator
2.62	February 16, 2012	Motion tracking improvement, further expansion of UV tools, cycles render engine, and remesh modifier
2.63	April 27, 2012	Bug fixes, B-mesh project: completely new mesh system with n-corners, plus new tools: dissolve, inset, bridge, vertex slide, vertex connect, and bevel
2.64	October 3, 2012	Green screen keying, node based compositing
2.65	December 10, 2012	Over 200 bug fixes, support for the Open Shading Language, and fire simulation
2.66	February 21, 2013	Rigid body simulation available outside of the game engine, dynamic topology sculpting, hair rendering now supported in cycles
2.67	May 7–30, 2013	Freestyle rendering mode for non-photographic rendering, subsurface scattering support added, the motion tracking solver is made more accurate and faster, and an add-on for 3D printing now comes bundled
2.68	July 18, 2013	Rendering performance is improved for CPUs and GPUs, support for NVIDIA Tesla K20, GTX Titan and GTX 780 GPUs. Smoke rendering improved to reduce blockiness.
2.69	October 31, 2013	Motion tracking now supports plane tracking, and hair rendering was improved
2.70	March 19, 2014	Initial support for volume rendering and small improvements to the user interface
2.71	June 26, 2014	Support for baking in cycles and volume rendering branched path tracing now renders faster
2.72	October 4, 2014	Volume rendering for GPUs, more features for sculpting and painting
2.73	January 8, 2015	New fullscreen mode, improved Pie Menus, 3D View can now display the world background.
2.74	March 31, 2015	Cycles got several precision, noise, speed, memory improvements, new Pointiness attribute.
2.75a	July 1, 2015	Blender now supports a fully integrated Multi-View and Stereo 3D pipeline, Cycles has much awaited initial support for AMD GPUs, and a new Light Portals feature.
2.76b	November 3, 2015	Cycles volume density render, Pixar OpenSubdiv mesh subdivision library, node inserting, video editing tools
2.77a	April 6, 2016	Improvements of Cycles, new features for the Grease Pencil, more support for OpenVDB, updated Python library and support for Windows XP removed
2.78c	February 28, 2017	Spherical stereo rendering for VR, Grease Pencil improvements for 2D animations, Freehand curves drawing over surfaces, Bendy Bones, Micropolygon displacements, Adaptive Subdivision. Cycles performance improvements.

Legend:

Old version   Older version, still supported   **Latest version**   Latest preview version   Future release

Suzanne

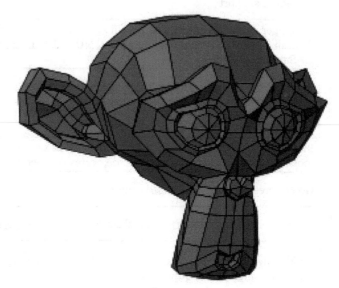

Suzanne

In January–February 2002 it was clear that NaN could not survive and would close the doors in March. Nevertheless, they put out one more release, 2.25. As a sort-of easter egg, a last personal tag, the artists and developers decided to add a 3D model of a chimpanzee head. It was created by Willem-Paul van Overbruggen (SLiD3), who named it Suzanne after the orangutan in the Kevin Smith film *Jay and Silent Bob Strike Back*.

Suzanne is Blender's alternative to more common test models such as the Utah Teapot and the Stanford Bunny. A low-polygon model with only 500 faces, Suzanne is often used as a quick and easy way to test material, animation, rigs, texture, and lighting setups and is also frequently used in joke images. Suzanne is still included in Blender. The largest Blender contest gives out an award called the Suzanne Award.

Clones

Due to Blender's open source nature, other programs have tried to take advantage of its success by repackaging and selling cosmetically-modified versions of it. Examples include IllusionMage, 3DMofun, 3DMagix, and Fluid Designer, the latter recognized as Blender-based.

Features

Official releases of Blender for Microsoft Windows, MacOS and Linux, as well as a port for FreeBSD, are available in both 32-bit and 64-bit versions. Though it is often distributed without extensive example scenes found in some other programs, the software contains features that are characteristic of high-end 3D software. Among its capabilities are:

- Support for a variety of geometric primitives, including polygon meshes, fast subdivision surface modeling, Bezier curves, NURBS surfaces, metaballs, icospheres, multi-res digital sculpting (including dynamic topology, maps baking, remeshing, resymetrize, decimation), outline font, and a new n-gon modeling system called B-mesh.

- Internal render engine with scanline rendering, indirect lighting, and ambient occlusion that can export in a wide variety of formats.

- A pathtracer render engine called Cycles, which can take advantage of the GPU for rendering. Cycles supports the Open Shading Language since Blender 2.65.

- Integration with a number of external render engines through plugins.

- Keyframed animation tools including inverse kinematics, armature (skeletal), hook, curve and lattice-based deformations, shape animations, non-linear animation, constraints, and vertex weighting.

- Simulation tools for soft body dynamics including mesh collision detection, LBM fluid dynamics, smoke simulation, Bullet rigid body dynamics, ocean generator with waves.

- A particle system that includes support for particle-based hair.

- Modifiers to apply non-destructive effects.

- Python scripting for tool creation and prototyping, game logic, importing/exporting from other formats, task automation and custom tools.

- Basic non-linear video/audio editing.

- The Blender Game Engine, a sub-project, offers interactivity features such as collision detection, dynamics engine, and programmable logic. It also allows the creation of stand-alone, real-time applications ranging from architectural visualization to video games.

- A fully integrated node-based compositor within the rendering pipeline accelerated with OpenCL.

- Procedural and node-based textures, as well as texture painting, projective painting, vertex painting, weight painting and dynamic painting.

- Real-time control during physics simulation and rendering.

- Camera and object tracking.

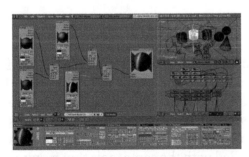  

| Using the node editor to create anisotropic metallic materials | The main character from the Blender Sintel open film | Rendering of a house |

User Interface

Blender's user interface underwent a significant update during the 2.5x series

Blender's user interface incorporates the following concepts:

Editing modes

> The two primary modes of work are *Object Mode* and *Edit Mode*, which are toggled with the Tab key. Object mode is used to manipulate individual objects as a unit, while Edit mode is used to manipulate the actual object data. For example, Object Mode can be used to move, scale, and rotate entire polygon meshes, and Edit Mode can be used to manipulate the individual vertices of a single mesh. There are also several other modes, such as Vertex Paint, Weight Paint, and Sculpt Mode.

Hotkey usage

> Most of the commands are accessible via hotkeys. There are also comprehensive GUI menus.

Numeric input

> Numeric buttons can be "dragged" to change their value directly without the need to aim at a particular widget, as well as being set using the keyboard. Both sliders and number buttons can be constrained to various step sizes with modifiers like the Ctrl and Shift keys. Python expressions can also be typed directly into number entry fields, allowing mathematical expressions to specify values.

Workspace management

> The Blender GUI builds its own tiled windowing system on top of one or multiple windows provided by the underlying platform. One platform window (often sized to fill the screen) is divided into sections and subsections that can be of any type of Blender's views or window-types. The user can define multiple layouts of such Blender windows, called *screens*, and switch quickly between them by selecting from a menu or with keyboard shortcuts. Each window-type's own GUI elements can be controlled with the same tools that manipulate 3D view. For example, one can zoom in and out of GUI-buttons using similar controls one zooms in and out in the 3D viewport. The GUI viewport and screen layout is fully us-

er-customizable. It is possible to set up the interface for specific tasks such as video editing or UV mapping or texturing by hiding features not used for the task.

Hardware Requirements

Blender hardware requirements			
Hardware	Minimum	Recommended	Production-standard
Processor	32-bit dual core 2 GHz CPU with SSE2 support	64-bit quad core CPU	64-bit eight core CPU
Memory	2 GB RAM	8 GB RAM	16 GB RAM
Graphics card	OpenGL 2.1 compatible card with 512 MB video RAM	OpenGL 3.2 compatible card with 2 GB video RAM (CUDA or OpenCL for GPU rendering)	Dual OpenGL 3.2 compatible cards with 4 GB video RAM
Display	1280×768 pixels, 24-bit color	1920×1080 pixels, 24-bit color	Dual 1920×1080 pixels, 24-bit color
Input	Mouse or trackpad	Three-button mouse	Three-button mouse and graphics tablet

Supported Platforms

Blender is available for Windows Vista and above, Mac OSX 10.6 and above, and Linux. Blender 2.76b is the last supported release for Windows XP.

File Format

Blender features an internal file system that can pack multiple scenes into a single file (called a ".blend" file).

- All of Blender's ".blend" files are forward, backward, and cross-platform compatible with other versions of Blender, with the following exceptions:

  o Loading animations stored in post-2.5 files in Blender pre-2.5. This is due to the reworked animation subsystem introduced in Blender 2.5 being inherently incompatible with older versions.

  o Loading meshes stored in post 2.63. This is due to the introduction of BMesh, a more versatile mesh format.

- All scenes, objects, materials, textures, sounds, images, post-production effects for an entire animation can be stored in a single ".blend" file. Data loaded from external sources, such as images and sounds, can also be stored externally and referenced through either an absolute or relative pathname. Likewise, ".blend" files themselves can also be used as libraries of Blender assets.

- Interface configurations are retained in the ".blend" files.

A wide variety of import/export scripts that extend Blender capabilities (accessing the object data via an internal API) make it possible to inter-operate with other 3D tools.

Blender organizes data as various kinds of "data blocks", such as Objects, Meshes, Lamps, Scenes, Materials, Images and so on. An object in Blender consists of multiple data blocks – for example, what the user would describe as a polygon mesh consists of at least an Object and a Mesh data block, and usually also a Material and many more, linked together. This allows various data blocks to refer to each other. There may be, for example, multiple Objects that refer to the same Mesh, and making subsequent editing of the shared mesh result in shape changes in all Objects using this Mesh. Objects, meshes, materials, textures etc. can also be linked to from other .blend files, which is what allows the use of .blend files as reusable resource libraries.

Video Editing

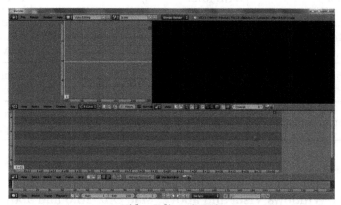
Video Editor (VSE)

Blender features a fully functional, production ready Non-Linear video editor called Video Sequence Editor or VSE for short. Blender's VSE has many features including effects like Gaussian Blur, color grading, Fade and Wipe transitions, and other video transformations. However, there is no multi-core support for rendering video with VSE.

WebGL Authoring

Blend4Web, an open source WebGL framework, can be used to convert whole Blender scenes with graphics, animation, sound and physics to work in standard web browsers. Export can be performed with a single click, even as a standalone web page.

Rendering and Ray Tracing

Cycles is the path-tracing render engine that is designed to be interactive and easy to use, while still supporting many production features. It comes installed as an add-on that is available by default and can be activated in the top header.

GPU Rendering

Cycles supports GPU rendering which is used to help speed up rendering times. There are two GPU rendering modes: CUDA, which is the preferred method for NVIDIA graphics cards; and OpenCL, which supports rendering on AMD graphics cards. Multiple GPUs are also supported, which can be used to create a render farm – although having multiple GPUs doesn't increase the available memory because each GPU can only access its own memory.

Supported features			
Feature	**CPU**	**CUDA**	**OpenCL**
Basic Shading	Yes	Yes	Yes
Transparent Shadows	Yes	Yes	Yes
Motion blur	Yes	Yes	Yes
Hair	Yes	Yes	Yes
Volume	Yes	Yes	Yes
Smoke/Fire	Yes	Yes	Yes
Subsurface Scattering	Yes	Yes	Yes
Open Shading Language	Yes	No	No
Correlated Multi-Jittered Sampling	Yes	Yes	Yes
Branched Path integrator	Yes	Yes	Yes
Displacement/Subdivision	Experimental	Experimental	Experimental

Integrator

The integrator is the rendering algorithm used for lighting computations. Cycles currently supports a path tracing integrator with direct light sampling. It works well for various lighting setups, but is not as suitable for caustics and some other complex lighting situations. Rays are traced from the camera into the scene, bouncing around until they find a light source such as a lamp, an object emitting light, or the world background. To find lamps and surfaces emitting light, both indirect light sampling (letting the ray follow the surface BSDF) and direct light sampling (picking a light source and tracing a ray towards it) are used.

There are two types of integrators:

1. The default path tracing integrator is a pure path tracer. At each hit it bounces light in one direction and picks one light to receive lighting from. This makes each individual sample faster to compute, but typically requires more samples to clean up the noise.

2. The alternative is a branched path tracing integrator which at the first hit splits the path for different surface components and takes all lights into account for shading instead of just one. This makes each sample slower, but reduces noise, especially in scenes dominated by direct or one-bounce lighting.

Open Shading Language

Blender users can create their own nodes using the Open Shading Language although it is important to note that there is no support for it on GPUs.

Materials

Materials define the look of meshes, NURBS curves and other geometric objects. They consist of three shaders, defining the mesh's appearance of the surface, volume inside, and displacement of the surface.

Surface Shader

The surface shader defines the light interaction at the surface of the mesh. One or more BSDFs can specify if incoming light is reflected back, refracted into the mesh, or absorbed.

Volume Shader

When the surface shader does not reflect or absorb light, it enters the volume. If no volume shader is specified, it will pass straight through to the other side of the mesh.

If one is defined, a volume shader describes the light interaction as it passes through the volume of the mesh. Light may be scattered, absorbed, or emitted at any point in the volume.

Displacement Shader

The shape of the surface may be altered by displacement shaders. This way, textures can be used to make the mesh surface more detailed.

Depending on the settings, the displacement may be virtual, only modifying the surface normals to give the impression of displacement (also known as bump mapping) or a combination of real and virtual displacement.

Demo Reels

The Blender website contains several demo reels that showcase various features of Blender.

Physics

Blender can be used to simulate smoke, rain, dust, cloth, water, hair and rigid bodies.

Cloth Simulation

A cloth is any piece of mesh that has been designated as 'cloth' in the physics tab.

Fluid Simulation

Physics fluid simulation

Physics Fluid Simulation

The fluid simulator can be used for simulating liquids, like water hitting a cup. It uses the Lattice Boltzmann methods to simulate the fluids and allows for lots of adjusting of the amount of particles and the resolution.

Particle Fluid Simulation

The particle physics fluid simulation creates particles that follow the Smoothed-particle hydrodynamics method.

Development

Game engine GLSL materials

Since the opening of the source, Blender has experienced significant refactoring of the initial codebase and major additions to its feature set.

Improvements include an animation system refresh; a stack-based modifier system; an updated particle system (which can also be used to simulate hair and fur); fluid dynamics; soft-body dynamics; GLSL shaders support in the game engine; advanced UV unwrapping; a fully recoded render pipeline, allowing separate render passes and "render to texture"; node-based material editing and compositing; and projection painting.

Part of these developments were fostered by Google's Summer of Code program, in which the Blender Foundation has participated since 2005.

Support

Blender is extensively documented on its website, with the rest of the support provided via community tutorials and discussion forums on the Internet. The Blender Network provides support and social services for Blender Professionals. Additionally, YouTube is known to have a great many video tutorials available for either Blender amateurs or professionals at no cost.

Use in the Media Industry

Blender started out as an inhouse tool for a Dutch commercial animation company NeoGeo. Blender has been used for television commercials in several parts of the world including Australia, Iceland, Brazil, Russia and Sweden.

Blender is used by *NASA* for publicly available 3D models. Many 3D models on NASA's 3D resources page are in a native .blend format.

Experience Curiosity: taking a Selfie

NASA also used Blender and Blend4Web to develop an interactive web application to celebrate the 3rd anniversary of the Curiosity rover landing on Mars. This app makes it possible to operate the rover, control its cameras and the robotic arm and reproduces some of the prominent events of the Mars Science Laboratory mission. The application was presented at the beginning of the WebGL section on SIGGRAPH 2015.

The first large professional project that used Blender was *Spider-Man 2*, where it was primarily used to create animatics and pre-visualizations for the storyboard department.

> *As an animatic artist working in the storyboard department of Spider-Man 2, I used Blender's 3D modeling and character animation tools to enhance the storyboards, re-creating sets and props, and putting into motion action and camera moves in 3D space to help make Sam Raimi's vision as clear to other departments as possible.*
> — Anthony Zierhut, Animatic Artist, Los Angeles.

The French-language film *Friday or Another Day* (*Vendredi ou un autre jour*) was the first 35 mm feature film to use Blender for all the special effects, made on Linux workstations. It won a prize at the Locarno International Film Festival. The special effects were by Digital Graphics of Belgium.

Blender has also been used for shows on the History Channel, alongside many other professional 3D graphics programs.

Tomm Moore's *The Secret of Kells*, which was partly produced in Blender by the Belgian studio Digital Graphics, has been nominated for an Oscar in the category "Best Animated Feature Film".

Plumíferos, a commercial animated feature film created entirely in Blender, was premiered in February 2010 in Argentina. Its main characters are anthropomorphic talking animals.

Special effects for episode 6 of Red Dwarf season X were confirmed being created using Blender by half of Gecko Animation, Ben Simonds. The company responsible for the special effects, Gecko Animation, uses Blender for multiple projects, including Red Dwarf. The episode screened in 2012.

Blender was used for both CGI and compositing for the movie *Hardcore Henry*.

The special effects for the TV series *The Man in the High Castle* were done in Blender, with some of the particle simulations relegated to Houdini.

Open Projects

Big Buck Bunny poster   *Sintel* promotional poster   *Tears of Steel* promotional poster

Every 1–2 years the Blender Foundation announces a new creative project to help drive innovation in Blender.

Elephants Dream (Open Movie Project: Orange)

In September 2005, some of the most notable Blender artists and developers began working on a short film using primarily free software, in an initiative known as the Orange Movie Project hosted by the Netherlands Media Art Institute (NIMk). The resulting film, *Elephants Dream*, premiered on March 24, 2006. In response to the success of *Elephants Dream*, the Blender Foundation founded the Blender Institute to do additional projects with two announced projects: *Big Buck Bunny*, also known as "Project Peach" (a 'furry and funny' short open animated film project) and *Yo Frankie*, also known as Project Apricot (an open game in collaboration with CrystalSpace that reused some of the assets created during Project Peach). This has later made its way to Nintendo 3DS's Nintendo Video between the years 2012 and 2013.

Big Buck Bunny (Open Movie Project: Peach)

On October 1, 2007, a new team started working on a second open project, "Peach", for the production of the short movie *Big Buck Bunny*. This time, however, the creative concept was totally different. Instead of the deep and mystical style of *Elephants Dream*, things are more "funny and furry" according to the official site. The movie had its premiere on April 10, 2008.

Yo Frankie! (Open Game Project: Apricot)

"Apricot" is a project for production of a game based on the universe and characters of the Peach movie (*Big Buck Bunny*) using free software. The game is titled *Yo Frankie*. The project started

February 1, 2008, and development was completed at the end of July 2008. A finalized product was expected at the end of August; however, the release was delayed. The game was released on December 9, 2008, under either the GNU GPL or LGPL, with all content being licensed under Creative Commons Attribution 3.0.

Sintel (Open Movie Project: Durian)

The Blender Foundation's Project Durian (in keeping with the tradition of fruits as code names) was this time chosen to make a fantasy action epic of about twelve minutes in length, starring a teenage girl and a young dragon as the main characters. The film premiered online on September 30, 2010. A game based on *Sintel* was officially announced on Blenderartists.org on May 12, 2010.

Many of the new features integrated into Blender 2.5 and beyond were a direct result of Project Durian.

Tears of Steel (Open Movie Project: Mango)

Derek de Lint in a scene from *Tears of Steel*

On October 2, 2011, the fourth open movie project, codenamed "Mango", was announced by the Blender Foundation. A team of artists assembled using an open call of community participation. It is the first Blender open movie to use live action as well as CG.

Filming for Mango started on May 7, 2012, and the movie was released on September 26, 2012. As with the previous films, all footage, scenes and models were made available under a free content compliant Creative Commons license.

According to the film's press release, "The film's premise is about a group of warriors and scientists, who gather at the 'Oude Kerk' in Amsterdam to stage a crucial event from the past, in a desperate attempt to rescue the world from destructive robots."

Cosmos Laundromat (Open Movie Project: Gooseberry)

On January 10, 2011, Ton Roosendaal announced that the fifth open movie project would be codenamed "Gooseberry" and that its goal would be to produce a feature-length animated film. He speculated that production would begin sometime between 2012 and 2014. The film was to be written and produced by a coalition of international animation studios. The studio lineup was announced on January 28, 2014, and production began soon thereafter. As of March 2014, a moodboard had been constructed and development goals had been set. The initial ten minute pilot was released on YouTube on August 10, 2015. It won the SIGGRAPH 2016 Computer Animation Festival Jury's Choice award.

Online Services

Blender Cloud

The Blender Cloud platform, launched in March 2014 and operated by the Blender Institute, is a subscription-based cloud computing platform and Blender client add-on which provides hosting and synchronization for backed-up animation project files. It was launched to promote and fundraise for *Project: Gooseberry*, and is intended to replace the selling of DVDs by the Blender Foundation with a subscription-based model for file hosting, asset sharing and collaboration. A feature of the Blender Cloud is Blender Sync, which provides synchronization between Blender clients for file changes, user preferences and other features.

Blender ID

The Blender ID is a unified login for Blender software and service users, providing a login for Blender Cloud, the Blender Store, the Blender Conference, Blender Network, Blender Development Fund and the Blender Foundation Certified Trainer Program.

BRL-CAD

BRL-CAD is a constructive solid geometry (CSG) solid modeling computer-aided design (CAD) system. It includes an interactive geometry editor, ray tracing support for graphics rendering and geometric analysis, computer network distributed framebuffer support, scripting, image-processing and signal-processing tools. The entire package is distributed in source code and binary form.

Although BRL-CAD can be used for a variety of engineering and graphics applications, the package's primary purpose continues to be the support of ballistic and electromagnetic analyses. In keeping with the Unix philosophy of developing independent tools to perform single, specific tasks and then linking the tools together in a package, BRL-CAD is basically a collection of libraries, tools, and utilities that work together to create, raytrace, and interrogate geometry and manipulate files and data. In contrast to many other 3D modelling applications, BRL-CAD primarily uses CSG rather than boundary representation. This means BRL-CAD can "study physical phenomena such as ballistic penetration and thermal, radiative, neutron, and other types of transport" It does also support boundary representation.

The BRL-CAD libraries are designed primarily for the geometric modeler who also wants to tinker with software and design custom tools. Each library is designed for a specific purpose: creating, editing, and raytracing geometry, and image handling. The application side of BRL-CAD also offers a number of tools and utilities that are primarily concerned with geometric conversion, interrogation, image format conversion, and command-line-oriented image manipulation.

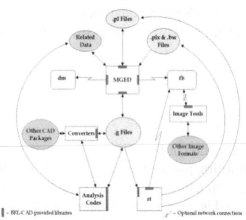

BRL-CAD data flow structure

History

Lead developer Mike Muuss works on the XM-1 tank in BRLCAD at a PDP11/70 terminal, circa 1980.

In 1979, the U.S. Army Ballistic Research Laboratory (BRL) – now the United States Army Research Laboratory – expressed a need for tools that could assist with the computer simulation and engineering analysis of combat vehicle systems and environments. When no CAD package was found to be adequate for this purpose, BRL software developers – led by Mike Muuss – began assembling a suite of utilities capable of interactively displaying, editing, and interrogating geometric models. This suite became known as BRL-CAD. Development on BRL-CAD as a package subsequently began in 1983; the first public release was made in 1984. BRL-CAD became an open-source project on December, 2004.

The BRL-CAD source code repository is the oldest known public version-controlled codebase in the world that's still under active development, dating back to 1983-12-16 00:10:31 UTC.

Archimedes (CAD)

Archimedes – "The Open CAD" – (also called Arquimedes) is a computer-aided design (CAD) program being developed with direct input from architects and architecture firms. With this design philosophy, the developers hope to create software better suited for architecture than the currently widely used AutoCAD, and other available CAD software. The program is free software released under the Eclipse Public License.

Features

- Basic drawing
    - Lines, Polylines, Arcs and Circles.
    - Editable Text
    - Explode
    - Offset
- Advanced CAD functions
    - Trimming
    - Filleting
    - Area measurement
- Miscellaneous
    - Autosave
    - SVG export
    - PDF export
    - English, Portuguese, and Italian language support

Integration with other CAD Systems

Archimedes uses its own XML-based open format, which resembles SVG. It does not yet include support for other CAD formats, but DXF support is planned.

Development

Archimedes is written in Java, and the latest version runs on Windows, Mac OS X, Linux/Unix based systems, and might run on platforms that have are supported by LWJGL and a Java Virtual machine on version 1.5.0 or later.

History

The Archimedes Project started as a collaboration between a group of programmers and architecture students at the University of São Paulo, in Brazil, in 2005. The project is currently being worked on as free and open source software. There is a team of students from the University working on it as collaborators under the coordination of Hugo (project leader) but everyone is free to contribute with plugins and/or patches.

Timeline

- Archimedes was registered as a SourceForge.net project on 12 July 2005.

- The last stable pre-RCP version was 0.16.0, released on 25 October 2000.

- The first stable version after the RCP migration was 0.50.0, released on 25 April 2007.

- The latest stable version is 0.64.2, which was released on 1 July 2012.

Migration to Eclipse RCP in Version 0.5x

A migration to the Eclipse Rich Client Platform in versions 0.5x has greatly improved the user interface model and stability, but some of the functionality from the last pre-RCP version is still being transferred. Version 0.58.0 moved this process a step closer by adding trimming, leader, svg and pdf exporting.

DesignSpark Mechanical

DesignSpark Mechanical is a free 3D CAD (computer-aided design) solid modeling software

DesignSpark Mechanical enables users to solid model in a 3D environment and create files for use with 3D printers. Using the direct modelling approach, it allows for unlimited and frequent design changes using an intuitive set of tools. This free 3D CAD software is offered as a payment free download, but requires a one-time registration with DesignSpark.com to receive the latest community news and product promotions.

Background

DesignSpark Mechanical is based on the SpaceClaim Engineer application and is the product of a collaboration between RS Components and SpaceClaim Corporation. An introductory brochure is available here as an interactive PDF. The goal to offer a free 3D CAD software with many features of high-end software is to engage with those who perhaps do not require or who cannot afford premium branded 3D CAD software, such as Engineering Students or small businesses. Add-on upgrade modules can be purchased later if required to release even more potential from this free 3D CAD software, making it on-par with many expensive high-end design software systems.

Rapid Prototyping

DesignSpark Mechanical supports the idea of Rapid Prototyping through SpaceClaim's 3D direct modelling methodology using the Pull, Move, Fill and Combine tools that allow a user to interact with digital 3D objects like modelling with clay, all available in the free 3D CAD version.

3D CAD Library

3D models for more than 45'000 products from the RS catalog are available for download within the software

Add-on Modules

Paid add-on modules are available and provide functionality for the free 3D CAD DesignSpark Mechanical software, such as full support of two popular 3D file formats (Export and import file type: STEP & IGES) and an associative drawing environment, adding many functions such as Threading, GD&T, Annotations and more.

Embroidermodder

Embroidermodder is a free machine embroidery software tool that supports a variety of formats and allows the user to add custom modifications to their embroidery designs.

History

Embroidermodder 1 was started by Mark Pontius in 2004 while staying up all night with his son in his first couple months. When Mark returned to his day job, he lacked the time to continue the project. Mark made the decision to focus on his family and work, and in 2005, Mark gave full control of the project to Josh Varga so that Embroidermodder could continue its growth.

Embroidermodder 2 was conceived in mid 2011 when Jonathan Greig and Josh Varga discussed the possibility of making a cross-platform version. It runs on Linux, Mac OS X, Microsoft Windows.

The Embroidermodder website and downloads are hosted on SourceForge. On July 18, 2013, The Embroidermodder 2 Source was moved to GitHub.

Embroidermodder 1 Features

- Runs under Microsoft Windows.

- Sourcecode (Visual C++) available.

- Reads/Writes Tajima .DST file format, which is compatible with most every commercial and vendor's software available.

- Also reads/writes Excel .CSV file format for hand editing using Excel or a text editor.

- Allows scaling designs to any size (not just +/- 20% like some software).

- Shows the design on-screen, with unlimited zoom to get up close and personal with any stitch. Zoom to actual size, fit to screen, selection, or just in/out. Scrollbars allow panning around the design.

- Multiple documents can be open, and each document may have multiple view windows, each at different zooms to allow fine detail editing, while still getting the big picture.

- Print design at actual size.

- Displays statistics like max/min/average stitch length, number of colors, etc.

- Select, move, insert, or delete either stitches, lines, or selection.

- Double click in select mode to select a region (stitches between Jumps or color changes).

- Cut/Copy/Paste selection.

- Cursor left/right steps selection point though individual stitches.

- Add text using any windows font.

- Toggle display of Jump stitches (as black dash-dot lines).

- Display updates are very fast using a combination of direct screen draw with efficient clipping and background rendering.

- Optional Debug mode (compile time option) with additional display and break capability, such as monitoring the background render progress in the status bar.

Embroidermodder 2 Features

- Runs under Linux, Mac OS X, Microsoft Windows and Raspberry Pi.

- CAD/CAM Graphical User Interface.

- Sourcecode (Qt4/Qt5 C++) available.

- Undo/Redo functionality.

- Reads over 45 different embroidery formats.

- Also reads/writes Excel .CSV file format for hand editing using Excel or a text editor or generating the .CSV data from an external program such as Mathematica.

- Cut/Copy/Paste selection between multiple documents.

- Scripting API.

- Add text using any installed system font.

- Customizable icon themes.

Libembroidery

One of the byproducts of Embroidermodder 2 was the creation of libembroidery library. libembroidery is written in C. It supports reading and writing of a variety of embroidery formats, and several vector formats which are not commonly used in embroidery.

The formats are as such (last updated January 2017):

'Stable' = Yes, supported and is considered stable. 'Unstable' = Yes, supported but may be unstable. No = Not supported.

Format	Read	Write	Description
.100	Unstable	No	Toyota Embroidery Format
.100	Unstable	No	Toyota Embroidery Format
.art	No	No	Bernina Embroidery Format
.bmc	No	No	Bitmap Cache Embroidery Format
.bro	Unstable	No	Bits & Volts Embroidery Format
.cnd	No	No	Melco Embroidery Format
.col	Unstable	Unstable	Embroidery Thread Color Format
.csd	Unstable	No	Singer Embroidery Format
.csv	Unstable	Unstable	Comma Separated Values
.dat	Unstable	No	Barudan Embroidery Format
.dem	No	No	Melco Embroidery Format
.dsb	Unstable	No	Barudan Embroidery Format
.dst	Unstable	Unstable	Tajima Embroidery Format
.dsz	Unstable	No	ZSK USA Embroidery Format
.dxf	No	No	Drawing Exchange Format
.edr	Unstable	Unstable	Embird Embroidery Format
.emd	Unstable	No	Elna Embroidery Format
.exp	Unstable	Unstable	Melco Embroidery Format
.exy	Unstable	No	Eltac Embroidery Format
.eys	No	No	Sierra Expanded Embroidery Format
.fxy	Unstable	No	Fortron Embroidery Format
.gc	No	No	Smoothie G-Code Format
.gnc	No	No	Great Notions Embroidery Format
.gt	Unstable	No	Gold Thread Embroidery Format
.hus	Unstable	Unstable	Husqvarna Viking Embroidery Format
.inb	Unstable	No	Inbro Embroidery Format
.inf	Unstable	Unstable	Embroidery Color Format
.jef	Unstable	Unstable	Janome Embroidery Format
.ksm	Unstable	Unstable	Pfaff Embroidery Format
.max	Unstable	Unstable	Pfaff Embroidery Format
.mit	Unstable	No	Mitsubishi Embroidery Format
.new	Unstable	No	Ameco Embroidery Format
.ofm	Unstable	No	Melco Embroidery Format
.pcd	Unstable	Unstable	Pfaff Embroidery Format
.pcm	Unstable	No	Pfaff Embroidery Format
.pcq	Unstable	Unstable	Pfaff Embroidery Format
.pcs	Unstable	Unstable	Pfaff Embroidery Format
.pec	Unstable	Unstable	Brother Embroidery Format
.pel	No	No	Brother Embroidery Format
.pem	No	No	Brother Embroidery Format
.pes	Unstable	Unstable	Brother Embroidery Format

Format	Read	Write	Description
.phb	Unstable	No	Brother Embroidery Format
.phc	Unstable	No	Brother Embroidery Format
.plt	Unstable	Unstable	AutoCAD Plot Drawing
.rgb	Unstable	Unstable	RGB Embroidery Format
.sew	Unstable	Unstable	Janome Embroidery Format
.shv	Unstable	No	Husqvarna Viking Embroidery Format
.sst	Unstable	No	Sunstar Embroidery Format
.stx	Unstable	No	Data Stitch Embroidery Format
.svg	Unstable	Unstable	Scalable Vector Graphics
.to1	Unstable	No	Pfaff Embroidery Format
.to9	Unstable	No	Pfaff Embroidery Format
.tap	Unstable	Unstable	Happy Embroidery Format
.thr	Unstable	Unstable	ThredWorks Embroidery Format
.txt	No	Unstable	Text File
.uoo	Unstable	No	Barudan Embroidery Format
.uo1	No	No	Barudan Embroidery Format
.vip	Unstable	No	Pfaff Embroidery Format
.vp3	Unstable	Unstable	Pfaff Embroidery Format
.xxx	Unstable	Unstable	Singer Embroidery Format
.zsk	Unstable	No	ZSK USA Embroidery Format

FreeCAD

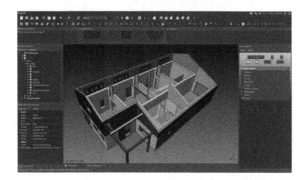

Interior of 3D house

Arduino board imported from Eagle PCB software

FreeCAD is a free and open-source (under the LGPLv2+ license) general-purpose parametric 3D CAD modeler and a building information modeling (BIM) software with finite-element-method (FEM) support. FreeCAD is aimed directly at mechanical engineering, BIM and product design but also fits in a wider range of uses around engineering, such as architecture or other engineering specialities. The program can be used interactively, or its functionality can be accessed and extended using the Python programming language. FreeCAD is currently in a beta stage of development.

Features

General

FreeCAD features tools similar to Autodesk Revit, CATIA, Creo, Autodesk Inventor, SolidWorks or Solid Edge, and therefore also falls into the category of BIM, Mechanical computer-aided design (MCAD), PLM, CAx and CAE. It is intended to be a feature-based parametric modeler with a modular software architecture, which makes it easy to provide additional functionality without modifying the core system.

As with many modern 3D CAD modelers, it will have a 2D component in order to extract design details from the 3D model to create 2D production drawings, but direct 2D drawing (like Auto-CAD LT) is not the focus, neither are animation or organic shapes (like Blender, Maya, 3ds Max or Cinema 4D), although, thanks to its wide adaptability, FreeCAD might become useful in a much broader area than its current focus.

FreeCAD is intended to make use of other open-source libraries from the field of scientific computing. Among them are Open CASCADE (a CAD kernel), Coin3D (an incarnation of Open Inventor), the Qt GUI framework, and Python, a popular scripting language. FreeCAD itself can also be used as a library by other programs.

There are moves to take FreeCAD into the architecture, engineering and construction (AEC) sector and add building information modeling (BIM) functionality with the Arch Module.

Supported File Formats

Freecad's own main file format is FreeCAD Standard file format (.FCStd). It is a standard zip file that holds files in a certain structure. Document.xml file has all geometric and parametric objects definitions. GuiDocument.xml then has visual representation details of objects. Other files include brep-files for objects and thumbnail of drawing.

Besides FreeCAD's own file format, files can be exported and imported in the following file formats: DXF, SVG (Scalable Vector Graphics), STEP, IGES, STL (STereoLithography), OBJ (Wavefront), DAE (Collada), SCAD (OpenSCAD), IV (Inventor) and IFC.

DWG Support

FreeCAD's support for the important DWG file format has been problematic due to software license compatibility problems with the GNU LibreDWG library. The GNU LibreDWG library started as a real open-source alternative to the source-available OpenDWG library (the later Teigha Converter) and is licensed under the GPLv3. As FreeCAD (and also LibreCAD) has dependencies on Open Cascade, which prior to version 6.7.0 was only compatible with GPLv2, it couldn't use the GNU LibreDWG library as GPLv2 and GPLv3 are essentially incompatible. Open CASCADE technologies were contacted by Debian team in 2009, and 2012 got a reply that Open CASCADE technologies was considering dual-licensing OCCT (the library), however they postponed that move. A request also went to the FSF to relicense GNU LibreDWG as GPLv2 or LGPLv3, which was rejected.

As of the 2014 the 0.14 release of FreeCAD, including the new LGPL release of Open Cascade, the

BSD-licensed version of Coin3D, and the removal of PyQT, FreeCAD is now completely GPL-free. However, LibreDWG has not been adopted. FreeCAD is able to import and export a limited subset of the DWG format via the Teigha Converter (the former OpenDWG library).

HeeksCAD

HeeksCAD is a free software Computer-aided design program written in C++. It uses Open CAS-CADE Technology internally for the modelling and wxWidgets as its widget toolkit.

HeeksCAD supports cuboids, spheres, cylinders and cones as basic 3D solids. Further geometric objects may be created by sweeping or connecting 2D-shapes.

HeeksCAD makes extensive use of local coordinate systems. For example, these are used to define the drawing plane and the direction of an extrusion.

The program can be extended with additional plugins. Plugins are available for Python scripting, milling and freeform surface modelling.

Magic (Software)

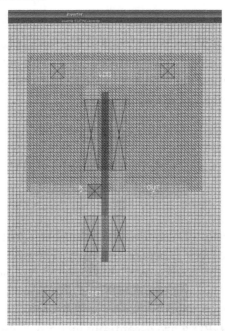

VLSI Layout of an Inverter Circuit using Magic software

Magic is a Very-large-scale integration (VLSI) layout tool originally written by John Ousterhout and his graduate students at UC Berkeley during the 1980s. As free and open-source software, subject to the requirements of the BSD license, Magic continues to be popular because it is easy to use and easy to expand for specialized tasks.

Differences

The main difference between Magic and other VLSI design tools is its use of "corner-stitched" geometry, in which all layout is represented as a stack of planes, and each plane consists entirely of "tiles" (rectangles). The tiles must cover the entire plane. Each tile consists of an (X, Y) coordinate of its lower left-hand corner, and links to four tiles: the right-most neighbor on the top, the top-most neighbor on the right, the bottom-most neighbor on the left, and the left-most neighbor on the bottom. With the addition of the type of material represented by the tile, the layout geometry in the plane is exactly specified. The corner-stitched geometry representation leads to the concept of layout as "paint" to be applied to, or erased from, a canvas. This is considerably different from other tools that use the concept of layout as "objects" to be placed and manipulated separately from one another. Each concept has its own strengths and weaknesses in terms of both practical use and speed of computation. The corner-stitched representation is particularly well suited to searches within a single plane, for which it excels in speed. It is not particularly well suited to extremely large databases: The need to maintain four pointers for each tile, as well as the need to store tiles representing the space between areas of material on a layout, makes it more memory-intensive than object-based representations.

An extension to the corner-stitched geometry representation called the "split tile" method, added in version 7.1, allows true representation of non-Manhattan geometry. This method allows each tile in the database to specify two material types, in which case the tile is regarded as being bisected by a diagonal line from corner to corner, with one material type on one side of the diagonal and the other material type on the other side of the diagonal. An additional flag specifies whether the diagonal runs from the top left corner to the bottom right, or the top right corner to the bottom left. The split-tile method has the advantange that nearly all rules that apply to corner-stitched geometry apply, unaltered, to split tiles. A further advantage is that all non-Manhattan geometry must have corners lying on the database internal grid. This makes it impossible to generate geometry that is off-grid within a single plane, a rule error for most fabrication processes that is a common problem with object-based representations.

Magic features real-time design rule checking, something that some costly commercial VLSI design software packages don't feature. Magic implements this by counting distance using Manhattan distance rather than Euclidean distance, which is much faster to compute. Magic versions from 7.3 properly compute Euclidean distance when given the drc euclidean on command. Euclidean distance checks are a trivial extension of the Manhattan distance checks, and require very little overhead. On a straight-line edge, the Manhattan and Euclidean distances are the same. Only on corners do the two distances diverge. When checking corners, it is only necessary to keep track of the direction of search from the corner point. Any geometry found inside the square representing the Manhattan distance from the corner undergoes an additional check to see if the same geometry lies outside the quarter-circle radius representing the Euclidean distance. Since this additional check is applied only to geometry found in violation of the Manhattan distance rule, it is not invoked often, so the computational overhead is very small.

Magic currently runs under Linux, although versions exist for DOS, OS/2, and other operating systems. Magic is frequently used in conjunction with IRSIM and other simulation programs.

OpenSCAD

OpenSCAD is a free software application for creating solid 3D CAD (computer-aided design) objects. It is a script-only based modeller that uses its own description language; parts can be previewed but cannot be interactively selected or modified by mouse in the 3D view. An OpenSCAD script specifies geometric primitives (such as spheres, boxes, cylinders etc.) and defines how they are modified and combined (for instance by intersection, difference, envelope combination and Minkowski sums) to render a 3D model. As such, the program does constructive solid geometry (CSG). OpenSCAD is available for Windows, Linux and OS X.

Previewing

For fast previewing of models using z-buffering, OpenSCAD employs OpenCSG and OpenGL.

The 3D model position can be interactively manipulated in the view with a mouse similarly to other 3D modellers. It is also possible to define a default 'camera' position in the script.

Part colors can be defined in the 3D view (including transparency).

Preview is relatively fast and allow interactive modifications while modifying the script.

The model renderer takes into account lighting, but the lighting source is not modifiable.

3D Volumes Computation

In contrast, CGAL is used for full 3D geometry rendering, which, as with other CSG geometry engines, can sometimes take several minutes or hours to complete.

Use

OpenSCAD allows a designer to create accurate 3D models and parametric designs that can be easily adjusted by changing the parameters.

OpenSCAD documents are human-readable scripts in plain ASCII text.

As such, OpenSCAD is a programmer-oriented solid-modeling tool, and has been recommended as an entry-level CAD tool for designing open-source hardware such as scientific tools for research and education.

It is mostly used to design 3D printed parts which are exported in STL format.

Exportation

- Views can be exported in png format

- 2D models can be exported in DXF

- 3D parts can be exported in AMF, OFF, STL, as simple volumes. There is no color, material nor parts definition in the exported model (July 2016).

Importation

- 2D drawings in DXF can be imported, then extruded as monolithic parts

- 3D parts can be imported in STL and can be scaled and submitted to subs-tractive or additive operations.

Animation

Animation is possible with a speed of a few images per seconds for simple models. The animation can have effect on any parameter, being it the camera position or the parts dimensions, position, shape or existence. It can be recorded as a set of images usable to build films.

Design

OpenScad is a wrapper to a CSG engine with a GUI interface and integrated editor, developed in C++. As of 2016, it uses the Computational Geometry Algorithms Library (CGAL) as its basic CSG engine.

Its script syntax is based upon functional programming philosophy and does not use real variables.

SAMoCAD

SAMoCAD is a free Computer Aided Design (CAD) application for 2D drawing. It works on all operating systems that are running Python 2.7.

SAMoCAD was developed as an independent project not based on another project. The GUI of SAMoCAD is based on WxPython library.

Most of the interface are analogous to AutoCAD, making it easier to use for users with experience of this CAD program. Available drawing features allow you to create simple architectural and engineering drawings.

SAMoCAD uses the DXF and SVG formats save drawings.

SolveSpace

SolveSpace is a free libre and open source 2D and 3D CAD (computer-aided design) program. It is a constraint-based parametric modeler with simple mechanical simulation capabilities. Version 2.1 onward runs on Windows, Linux and macOS. It is developed by Jonathan Westhues and a community of volunteers.

Features

Applications include:

- Modeling 3D parts – Draw with extrudes, revolves, and Boolean (union / difference) operations

- Modeling 2D parts – Draw the part as a single section, and export as a DXF, PDF or SVG; use 3D assembly to verify fit

- Preparing CAM data – Export 2D vector art for a waterjet machine or laser cutter; or generate STEP or STL, for import into third-party CAM software

- Mechanism design – Use the constraint solver to simulate planar or spatial linkages, with pin, ball, or slide joints

- Plane and solid geometry – Replace hand-solved trigonometry and spreadsheets with a live dimensioned drawing

SolveSpace is free software distributed under GPLv3. Files to open need to be in its own text-based SolveSpace Models (*.slvs) format. Various export formats are provided, including 2D vector drawing as DXF, EPS, PDF, SVG, HPGL, STEP; 3D wireframe as DXF and STEP; triangle mesh as STL and Wavefront OBJ; and NURBS surfaces as STEP.

Appearances

A brief review and interview with the developer appeared in Libre Graphics World. This review praises SolveSpace for its small executable file size, its advanced constraints solver and range of output formats. The same review notes some drawbacks, mainly its slow and limited processing of NURBS booleans and lack of native Linux support. However, native Linux support has since been added.

A third-party video demonstration by Chris Madsen for an earlier version of SolveSpace is available on YouTube as Using SolveSpace to draw Sonex flap detent.

SketchFlat

A previous software package called SketchFlat, also developed by Westhues, has been replaced by SolveSpace.

LibreCAD

LibreCAD is a free Computer-aided design (CAD) application for 2D design. It works on Linux, OS X, Unix and Windows operating systems.

LibreCAD was developed as a fork of QCad Community Edition. The GUI of LibreCAD is based on Qt4 libraries, so it runs on several platforms in the same way.

Most of the interface and handle concepts are analogous to AutoCAD, making it easier to use for users with experience of this type of commercial CAD application.

LibreCAD uses the AutoCAD DXF file format internally for import and save files, as well as allowing export to many other file formats.

GPLv3 vs GPLv2 Controversy

As the GNU LibreDWG library is released under GPLv3 it can't be used by GPLv2 licensed LibreCAD (and FreeCAD) as their licenses are incompatible. A request also went to the FSF to re-license GNU LibreDWG as GPLv2, which was rejected. This controversy has been resolved by writing a new GPLv2 licensed library called *libdxfrw*, with more complete DWG support.

References

- Evans, Brian (2012), Practical 3D Printers: The Science and Art of 3D Printing, Apress, p. 113, ISBN 9781430243922

- Kassenaar, Joeri (May 21, 2005). "Brief history of the Blender logo". Archived from the original on October 23, 2007. Retrieved January 18, 2007

- Pearce, Joshua M. (2014), "Chapter 6: „Digital Designs and Scientific Hardware"", Open-Source Lab: How to Build Your Own Hardware and Reduce Research Costs, Elsevier, pp. 165–254, ISBN 9780124104624

- Prokoudine, Alexandre. "SolveSpace 2D/3D CAD software released under terms of GPL". Libre Graphics World, June 2013. Retrieved 12 June 2016

- Pettis, Bre; France, Anna Kaziunas; Shergill, Jay (2012), Getting Started with MakerBot, O'Reilly Media, Inc., p. 131, ISBN 9781449338657

- "Frequently Asked Questions about the GNU Licenses – Is GPLv3 compatible with GPLv2?". The official site. Retrieved 13 April 2011

Electronic Design Automation Software

Circuits cloud is a cloud computing based application that is available online. It is used to design electronic circuits. CircuitMaker, Electric, gEDA, KiCad, and PCB are the other software mentioned in this section. Computer-aided design is best understood in confluence with the major topics listed in the following chapter.

CircuitMaker

CircuitMaker is electronic design automation software for printed circuit board design targeted at the hobby, hacker, and maker community. CircuitMaker is available as freeware, and the hardware designed with it may be used for commercial and non-commercial purposes without limitations. It is currently available publicly as version 1.3 by Altium Limited, with the first non-beta release on January 17, 2016.

History

CircuitMaker 2000

Electronic design automation software (EDA) developer Protel marketed CircuitMaker 2000 as a schematic capture tool, together with Traxmaker as its PCB layout counterpart, as a powerful yet affordable solution for circuit board needs. Its ease of use and comparatively low cost quickly gained it popularity among students, and the software suite was commonly used to teach circuit board design to engineering students in universities. The wide availability of plug-ins and component libraries have accelerated adoption, and quickly amassed a worldwide community. When Protel was acquired by Altium Limited in the early 2000s, engineering efforts were redirected towards the development of DXP2004, and CircuitMaker 2000 was eventually discontinued. Due to its new status as abandonware, CircuitMaker 2000 remained popular among hobby users and students. This popularity has been observed by Altium, and the most successful features of CircuitMaker 2000 have since been integrated in DXP2004 and later found their way into Altium Designer.

Rebirth

Open source hardware and easy-to-use development boards such as the Arduino and the Raspberry Pi have increased community interest in electronics, particularly in fablabs, hackerspaces and makerspaces. The leading EDA software vendors traditionally lack free versions, and professional licenses are unaffordable for amateurs. This resulted in high piracy rates for professional software packages, or users sticking to outdated software, including CircuitMaker 2000. Several initiatives such as Eagle have attempted to fill this void, releasing restricted versions of semi-professional EDA tools. The rise of KiCAD further fragmented the market. This pressure eventually provided the incentive for Altium to release a simplified and more user friendly version of their professional EDA software package and flagship product, Altium Designer, targeted at less complex circuit board projects, culminating in the rebirth of CircuitMaker as schematic capture and PCB design software.

Despite the resemblance in naming, the current CircuitMaker differs entirely from CircuitMaker 2000 regarding features and graphical user interface: the SPICE simulation module has been removed, the library system has been overhauled, and the controls changed from classic menus to a more modern and visually appealing ribbon interface.

Features

CircuitMaker implements schematic capture and PCB design using the same engine as Altium Designer, providing an almost identical user experience. The schematic editor includes basic component placement and circuit design as well as advanced multi-channel design and hierarchical schematics. All schematics are uploaded to the Altium server and can be viewed by anyone with a CircuitMaker account, stimulating design re-use. CircuitMaker supports integration with the Octopart search engine and allows drag and drop placement of components from the Octopart search results if schematic models are attached to them. Users can build missing schematic symbols and commit them to the server, called the *Community Vault*, making them available for other users. The continuously growing part database eliminates the need for a custom schematic symbol or footprint design for common parts, increasing user-friendliness for beginners.

Concurrency editing was added in version 1.3

Transfer of schematics to a PCB is a straightforward process in CircuitMaker since PCB footprints are automatically attached to any component on the schematic that was picked from the Octopart library. PCB footprints may have simple 3D models or complex STEP models attached to them, enabling real time 3D rendering of the PCB during development. CircuitMaker supports design rule configuration and real time design rule checking. Some advanced features, including differential pair routing and polygon pour management, are also available. Production files can be exported directly, although an external Gerber viewer must be used to check the exports. The entire PCB can also be exported as a 3D STEP model for further use in mechanical 3D CAD software.

Open Source Hardware

CircuitMaker requires a free account to represent its users in the community. An active internet connection is required to start and use the software. Users are allowed to have 2 *private* projects, the so-called *sandbox mode* for practicing. By default, all schematics and PCBs are uploaded to the server and can be viewed by other users as soon as they are committed through the internal git engine. While this renders CircuitMaker undesirable for *closed source* projects, it encourages collaboration in the community. Users are allowed to fork existing projects, or request permission to collaborate in existing projects. Importing schematic documents and PCBs from other EDA packages (OrCAD, PADS, P-CAD, EAGLE) is supported. Users are allowed to own unlimited projects, and there is no hard limit on board complexity. However, Altium warns that users may experience a performance drop for large projects.

All documents are under version control by default, allowing users to revert changes made in their projects, and build new versions of existing schematic symbols or footprints in the Community Vault. Users can comment on each others projects and parts, rate them, and propose improvements.

CircuitMaker supports direct generation of production files in industry standard formats such as Gerber and NC Drill, as well as printing of stencils for DIY circuit board etching.

Online Community

As of April 2017, there are over 110 000 registered users within the CircuitMaker Community, together authoring over 12 000 PCB projects. The ease of use has led to rapid adoption of Circuit-Maker by schools and universities to teach PCB design.

Criticism

As a result of its reliance on the Altium Designer schematic capture and PCB design engine, CircuitMaker is only available for the Windows operating system. This requires users to have access to a Windows license to use CircuitMaker. Dependence on Windows has been cited as a weakness of the CircuitMaker project, and Altium has reported to current users that a cross-platform solution is in development. As of 2017, CircuitMaker can be run in Wine on Ubuntu, with limitations, but the installation procedure is cumbersome, and many users reported it does not work on their linux distribution. This currently forces most users to fall back to a complete virtual machine. Unofficial support for Linux and BSD users is provided by Altium staff and volunteers on the CircuitMaker forum. CircuitMaker currently does not install or run on ReactOS due to a .NET Framework related error.

A second concern is the lock-in resulting from CircuitMaker's cloud centric approach. While users can import resources from competing EDA software packages, CircuitMaker does not support exporting design resources itself. Reviewers consider this in conflict with the open source ideology. However, a workaround for this issue is provided by Altium Designer 15 and 16 which do support the import of CircuitMaker files. A trial version of Altium Designer can be requested free of charge from Altium for this purpose.

Circuits Cloud

Circuits Cloud is an online free analog/digital circuits simulator. It is a NGSPICE-based simulator. Circuits Cloud is a cloud-computing-based application, where the user can access the application through the internet, while all their data are stored online. The Circuits Cloud project cost about BD 7000 (around $18.6K). Total development time until the first release was 4 years.

History

Circuits Cloud was created and developed for educational purposes, by Eng. Shaffee Mayoof. The initial release was on 20 June 2014. Circuits Cloud was initially developed as an online digital circuits simulator, but updated later on by Eng. Mayoof and computer engineering students who were candidates in the industrial training program provided by the application owner, Script For Information Technology Solutions, to support analog circuits simulation.

Electric (Software)

The Electric VLSI Design System is an EDA tool written in the early 1980s by Steven M. Rubin. Electric is used to draw schematics and to do integrated circuit layout. It can also handle hardware description languages such as VHDL and Verilog. The system has many analysis and synthesis tools, including Design rule checking, Simulation, Routing, Layout vs. Schematic, Logical Effort, and more.

Electric is currently part of the GNU project and has been developed in Java and distributed as free and open-source software, subject to the requirements of the GNU General Public License (GPL), version 3 or any later.

Alternative Design Style for Integrated Circuits

Unlike other systems that design integrated circuits (ICs) by manipulating polygons on different layers of the wafer, Electric views IC layout as connected circuitry, similar to the way schematic capture systems work. In Electric, designers place nodes (transistors, contacts, etc.) and connect them with arcs (wires). This has advantages and disadvantages.

One advantage is that circuits are always extracted, so analyses that need to know the topology (Layout vs. Schematic, Simulation, etc.) can run faster. Also, by presenting a schematic-capture-like user interface, the system offers a uniform user experience for both IC layout and schematic design. And finally, the nodes-and-arcs view of a circuit makes it easy to add layout constraints to the arcs which allow the designer to "program" the layout so that it stays connected as changes are made.

This style of design also has disadvantages. One disadvantage is that designers are not used to such an interaction and require training in order to use it. It has been observed that people with no previous experience in IC layout are comfortable with Electric's unusual style, but those who have done IC layout on other systems find Electric difficult to use. Another disadvantage is that it is hard to import polygons from traditional systems because they have to be node-extracted, and the polygons don't always match the set of nodes and arcs provided by Electric.

History

Electric was written in the C programming language in the early 1980s (the earliest internal memo on Electric is dated November 19, 1982). For some time after that, Electric was distributed free of charge to universities and research institutions, and found widespread international use.

In the mid 1980s, Electric was sold commercially by Applicon, under the name "Bravo3VLSI".

In 1988, Electric Editor Incorporated was founded, and sold the system commercially. The company released the source code through the Free Software Foundation in 1998.

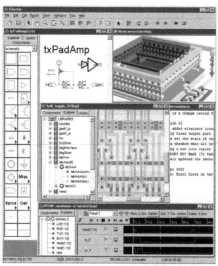

Screenshot Electric VLSI Design System

In 2000, Static Free Software was created to manage Electric's distribution.

In September, 2003 the C version of Electric was abandoned, and the system was translated into the Java language. The work was completed in June, 2005. Although the C code is still available, it is no longer developed or supported. The new and improved Java code remains free to all users.

gEDA

The word "gEDA" is a conjunction of "GPL" and "EDA". The names of some of the individual tools in the gEDA Suite are prefixed with the letter "g" to emphasize that they are released under the GNU General Public License.

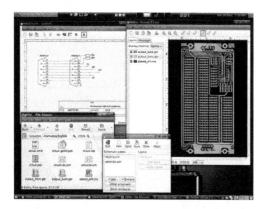

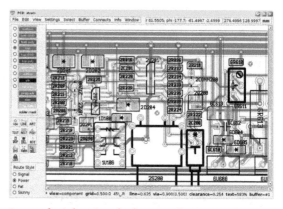

Gschem and gerbv showing a simple connector design under creation using components from the gEDA Suite.

Screenshot showing the layout editor PCB in action.

The term gEDA refers to two things:

1. A set of software applications (CAD tools) used for electronic design released under the GPL. As such, gEDA is an ECAD (electronic CAD) or EDA (electronic design automation)

application suite. gEDA is mostly oriented towards printed circuit board design (as opposed to integrated circuit design). The gEDA applications are often referred to collectively as "the gEDA Suite".

2. The collaboration of free software/open-source developers who work to develop and maintain the gEDA toolkit. The developers communicate via gEDA mailing lists, and have participated in the annual "Google Summer of Code" event as a single project. This collaboration is often referred to as "the gEDA Project".

History

The gEDA project was started by Ales Hvezda in an effort to remedy the lack of free software EDA tools for Linux/UNIX. The first software was released on 1 April 1998, and included a schematic capture program and a netlister. At that time, the gEDA Project website and mailing lists were also set up.

Originally, the project planned to also write a PCB layout program. However, an existing open-source layout program, "PCB", was soon discovered by the project. Thereafter, the ability to target netlists to PCB was quickly built into the gEDA Project's netlister, and plans to write a new layout program from scratch were scrapped. Meanwhile, developers working on PCB became affiliates of the gEDA Project.

Other open-source EDA programs were created at about the same time. The authors of those programs became affiliated with the gEDA website and mailing lists, and the collaborative gEDA Project was born.

At present, the gEDA Project remains a federation of software tools developed by different (but sometimes overlapping) programmers. The thread which holds the project together is the shared vision of creating a powerful, community-based, open-source EDA toolkit.

Detailed Description

Loosely speaking, the term "gEDA Suite" refers to all free software projects and applications that have associated themselves with the gEDA Project via the geda-dev/geda-user mailing lists. These include:

- gEDA/gaf - gschem and friends (the original project)
- PCB - PCB layout program
- Gerbv - Gerber file viewer
- ngspice - a port of Berkeley SPICE
- GnuCap - A modern electronic circuit simulation program
- gspiceui - A GUI front end for ngspice/GnuCap
- gwave - An analog waveform viewer
- gaw - An analog waveform viewer a rewrite of gwave. Works with gspiceui.

- Icarus Verilog - A Verilog simulator
- GTKWave - A digital waveform viewer
- wcalc - Transmission line and electromagnetic structure analysis

Within the gEDA Suite, gEDA/gaf ("gaf" stands for "gschem and friends") is the smaller subset of tools grouped together under the gEDA name and maintained directly by the gEDA project's founders. GEDA/gaf includes:

- gschem - A schematic capture program
- gnetlist - A netlist generation program
- gsymcheck - A syntax checker for schematic symbols
- gattrib - A spreadsheet program for editing symbol attributes on a schematic.
- libgeda - Libraries for gschem, gnetlist, and gsymcheck
- gsch2pcb - Forward annotation from schematic to layout using pcb
- Assorted utility programs

Platforms

Linux

Because one of the gEDA Project's longstanding goals is to provide a suite of EDA applications for Linux, all applications in the gEDA Suite compile and run on Linux. Besides building the programs from source, binary executables for all programs in the gEDA Suite are available from popular package archives; the programs may be installed on many common Linux distributions using package management tools such as apt or dnf.

Unix

All gEDA applications will also compile and run on other Unix-like operating systems, such as OpenBSD, FreeBSD and NetBSD. Some of these distributions also support installation of pre-packaged binaries using package management utilities.

Mac OS X

Most gEDA applications also install and run successfully on Mac OS X, typically using the Fink package manager and Macports. Since few commercial EDA tools run on the Mac, this feature has made gEDA a popular electronic design package amongst Mac users.

Microsoft Windows

Microsoft Windows support is currently not a primary project goal. Nonetheless, some programs in the gEDA Suite have built-in hooks for Windows support, and those programs will build and run under Windows. However, binary executables for most of the gEDA Suite are not distributed by the gEDA Project.

Community

An important feature of the gEDA project is the strong user community it has created. The gEDA mailing lists have several hundred subscribers, and many subscribers are electronics experts. Thus, the gEDA mailing lists have become a source not only for information related to the gEDA applications, but also for exchange of general electronic design information.

As a consequence of the project's openness, schematic symbols, footprints, and utility scripts are freely created and shared amongst the members of the gEDA community.

KiCad

KiCad is a free software suite for electronic design automation (EDA). It facilitates the design of schematics for electronic circuits and their conversion to PCB designs. KiCad was originally developed by Jean-Pierre Charras, and features an integrated environment for schematic capture and PCB layout design. Tools exist within the package to create a bill of materials, artwork, Gerber files, and 3D views of the PCB and its components. KiCad's popularity is fueled by its GerbView component, used as Gerber viewer by users of other EDA software that does not support this feature such as CircuitMaker. Olimex has announced to have switched from EAGLE to KiCad as their primary EDA tool.

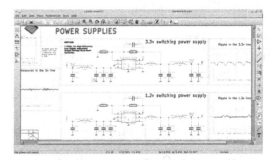

KiCad Eeschema for Schematic capture.

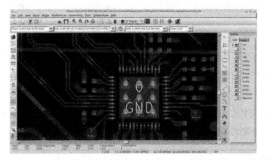

KiCad Pcbnew for layout design.

KiCad 3D Viewer showing both VRML and IDF features on a demo board.

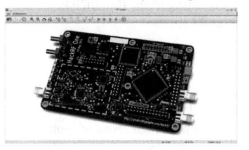

KiCad 3D Viewer

History

KiCad was created in 1992 by Jean-Pierre Charras while working at IUT de Grenoble. Since then KiCad has gained a number of both volunteer and paid contributors. Notably in 2013 the CERN

BE-CO-HT section started contributing resources towards KiCad to help foster open hardware development by helping improve KiCad to be on par with commercial EDA tools.

KiCad adopted a point release versioning scheme in December 2015 starting with KiCad 4.0.0. This was the first release featuring the more advanced tools implemented by CERN developers. CERN hopes to contribute further to the development of KiCad by hiring a developer through donations. Contributions may be made through the links on KiCad's website.

Parts

The KiCad suite has five main parts:

- `KiCad` - the project manager.
- `Eeschema` - the schematic capture editor.
- `Pcbnew` - the PCB layout program. It also has a 3D view.
- `GerbView` - the Gerber viewer.
- `Bitmap2Component` - tool to convert images to footprints for PCB artwork.

Features

KiCad uses an integrated environment for all of the stages of the design process: Schematic capture, PCB layout, Gerber file generation/visualization, and library editing.

KiCad is a cross-platform program, written in C++ with wxWidgets to run on FreeBSD, Linux, Microsoft Windows and Mac OS X. Many component libraries are available, and users can add custom components. The custom components can be available on a per-project basis, or installed for use in any project. There are also tools to help with importing components from other EDA applications, for instance EAGLE. Configuration files are in well documented plain text, which helps with interfacing version control systems, as well as with automated component generation scripts.

Multiple languages are supported, such as English, Catalan, Czech, German, Greek, Spanish, Finnish, French, Hungarian, Italian, Japanese, Korean, Dutch, Polish, Portuguese, Russian, Slovene, Swedish, and Chinese.

Eeschema

Eeschema has features including hierarchical schematic sheets, custom symbol creation, and an ERC (electrical rules check). Schematic symbols in Eeschema are very loosely coupled to footprints in Pcbnew to encourage reuse of footprints and symbols (e.g. a single 0805 footprint can be used for capacitors, resistors, inductors, etc.).

Pcbnew

Internally Pcbnew supports up to 32 copper layers and 32 technical layers. Dimensions are stored with nanometer precision in signed 32 bit integers making the theoretical maximum PCB dimension 2^{31} nm or approximately 2.14 meters.

Currently Pcbnew is being heavily refactored including getting a new rendering engine (called the graphics abstraction layer or GAL) with OpenGL and Cairo back ends. Pcbnew is also getting a new tool framework to more easily allow developers to add tools without having to deal with supporting multiple renderers. Due to this some tools are only available on the legacy XOR based renderer and some are only available with the GAL renderers.

KiCad has a built-in autorouter for basic, single connections. Alternatively, the open source (but discontinued) Java-based FreeRouting can be used to externally autoroute boards.

A DRC (design rules check) is available to check for common logical errors.

The 3D PCB viewing function is based on VRML models and the board model can be exported for CAD integration.

Some recent additions follow.

An interactive router which features the ability to walk around existing traces in the way, or shove existing traces into a different position while maintaining their connectivity.

High speed PCB routing tools such as track length matching and differential pair support.

Python scripting support.

PCB (Software)

PCB is a free and open-source software suite for electronic design automation (EDA) - for printed circuit boards (PCB) layout. It uses GTK+ for its GUI widgets.

History

PCB was first written by Thomas Nau for an Atari ST in 1990 and ported to UNIX and X11 in 1994. Initially PCB was not intended to be a professional layout system but as a tool for individuals to do small-scale development of hardware. The second release 1.2 introduced user menus. This made PCB easier to use and increased its popularity. Harry Eaton took over PCB development beginning with Release 1.5, although he contributed some code from Release 1.4.3

Features

- Scalable fonts
- Layer groups to keep signals together
- Add on device drivers
- Gerber RS-274X and NC Drill output support
- Centroid (X-Y) data output
- PostScript and Encapsulated PostScript output

- Rats-nest generation from simple net lists
- Automatic clearance around pins that pierce a polygon
- Flags for pins and vias
- Groups of action commands can be undone by a single undo
- Simple design rule checker (DRC) - checks for minimum spacing and overlap rules
- Drawing directly on the silk layer
- Viewable solder-mask layers and editing
- Netlist window
- Netlist entry by drawing rats
- Auto router
- Snap to pins and pads
- Element files and libraries that can contain whole sub-layouts, metric grids
- Up to 16 copper layer designs by default
- Trace optimizer
- Rats nest
- Connectivity verification
- Can interoperate with free schematic capture tools such as gEDA and XCircuit
- GNU autoconf/automake based build system
- PCB is Free Software

References

- Fijolek, Rafal (5 August 2016). "Collaboration in CircuitMaker extends to real time concurrency editing!". Circuitmaker. Retrieved 5 August 2016
- Verbelen, Yannick; Van Belle, Davy; Tiete, Jelmer (2013). "Experimental Analysis of Small Scale PCB Manufacturing Techniques for Fablabs" (PDF). International Journal of Engineering Innovation & Research. IJEIR. 2 (2): 134–143. Retrieved 22 November 2015
- "In Collaboration With University of Bahrain: Script Launches Electronic Circuits Simulation System" (2162). Dar Albilad Press and Publishing. Albilad Press. 15 December 2014. Retrieved 1 August 2015
- Onwubolu, Godfrey (2005). Mechatronics: Principles and Applications. Elsevier Ltd. pp. 637–640. ISBN 978-0-7506-6379-3
- "(Script For Information Technology) Launches Electronic Circuits Simulation Cloud System" (4397). Dar Alwasat Publishing and Distribution. Alwasat. 21 September 2014. Retrieved 1 August 2015

An Integrated Study of CAD File Formats

The topics discussed in the chapter are of great importance to broaden the existing knowledge of CAD file formats. The file format used in Autodesk 3ds max 3D modeling and rendering software is known as 3DS. Additive manufacturing file format, COLLADA, KernelCAD and PLY are other file formats discussed in this section. The aspects elucidated in this chapter are of vital importance, and provide a better understanding of computer-aided design.

.3DS

3DS is one of the file formats used by the Autodesk 3ds Max 3D modeling, animation and rendering software.

It was the native file format of the old Autodesk 3D Studio DOS (releases 1 to 4), which was popular until its successor (3D Studio MAX 1.0) replaced it in April 1996. Having been around since 1990 (when the first version of 3D Studio DOS was launched), it has grown to become a *de facto* industry standard for transferring models between 3D programs, or for storing models for 3D resource catalogs (along with OBJ, which is more frequently used as a model archiving file format).

While the 3DS format aims to provide an import/export format, retaining only essential geometry, texture and lighting data, the related MAX format (now superseded by the PRJ format) also contains extra information specific to Autodesk 3ds Max, to allow a scene to be completely saved/loaded.

Structure

3ds is a binary file format.

The format is based in chunks, where each section of data is embedded in a block that contains a chunk identifier and the length of the data (to provide the location of the next main block), as well as the data itself. This allows parsers to skip chunks they don't recognize, and allows for extensions to the format.

The chunks form a hierarchical structure, similar to an xml DOM tree. The first two bytes of the chunk are its ID. From that value the parser can identify the chunk and decide whether it will parse it or skip it. The next four bytes contain a little-endian integer that is the length of the chunk, including its data, the length of its sub-blocks and the 6-byte header. The next bytes are the chunk's data, followed by the sub-chunks, in a structure that may extend to several levels deep.

Below is a list of the most common IDs for chunks, represented in a hierarchical fashion depicting their dependencies:

```
0x4D4D // Main Chunk
├─ 0x0002 // M3D Version
├─ 0x3D3D // 3D Editor Chunk
│    ├─ 0x4000 // Object Block
│    │    ├─ 0x4100 // Triangular Mesh
│    │    │    ├─ 0x4110 // Vertices List
│    │    │    ├─ 0x4120 // Faces Description
│    │    │    │    ├─ 0x4130 // Faces Material
│    │    │    │    └─ 0x4150 // Smoothing Group List
│    │    │    ├─ 0x4140 // Mapping Coordinates List
│    │    │    └─ 0x4160 // Local Coordinates System
│    │    ├─ 0x4600 // Light
│    │    │    └─ 0x4610 // Spotlight
│    │    └─ 0x4700 // Camera
│    └─ 0xAFFF // Material Block
│         ├─ 0xA000 // Material Name
│         ├─ 0xA010 // Ambient Color
│         ├─ 0xA020 // Diffuse Color
│         ├─ 0xA030 // Specular Color
│         ├─ 0xA200 // Texture Map 1
│         ├─ 0xA230 // Bump Map
│         └─ 0xA220 // Reflection Map
│              │  /* Sub Chunks For Each Map */
│              ├─ 0xA300 // Mapping Filename
│              └─ 0xA351 // Mapping Parameters
└─ 0xB000 // Keyframer Chunk
     ├─ 0xB002 // Mesh Information Block
     ├─ 0xB007 // Spot Light Information Block
     └─ 0xB008 // Frames (Start and End)
          ├─ 0xB010 // Object Name
          ├─ 0xB013 // Object Pivot Point
          ├─ 0xB020 // Position Track
          ├─ 0xB021 // Rotation Track
          ├─ 0xB022 // Scale Track
          └─ 0xB030 // Hierarchy Position
```

Shortcomings

It has been pointed out that, despite its popularity, the format may not be the most suitable for 3D data exchange. Some of the disadvantages mentioned are:

- All meshes must be made of triangles.

- All texture filenames are limited to the 8.3 DOS format.

- The number of vertices and polygons per mesh is limited to 65536.

- Accurate vertex normals cannot be stored in the .3ds file. Instead "smoothing groups" are used so that the receiving program can recreate a (hopefully good) representation of the vertex normals. This is still a hold-over legacy for many animation programs today which started in the 1980s (3DS MAX, Lightwave and trueSpace still use smoothing groups, and Maya did up to v2.51).

- Object, light and camera names are limited to 10 characters. Material names are limited to 16 characters.

- Directional light sources are not supported.

Additive Manufacturing File Format

Additive Manufacturing File Format (AMF) is an open standard for describing objects for additive manufacturing processes such as 3D printing. The official ISO/ASTM 52915:2013standard is an XML-based format designed to allow any computer-aided design software to describe the shape and composition of any 3D object to be fabricated on any 3D printer. Unlike its predecessor STL format, AMF has native support for color, materials, lattices, and constellations.

Structure

An AMF can represent one object, or multiple objects arranged in a constellation. Each object is described as a set of non-overlapping volumes. Each volume is described by a triangular mesh that references a set of points (vertices). These vertices can be shared among volumes belonging to the same object. An AMF file can also specify the material and the color of each volume, as well as the color of each triangle in the mesh. The AMF file is compressed using the zip compression format, but the ".amf" file extension is retained. A minimal AMF reader implementation must be able to decompress an AMF file and import at least geometry information (ignoring curvature).

Basic File Structure

The AMF file begins with the XML declaration line specifying the XML version and encoding. The remainder of the file is enclosed between an opening <amf> element and a closing </amf> element. The unit system can also be specified (millimeter, inch, feet, meter or micrometer). In absence of a units specification, millimeters are assumed.

Within the AMF brackets, there are five top level elements. Only a single object element is required for a fully functional AMF file.

1. `<object>` The object element defines a volume or volumes of material, each of which are associated with a material ID for printing. At least one object element must be present in the file. Additional objects are optional.

2. `<material>` The optional material element defines one or more materials for printing with an associated material ID. If no material element is included, a single default material is assumed.

3. `<texture>` The optional texture element defines one or more images or textures for color or texture mapping, each with an associated texture ID.

4. `<constellation>` The optional constellation element hierarchically combines objects and other constellations into a relative pattern for printing.

5. `<metadata>` The optional metadata element specifies additional information about the object(s) and elements contained in the file.

Geometry Specification

The format uses a Face-vertex polygon mesh layout. Each top-level `<object>` element specifies a unique id. The `<object>` element can also optionally specify a material. The entire mesh geometry is contained in a single mesh element. The mesh is defined using one `<vertices>` element and one or more `<volume>` elements. The required `<vertices>` element lists all vertices that are used in this object. Each vertex is implicitly assigned a number in the order in which it was declared, starting at zero. The required child element <coordinates> gives the position of the point in 3D space using the `<x>`, `<y>` and `<z>` elements. After the vertex information, at least one `<volume>` element must be included. Each volume encapsulates a closed volume of the object, Multiple volumes can be specified in a single object. Volumes may share vertices at interfaces but may not have any overlapping volume. Within each volume, the child element `<triangle>` is used to define triangles that tessellate the surface of the volume. Each `<triangle>` element will list three vertices from the set of indices of the previously defined vertices given in the <vertices> element. The indices of the three vertices of the triangles are specified using the `<v1>`, `<v2>` and `<v3>` elements. The order of the vertices must be according to the right-hand rule, such that vertices are listed in counter-clockwise order as viewed from the outside. Each triangle is implicitly assigned a number in the order in which it was declared, starting at zero.

Color Specification

Colors are introduced using the `<color>` element by specifying the red, green, blue and alpha (transparency) channels in the sRGB color space as numbers in the range of 0 to 1. The `<color>` element can be inserted at the material, object, volume, vertex, or triangle levels, and takes priority in reverse order (triangle color is highest priority). The transparency channel specifies to what degree the color from the lower level is blended in. By default, all values are set to zero.

A color can also be specified by referring to a formula that can use a variety of coordinate-dependent functions.

Texture Maps

Texture maps allow assigning color or material to a surface or a volume, borrowing from the idea of Texture mapping in graphics. The `<texture>` element is first used to associate a `texture-id` with particular texture data. The data can be represented as either a 2D or a 3D array, depending on whether the color or material need to be mapped to a surface or a volume. The data is represented as a string of bytes in Base64 encoding, one byte per pixel specifying the grayscale level in the 0-255 range.

Once the texture-id is assigned, the texture data can be referenced in a color formula, such as in the example below.

Usually, however, the coordinated will not be used directly as shown above, but transformed first to bring them from object coordinates to texture coordinates. For example, `tex(1,f1(x,y,z),f2(x-,y,z),f3(x,y,z))` where `f1()`, `f2()`, `f3()` are some functions, typically linear.

Material Specification

Materials are introduced using the `<material>` element. Each material is assigned a unique id. Geometric volumes are associated with materials by specifying a material-id within the `<volume>` element.

Mixed, Graded, Lattice, and Random Materials

New materials can be defined as compositions of other materials. The element `<composite>` is used to specify the proportions of the composition, as a constant or as a formula dependent of the x, y, and z coordinates. A constant mixing proportion will lead to a homogenous material. A coordinate-dependent composition can lead to a graded material. More complex coordinate-dependent proportions can lead to nonlinear material gradients as well as periodic and non-periodic substructure. The proportion formula can also refer to a texture map using the `tex(textureid,x-,y,z)` function. Reference to material-id "0" (void) is reserved and may be used to specify porous structures. Reference to the rand(x,y,z) function can be used to specify pseudo-random materials. The `rand(x,y,z)` function returns a random number between 0 and 1 that is persistent for that coordinate.

Print Constellations

Multiple objects can be arranged together using the `<constellation>` element. A constellation can specify the position and orientation of objects to increase packing efficiency and to describe large arrays of identical objects. The `<instance>` element specifies the displacement and rotation an existing object needs to undergo to arrive into its position in the constellation. The displacement and rotation are always defined relatively to the original position and orientation in which the object was defined. A constellation can refer to another constellation as long as cyclic references are avoided.

If multiple top-level constellations are specified, or if multplie objects without constellations are specified, each of them will be imported with no relative position data. The importing program can then freely determine the relative positioning.

Meta-data

The <metadata> element can optionally be used to specify additional information about the objects, geometries and materials being defined. For example, this information can specify a name, textual description, authorship, copyright information and special instructions. The <metadata> element can be included at the top level to specify attributes of the entire file, or within objects, volumes and materials to specify attributes local to that entity.

Optional Curved Triangles

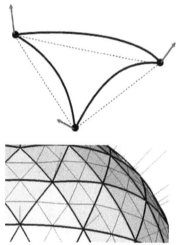

A curved triangle patch. Normals at vertices are used to recursively subdivide the triangle into four sub-triangles

In order to improve geometric fidelity, the format allows curving the triangle patches. By default, all triangles are assumed to be flat and all triangle edges are assumed to be straight lines connecting their two vertices. However, curved triangles and curved edges can optionally be specified in order to reduce the number of mesh elements required to describe a curved surface. The curvature information has been shown to reduce the error of a spherical surface by a factor of 1000 as compared to a surface described by the same number of planar triangles. Curvature should not create a deviation from the plane of the flat triangle that exceeds 50% of the largest dimension of the triangle.

To specify curvature, a vertex can optionally contain a child element <normal> to specify desired surface normal at the location of the vertex. The normal should be unit length and pointing outwards. If this normal is specified, all triangle edges meeting at that vertex are curved so that they are perpendicular to that normal and in the plane defined by the normal and the original straight edge. When the curvature of a surface at a vertex is undefined (for example at a cusp, corner or edge), an <edge> element can be used to specify the curvature of a single non-linear edge joining two vertices. The curvature is specified using the tangent direction vectors at the beginning and end of that edge. The <edge> element will take precedence in case of a conflict with the curvature implied by a <normal> element.

When curvature is specified, the triangle is decomposed recursively into four sub-triangles. The recursion must be executed five levels deep, so that the original curved triangle is ultimately replaced by 1024 flat triangles. These 1024 triangles are generated "on the fly" and stored temporarily only while layers intersecting that triangle are being processed for manufacturing.

Formulas

In both the `<color>` and `<composite>` elements, coordinate-dependent formulas can be used instead of constants. These formulas can use various standard algebraic and mathematical operators and expressions.

Compression

An AMF can be stored either as plain text or as compressed text. If compressed, the compression is in ZIP archive format. A compressed AMF file is typically about half the size of an equivalent compressed binary STL file. The compression can be done manually using compression software such as WinZip, 7-Zip, or automatically by the exporting software during write. Both the compressed and uncompressed files have the AMF extension and it is the responsibility of the parsing program to determine whether or not the file is compressed, and if so to perform decompression during import.

Design Considerations

When the ASTM Design subcommittee began developing the AMF specifications, a survey of stakeholders revealed that the key priority for the new standard was the requirement for a non-proprietary format. Units and buildability issues were a concern lingering from problems with the STL format. Other key requirements were the ability to specify geometry with high fidelity and small file sizes, multiple materials, color, and microstructures. In order to be successful across the field of additive manufacturing, this file format was designed to address the following concerns:

1. Technology independence: The file format must describe an object in a general way such that any machine can build it to the best of its ability. It is resolution and layer-thickness independent, and does not contain information specific to any one manufacturing process or technique. This does not negate the inclusion of properties that only certain advanced machines support (for example, color, multiple materials, etc.), but these are defined in such a way as to avoid exclusivity.

2. Simplicity: The file format must be easy to implement and understand. The format should be readable and editable in a simple text viewer, in order to encourage understanding and adoption. No identical information should be stored in multiple places.

3. Scalability: The file format should scale well with increase in part complexity and size, and with the improving resolution and accuracy of manufacturing equipment. This includes being able to handle large arrays of identical objects, complex repeated internal features (e.g. meshes), smooth curved surfaces with fine printing resolution, and multiple components arranged in an optimal packing for printing.

4. Performance: The file format must enable reasonable duration (interactive time) for read and write operations and reasonable file sizes for a typical large object.

5. Backwards compatibility: Any existing STL file should be convertible directly into a valid AMF file without any loss of information and without requiring any additional information. AMF files are also easily convertible back to STL for use on legacy systems, although advanced features will be lost.

6. Future compatibility: In order to remain useful in a rapidly changing industry, this file format must be easily extensible while remaining compatible with earlier versions and technologies. This allows new features to be added as advances in technology warrant, while still working flawlessly for simple homogenous geometries on the oldest hardware.

History

Since the mid-1980s, the STL file format has been the *de facto* industry standard for transferring information between design programs and additive manufacturing equipment. The STL format only contained information about a surface mesh, and had no provisions for representing color, texture, material, substructure, and other properties of the fabricated target object. As additive manufacturing technology evolved from producing primarily single-material, homogenous shapes to producing multi-material geometries in full color with functionally graded materials and microstructures, there was a growing need for a standard interchange file format that could support these features. A second factor that ushered the development of the standard was the improving resolution of additive manufacturing technologies. As the fidelity of printing processes approached micron scale resolution, the number of triangles required to describe smooth curved surfaces resulted in unacceptably large file sizes.

During the 1990s and 2000s, a number of proprietary file formats have been in use by various companies to support specific features of their manufacturing equipment, but the lack of an industry-wide agreement prevented widespread adoption of any single format. In January 2009, a new ASTM Committee F42 on Additive Manufacturing Technologies was established, and a design subcommittee was formed to develop a new standard. A survey was conducted in late 2009 leading to over a year of deliberations on the new standard. The resulting first revision of the AMF standard became official on May 2, 2011.

During the July 2013 meetings of ASTM's F42 and ISO's TC261 in Nottingham (UK), the Joint Plan for Additive Manufacturing Standards Development was approved. Since then, the AMF standard is managed jointly by ISO and ASTM.

Sample File

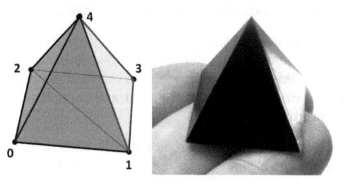

Object produced by the sample AMF code.

Below is a simple AMF file describing a pyramid made of two materials, adapted from the AMF tutorial (548 bytes compressed). To create this AMF file, copy and paste the text below text into a text editor or an xml editor, and save the file as "pyramid.amf". Then compress the file with ZIP, and rename the file extension from ".zip" to ".zip.amf".

```xml
<?xml version="1.0" encoding="utf-8"?>
<amf unit="inch" version="1.1">
  <metadata type="name">Split Pyramid</metadata>
  <metadata type="author">John Smith</metadata>
  <object id="1">
    <mesh>
      <vertices>
        <vertex><coordinates><x>0</x><y>0</y><z>0</z></coordinates></vertex>
        <vertex><coordinates><x>1</x><y>0</y><z>0</z></coordinates></vertex>
        <vertex><coordinates><x>0</x><y>1</y><z>0</z></coordinates></vertex>
        <vertex><coordinates><x>1</x><y>1</y><z>0</z></coordinates></vertex>
        <vertex><coordinates><x>0.5</x><y>0.5</y><z>1</z></coordinates></vertex>
      </vertices>
      <volume materialid="2">
        <metadata type="name">Hard side</metadata>
        <triangle><v1>2</v1><v2>1</v2><v3>0</v3></triangle>
        <triangle><v1>0</v1><v2>1</v2><v3>4</v3></triangle>
        <triangle><v1>4</v1><v2>1</v2><v3>2</v3></triangle>
        <triangle><v1>0</v1><v2>4</v2><v3>2</v3></triangle>
      </volume>
      <volume materialid="3">
        <metadata type="name">Soft side</metadata>
        <triangle><v1>2</v1><v2>3</v2><v3>1</v3></triangle>
        <triangle><v1>1</v1><v2>3</v2><v3>4</v3></triangle>
        <triangle><v1>4</v1><v2>3</v2><v3>2</v3></triangle>
        <triangle><v1>4</v1><v2>2</v2><v3>1</v3></triangle>
      </volume>
    </mesh>
  </object>
  <material id="2">
    <metadata type="name">Hard material</metadata>
    <color><r>0.1</r><g>0.1</g><b>0.1</b></color>
  </material>
```

```
<material id="3">
  <metadata type="name">Soft material</metadata>
  <color><r>0</r><g>0.9</g><b>0.9</b><a>0.5</a></color>
</material>
</amf>
```

COLLADA

COLLADA (*COLLAborative Design Activity*) is an interchange file format for interactive 3D applications. It is managed by the nonprofit technology consortium, the Khronos Group, and has been adopted by ISO as a publicly available specification, ISO/PAS 17506.

COLLADA defines an open standard XML schema for exchanging digital assets among various graphics software applications that might otherwise store their assets in incompatible file formats. COLLADA documents that describe digital assets are XML files, usually identified with a .dae (digital asset exchange) filename extension.

History

Originally created at Sony Computer Entertainment by Rémi Arnaud and Mark C. Barnes, it has since become the property of the Khronos Group, a member-funded industry consortium, which now shares the copyright with Sony. The COLLADA schema and specification are freely available from the Khronos Group. The COLLADA DOM uses the SCEA Shared Source License.

Several graphics companies collaborated with Sony from COLLADA's beginnings to create a tool that would be useful to the widest possible audience, and COLLADA continues to evolve through the efforts of Khronos contributors. Early collaborators included Alias Systems Corporation, Criterion Software, Autodesk, Inc., and Avid Technology. Dozens of commercial game studios and game engines have adopted the standard.

In March 2011, Khronos released the COLLADA Conformance Test Suite (CTS). The suite allows applications that import and export COLLADA to test against a large suite of examples, ensuring that they conform properly to the specification. In July 2012, the CTS software was released on GitHub, allowing for community contributions.

ISO/PAS 17506:2012 *Industrial automation systems and integration -- COLLADA digital asset schema specification for 3D visualization of industrial data* was published in July 2012.

Software Tools

COLLADA was originally intended as an intermediate format for transporting data from one digital content creation (DCC) tool to another application. Applications exist to support the usage of several DCCs, including:

- 3ds Max (ColladaMax)

- Adobe Photoshop
- ArtiosCAD
- Blender
- Bryce
- Carrara
- Cheddar Cheese Press (model processor)
- Chief Architect Software
- Cinema 4D (MAXON)
- CityEngine
- Clara.io
- DAZ Studio
- Delphi
- E-on Vue 9 xStream
- FreeCAD
- FormZ
- Houdini
- iBooks Author
- LightWave 3D (v 9.5)
- MakeHuman
- Maya (ColladaMaya)
- MeshLab
- Modo
- OpenRAVE
- Poser Pro (v 7.0)
- Robot Operating System
- Shade 3D (E Frontier, Mirye)
- SketchUp (v 8.0) – KMZ file is a zip file containing a KML file, a COLLADA file, and texture images
- Softimage|XSI

- Strata 3D

- Vectorworks

- Visual3D Game Development Tool for Collada scene and model viewing, editing, and exporting

- Wings 3D

- Xcode (v 4.4+)

Game Engines

Although originally intended as an interchange format, many game engines now support COLLADA natively, including:

- Ardor3D

- Blender Game Engine

- C4 Engine

- CryEngine 2

- EON Studio

- FireMonkey

- GamePlay

- Godot

- GLGE

- Irrlicht Engine

- OpenSimulator

- Panda3d

- SceneKit

- ShiVa

- Spring

- Torque 3D

- Turbulenz

- Unigine

- Unity

- Unreal Engine

- Vanda Engine

- Visual3D Game Engine
- Neoaxis 3d Game Engine
- HPL Engine 1

Applications

Some games and 3D applications have started to support COLLADA:

- ArcGIS
- Autodesk InfraWorks
- Chief Architect Software supports import and export .dae files.
- EON Professional
- Google Earth (v 4) – users can simply drag and drop a COLLADA file on top of the virtual Earth
- JanusVR
- Kerbal Space Program - .dae files for 3d model mods.
- Maple (software) - 3D plots can be exported as COLLADA
- Open Wonderland
- OpenSimulator
- Mac OS X 10.6's Preview
- NASA World Wind
- SAP Visual Enterprise Author – supports import and export .dae files.
- Second Life
- SketchUp - import .dae files.
- Systems Tool Kit (STK) - utilizes .dae files for 3d models
- TNTmips

Libraries

There are several libraries available to read and write COLLADA files under programmatic control:

- COLLADA DOM (C++) - The COLLADA DOM is generated at compile-time from the COLLADA schema. It provides a low-level interface that eliminates the need for hand-written parsing routines, but is limited to reading and writing only one version of COLLADA, making it difficult to upgrade as new versions are released.
- FCollada (C++) - A utility library available from Feeling Software. In contrast to the COLLADA DOM, Feeling Software's FCollada provides a higher-level interface. FCollada is used

in ColladaMaya, ColladaMax, and several commercial game engines. The development of the open source part was discontinued by Feeling Software in 2008. The company continues to support its paying customers and licenses with improved versions of its software.

- OpenCOLLADA (C++) - The OpenCOLLADA project provides plugins for 3ds Max and Maya and the sources of utility libraries which were developed for the plugins.

- pycollada (Python) - A Python module for creating, editing and loading COLLADA. The library allows the application to load a COLLADA file and interact with it as a Python object. In addition, it supports creating a COLLADA Python object from scratch, as well as in-place editing.

- Scene Kit (Objective-C) - An Objective-C framework introduced in OS X 10.8 Mountain Lion that allows reading, high-level manipulation and display of COLLADA scenes.

- GLGE (JavaScript) - a JavaScript library presenting COLLADA files in a web browser using WebGL.

- Three.js (JavaScript) - a 3D Javascript library capable of loading COLLADA files in a web browser.

- StormEngineC (JavaScript) - Javascript 3D graphics library with option of loading COLLADA files.

Physics

As of version 1.4, physics support was added to the COLLADA standard. The goal is to allow content creators to define various physical attributes in visual scenes. For example, one can define surface material properties such as friction. Furthermore, content creators can define the physical attributes for the objects in the scene. This is done by defining the rigid bodies that should be linked to the visual representations. More features include support for ragdolls, collision volumes, physical constraints between physical objects, and global physical properties such as gravitation.

Physics middleware products that support this standard include Bullet Physics Library, Open Dynamics Engine, PAL and NVIDIA's PhysX. These products support by reading the abstract found in the COLLADA file and transferring it into a form that the middleware can support and represent in a physical simulation. This also enables different middleware and tools to exchange physics data in a standardized manner.

The Physics Abstraction Layer provides support for COLLADA Physics to multiple physics engines that do not natively provide COLLADA support including JigLib, OpenTissue, Tokamak physics engine and True Axis. PAL also provides support for COLLADA to physics engines that also feature a native interface.

Versions

- 1.0: October 2004

- 1.2: February 2005

- 1.3: June 2005

- 1.4.0: January 2006; added features such as character skinning and morph targets, rigid body dynamics, support for OpenGL ES materials, and shader effects for multiple shading languages including the Cg programming language, GLSL, and HLSL. First release through Khronos.

- 1.4.1: July 2006; primarily a patch release.

- 1.5.0: August 2008; added kinematics and B-rep as well as some FX redesign and OpenGL ES support. Formalised as ISO/PAS 17506:2012.

JT (Visualization Format)

JT (Jupiter Tesselation) is an ISO-standardized 3D data format and is in industry used for product visualization, collaboration, CAD data exchange, and in some also for long-term data retention. It can contain any combination of approximate (faceted) data, boundary representation surfaces (NURBS), Product and Manufacturing Information (PMI), and Metadata (textual attributes) either exported from the native CAD system or inserted by a product data management (PDM) system.

Overview

JT files are used in product lifecycle management (PLM) software programs and their respective CAD solutions, by engineers and other professionals that need to analyze the geometry of complex products. The format and associated software is structured so that extremely large numbers of components can be quickly loaded, shaded and manipulated in real-time. Because all major 3D CAD formats are supported, a JT assembly can contain a mixture of any combination which has led to the term "multi-CAD". As JT is typically implemented as an integral part of a PLM solution, the resulting multi-CAD assembly is managed such that changes to the original CAD product definition files can be automatically synchronized with their associated JT files resulting in a multi-CAD assembly that is always up-to-date.

Because JT files are inherently "lightweight" (~1-10% of the size of a CAD file) they are ideal for internet collaboration. With the growing trend toward globalization, more companies are leveraging resources wherever they are available in the world. Collaboration using JT allows companies to send 3D visualization data to suppliers and partners much more easily than sending the associated "heavy" CAD files. In addition, real-time, on-line collaboration is easier because the amount of information sent back-and-forth across the internet is reduced. Finally, JT provides an inherent security feature such that intellectual property does not have to be shared with inappropriate parties. As indicated above, JT can contain any combination of data such that the right amount of information can be shared without exposing the underlying proprietary design definition information.

JT is often used for Digital mockup (DMU) work, which allows engineers to validate that a product can be assembled without interferences long before a physical prototype could be produced. This "spatial validation" is enabled by precise measurements and cross-sectioning as well as sophisti-cated clearance/interference detection. Leveraging JT for digital mockup allows users to reduce or eliminate costly physical prototypes and enables decision-making to occur much earlier in the development process.

Finally, JT is used as a CAD interoperability format for exchanging design data for Collaborative Product Development, where JT files are created by translating data from CAD systems such as NX (Unigraphics), Creo Elements/Pro, I-DEAS, Solid Edge, Catia, Microstation or Autodesk Inventor.

History and Status in Standardization

JT was originally developed by Engineering Animation, Inc. and Hewlett Packard as the Direct-Model toolkit (initially Jupiter). JT is the abbreviation for Jupiter Tesselation. When EAI was purchased by UGS Corp., JT became a part of UGS's suite of products. Early in 2007 UGS an-nounced the publication of the JT data format easing the adoption of JT as a master 3D format. Also in 2007, UGS was acquired by Siemens AG and became Siemens PLM Software. JT is the common interoperability format in use across all of Siemens PLM Software and has been adopted as the long term data archival format across all of Siemens.

On 2009 September 18 the ISO stated officially that the JT specification has been accepted for pub-lication as an ISO Publicly Available Specification (PAS). End of August 2010 the Ballot for the new Work Item Proposal for JT as ISO International Standard was started by ProSTEP iViP. ProSTEP iViP thereby aimed on the one hand to publish the JT file format specification as ISO Standard and, on the other hand, to harmonize this undertaking with the new STEP AP 242 development, so that JT and STEP (especially STEP AP 242 XML) can be used together to assure major benefits within industrial data exchange scenarios.

On 2012 December, JT has been officially published as ISO 14306:2012 (ISO JT V1) as a 3D vi-sualization format, based on version 9.5 of JT specifications released by Siemens PLM Software. Through this publication via ISO, for the first time a completely neutral and royalty-free specifica-tion of JT was available.

Beginning of 2013, in ISO the specification of ISO JT V2 was started. The ISO/DIS 14306 V2 was accepted by ISO in November 2016. The publication as ISO International Standard is expected within the first half of 2017. Main difference between V1 and V2 is the incorporation of a STEP B-rep as an additional B-rep segment.

For providing additional functionalities and innovations required by industry, ProSTEP iViP and VDA decided mid of 2015 to specify a so-called JT Industrial Application Package (JTIAP), which is a JT file format specification completely compatible to ISO 14306 (V1 as well as the future V2) and currently existing JT-Open-based implementations. Thereby, JTIAP provide a more compre-hensive compression algorithm (LZMA), specifies XT B-rep as recommended representation of exact geometry and allows the neutral and royalty-free implementation of JT.

Large Model Rendering

JT was created to support the interactive display of very large assemblies (i.e. those containing tens of thousands of components). The JT file format is capable of storing an arbitrary number of faceted representations with varying levels of detail (LODs). When the whole product is displayed on the computer screen the hosting application displays only a simple, coarse, model. However, as the user zooms into a particular area, progressively finer representations are loaded and displayed. Over time, unused representations are unloaded to save memory.

Data Model

The JT data model is capable of representing a wide range of engineering data. This data can be very lightweight, holding little more than facet data or it can be quite rich, containing complete NURBS geometry representations along with product structure, attributes, meta data and PMI. It also supports multiple tessellations and level-of-detail (LOD) generation.

- Product Structure - assembly, part, instance

- Facet - polygon, polygon set

- Lighting - light set, point light, infinite light

- Textures

- Precise Geometry and Topology - point, curve, surface, face, loop, edge, vertex

- Boundary representation (B-rep) could used either JT B-rep and XT B-rep (Parasolid) format, STEP B-rep will be supported by ISO JT V2

- Geometry Primitives - box, cylinder, pyramid, sphere

- Product Manufacturing Information (PMI) - GD&T, 3D annotations

- Attributes / Properties - text, integer, float, date, layers

File Structure

The relationship of product structure hierarchy to exported JT file structure is arbitrary. Any node in the hierarchy may be specified as the start of a new JT file. Thus, product structure may be represented in a variety of JT file configurations.

JT supports common product structure-to-file structure mappings. These include:

- Per part - All assembly nodes in a product structure hierarchy are stored in a single JT file, and each part node in the hierarchy is stored in an individual JT file in a subdirectory that is of the same name as the assembly JT file.

- Fully shattered - Each product structure node in the hierarchy is stored in an individual JT file.

- Monolithic - All product structure is stored in a single JT file.

- PLMXML - An open XML-based file format, specified by Siemens PLM Software. A PLMXML-structure could link to the model data in another file (an External Representation), or the data can be embedded within the Representation element in the XML file (an Internal-Representation).

- STEP AP 242 XML - An ISO Standard, with allows to represent assembly, meta, kinematic data etc. and to link to the model data as external references (leaves on a STEP-tree). In global automotive industry, for realizing cross-company data exchange scenarios the application of STEP AP 242 XML and JT is recommended.

Client applications may use these mappings, or choose to define their own custom mapping.

Compression

To help shrink the storage and transmission bandwidth requirements of 3D models, JT files may take advantage of compression. Use of compression is transparent to the user of the JT data, and a given model may be composed of JT files using different compression settings (including none).

To date, the JT file format has evolved through two forms of compression, exposed in JT Open Toolkit as standard and advanced compression. These differ in that the former employs a simple, lossless compression algorithm, while the latter employs a more sophisticated, domain-specific compression scheme supporting lossy geometry compression. Client applications are encouraged to take advantage of advanced compression over standard compression, as attainable compression ratios are much greater. Support for standard compression is maintained only in the interest of backward compatibility with legacy JT file viewing applications.

The compression form used by a JT file is related to the JT file format version in which it was written. This version is readily viewable by opening a JT file in a text editor and looking at its ASCII header information.

KernelCAD

KernelCAD is a software development framework and set of components for enabling 3D/CAD functionality in Windows applications. KernelCAD was first developed by DInsight in 2001.

DInsight promotes KernelCAD as quick way to add 3D/CAD functionality without significant knowledge about the subject. It targets software engineers.

Architecture

Although it can be used directly as a set of Windows DLLs its main interface is implemented as Microsoft ActiveX controls. As such it can be added to forms or dialogs using development environments such as Microsoft Visual Studio (native and .NET languages are supported) or Borland Delphi. Some functionality can be used in background without creating a window. KernelCAD Viewer control is optimised for adding 3D solid render-only views to Microsoft Office documents and HTML, including compiled help.

The Modeling Studio application, included in the main product, acts mostly as a utility for operations like import/export, modeling of 3DS type of objects using arc and line splines and 3D debugger service.

Basic operations (Boolean Subtract, Cut Surface, measurements, etc.) are available in context menus of the component, but mostly functionality is expected to be programmed using an interface hierarchy.

As of version 4.1, the core of KernelCAD is released as free software. Some parts of the source code are open. AutoCAD data exchange and Euclidean shortest path modules are licensed.

Versions released in 2012 bifurcated into Standard Edition (v4.0) based on Open CASCADE Technology and KernelCAD Light (v3.2), which does not include bspline modelling and Step support.

Supported Formats

- GLM (native)
- DWG
- DXF
- STEP
- IGES
- SAT
- VRML
- STL
- CSFDB
- BREP
- CSV
- XYZ

PLY (File Format)

PLY is a computer file format known as the Polygon File Format or the Stanford Triangle Format. It was principally designed to store three-dimensional data from 3D scanners. The data storage format supports a relatively simple description of a single object as a list of nominally flat polygons. A variety of properties can be stored, including: color and transparency, surface normals, texture coordinates and data confidence values. The format permits one to have different properties for the front and back of a polygon. There are two versions of the file format, one in ASCII, the other in binary.

The Digital Michelangelo Project at Stanford University used the PLY format for an extremely high resolution 3D scan of the Michelangelo "David" sculpture.

The File Format

Files are organised as a header, that specifies the elements of a mesh and their types, followed by the list of elements itself. The elements are usually vertices and faces, but may include other entities such as edges, samples of range maps, and triangle strips.

The header of both ASCII and binary files is ASCII text. Only the numerical data that follows the header is different between the two versions. The header always starts with a "magic number", a line containing

```
ply
```

which identifies the file as a PLY file. The second line indicates which variation of the PLY format this is. It should be one of:

```
format ascii 1.0
format binary_little_endian 1.0
format binary_big_endian 1.0
```

Future versions of the standard will change the revision number at the end - but 1.0 is the only version currently in use.

Comments may be placed in the header by using the word `comment` at the start of the line. Everything from there until the end of the line should then be ignored. e.g.:

```
comment This is a comment!
```

The 'element' keyword introduces a description of how some particular data element is stored and how many of them there are. Hence, in a file where there are 12 vertices, each represented as a floating point (X,Y,Z) triple, one would expect to see:

```
element vertex 12
```

```
property float x
property float y
property float z
```

Other 'property' lines might indicate that colours or other data items are stored at each vertex and indicate the data type of that information. Regarding the data type there are two variants, depending on the source of the ply file. The type can be specified with one of *char uchar short ushort int uint float double*, or one of *int8 uint8 int16 uint16 int32 uint32 float32 float64*. For an object with ten polygonal faces, one might see:

```
element face 10
property list uchar int vertex_indices
```

The word 'list' indicates that the data is a list of values, the first of which is the number of entries in the list (represented as a 'uchar' in this case). In this example each list entry is represented as an 'int'. At the end of the header, there must always be the line:

```
end_header
```

ASCII or Binary Format

In the ASCII version of the format, the vertices and faces are each described one to a line with the numbers separated by white space. In the binary version, the data is simply packed closely together at the 'endianness' specified in the header and with the data types given in the 'property' records. For the common "property list…" representation for polygons, the first number for that element is the number of vertices that the polygon has and the remaining numbers are the indices of those vertices in the preceding vertex list.

History

The PLY format was developed in the mid-90s by Greg Turk and others in the Stanford graphics lab under the direction of Marc Levoy. Its design was inspired by the Wavefront .obj format, but the Obj format lacked extensibility for arbitrary properties and groupings, so the "property" and "element" keywords were devised to generalize the notions of vertices, faces, associated data, and other groupings.

Permissions

We would like to thank the editorial team for lending their expertise to make the book truly unique. They have played a crucial role in the development of this book. Without their invaluable contributions this book wouldn't have been possible. They have made vital efforts to compile up to date information on the varied aspects of this subject to make this book a valuable addition to the collection of many professionals and students.

This book was conceptualized with the vision of imparting up-to-date and integrated information in this field. To ensure the same, a matchless editorial board was set up. Every individual on the board went through rigorous rounds of assessment to prove their worth. After which they invested a large part of their time researching and compiling the most relevant data for our readers.

The editorial board has been involved in producing this book since its inception. They have spent rigorous hours researching and exploring the diverse topics which have resulted in the successful publishing of this book. They have passed on their knowledge of decades through this book. To expedite this challenging task, the publisher supported the team at every step. A small team of assistant editors was also appointed to further simplify the editing procedure and attain best results for the readers.

Apart from the editorial board, the designing team has also invested a significant amount of their time in understanding the subject and creating the most relevant covers. They scrutinized every image to scout for the most suitable representation of the subject and create an appropriate cover for the book.

The publishing team has been an ardent support to the editorial, designing and production team. Their endless efforts to recruit the best for this project, has resulted in the accomplishment of this book. They are a veteran in the field of academics and their pool of knowledge is as vast as their experience in printing. Their expertise and guidance has proved useful at every step. Their uncompromising quality standards have made this book an exceptional effort. Their encouragement from time to time has been an inspiration for everyone.

The publisher and the editorial board hope that this book will prove to be a valuable piece of knowledge for students, practitioners and scholars across the globe.

Index